MILES OF SMILES

Frontispiece: George Wilkie (1875 – 1944). Champion of Cleethorpes and father of Wonderland. The man in whose enterprise vowed to make Cleethorpes the Blackpool of the East Coast; or was it to have Blackpool regarded as the Cleethorpes of the Lancashire Coast? He was a pioneer of the British fairground, founded the Cleethorpes Advancement Association, was a long standing member of the Freemasons, a Cleethorpes Councillor and was largely responsible either directly or indirectly, for the development of the North Promenade.

Grimsby Evening Telegraph.

CLEETHORPES

MILES
—OF—
SMILES

The Story of Wonderland and
the North Promenade

Rob Foxon

ROB FOXON

Copyright © 2023 Rob Foxon

The moral right of the author has been asserted.

Apart from any fair dealing for the purposes of research or private study, or criticism or review, as permitted under the Copyright, Designs and Patents Act 1988, this publication may only be reproduced, stored or transmitted, in any form or by any means, with the prior permission in writing of the publishers, or in the case of reprographic reproduction in accordance with the terms of licences issued by the Copyright Licensing Agency. Enquiries concerning reproduction outside those terms should be sent to the publishers.

Illustrations are credited throughout the text. The author gratefully acknowledges the permissions granted to reproduce any copyright material in this book. The quality of images included varies, but are chosen to capture the widest possible vision of the atmosphere and detail of the North Promenade from its earliest days.

Whilst every effort has been made to trace copyright holders and to obtain their permission for the use of copyright material, the author apologises for any errors or omissions that may come to light and would be grateful to be notified of any corrections that should be incorporated in a future reprint or edition of this book.

Matador
Unit E2 Airfield Business Park,
Harrison Road, Market Harborough,
Leicestershire. LE16 7UL
Tel: 0116 2792299
Email: books@troubador.co.uk
Web: www.troubador.co.uk/matador
Twitter: @matadorbooks

ISBN 978 1803136 363

British Library Cataloguing in Publication Data.
A catalogue record for this book is available from the British Library.

Printed and bound in the UK by TJ Books Limited, Padstow, Cornwall
Typeset in 10pt Minion Pro by Troubador Publishing Ltd, Leicester, UK

Matador is an imprint of Troubador Publishing Ltd

"In less than twenty miles of coastline, the Great Central Railway Co. owned and operated a paddle steamer service, two major docks, an electric tramway and handled considerable seaside excursion traffic"

Dedicated to the memory of

Doug Best

Friend and Mentor

Who passed away in his 99th year

just prior to this book going to press.

ABOUT THE AUTHOR

Rob Foxon was born in 1947 and brought up in the twin towns of Grimsby & Cleethorpes. It was here his interest in railways developed, for railways have always been his first calling. At that time Cleethorpes was a thriving seaside resort. Situated at the end of the North Promenade was Wonderland, established in the 1920's and said to be the largest covered amusement park on the East Coast. It was there he spent his weekends and school holidays as a schoolboy helper on the live steam operated Lakeside Miniature Railway that ran twice around the Boating Lake and under the Big Dipper for 6d. He spent six gloriously happy summer seasons from 1957 to 1962 working on the miniature railway at first under engineering manager Jack Newbutt and later, Doug Best who introduced his son, Armas, to the line.

A few years ago, Rob welcomed 'Henrietta' to the Foxon family. Another granddaughter many will have thought, but 'Henrietta' is actually one of the miniature railway steam locomotives he worked with at Wonderland over 60 years ago! She ended up on the Coniston Miniature Railway and when this closed following the passing of the owner, he purchased her at the dispersal sale and re-acquainted himself with a happy part of his childhood.

An impression of the atmosphere of Wonderland can be gained from the compact nature of the site. The whole area was packed with happy holidaymakers determined to have a good time. Next to the miniature railway was a magnificent set of Gallopers complete with Gavioli fairground organ which played rousing music all day, every day. Then there were the sounds of Wonderland. Interrupting the fairground organ was the groaning of the giant electric motor in the powerhouse hauling the Big Dipper cars up the lift hill to the highest point on the ride. The light tapping noise that could be heard was of the safety device to prevent runaways in case the car stalled or the rope failed. This was soon followed by screams from the riders as the cars descended the deepest dip at speeds of up to 40mph! There was the pop-pop sound from the motor boats, the crashing of the speedway cars, bell ringing from the Peter Pan railway and of course the sight and smell of real steam on the miniature railway. All this was repeated day after day during the summer season and made an indelible impression on a young mind!

His time at the miniature railway came to an end at the close of the 1962 summer season. Rob's professional career was in medical electronics and instrumentation, but his passion for railways never diminished. He developed a specialist interest as a railway film historian by presenting archive railway film shows under the banner Railways Remembered to audiences in theatres and public halls nationwide. The Railway Film Archive is probably the largest single collection of historic railway film footage in the country.

In 2008 he presented a Railways Remembered film show at the Memorial Hall in Cleethorpes and as a result of the publicity was astonished to be contacted by Doug Best who re-introduced him to others from Wonderland days, all of whom he had lost contact with for some 40 years! Doug's remarkable memory was still very clear and they have shared memories and reminisced for many hours since. Their first-hand accounts of Wonderland, its people and the North Promenade, are the foundations of this book.

CONTENTS

Foreword ... xiii
Acknowledgements ... xv
Abbreviations used in this book ... xvii
Prologue: The Cleethorpes Experience ... xix

Chapter One ... 1
The Railway Comes to Cleethorpes

Chapter Two ... 6
The Victorian and Edwardian North Promenade

Chapter Three ... 33
Wish You Were Here

Chapter Four ... 40
Cleethorpes and the Great War 1914 – 1918

Chapter Five ... 44
Exciting Times Ahead!

Chapter Six ... 61
The North Promenade between the Wars

Chapter Seven ... 89
Wonderland in the Thirties

Chapter Eight ... 105
The North Promenade and the Second World War

Miles of Smiles

Chapter Nine 107
The Post-War North Promenade

Chapter Ten 126
Post-War Wonderland

Chapter Eleven 150
Wonderland Rides – A Closer Look

Chapter Twelve 174
Wonderland Side Stalls and Attractions

Chapter Thirteen 180
Some Amusement Machines on the North Promenade

Chapter Fourteen 184
Wondersnaps

Chapter Fifteen 190
Wonderland People

Chapter Sixteen 200
Seaside Excursions or 'Trip' Trains

Chapter Seventeen 207
Sale of Commercial Sea Front Property on the North Promenade

Chapter Eighteen 224
Wonderland Finale

Chapter Nineteen 230
The North Promenade Today

Chapter Twenty 242
Visions of the Future

Appendix One 247
Alternative Names

Contents

Appendix Two — 249
Timeline of Wonderland Rides

Appendix Three — 251
The Hotchkiss Patent Bicycle Rail Road

Appendix Four — 253
The Great Central Railway Journal 1906

Appendix Five — 257
The Cagney Railway at Wonderland

Appendix Six — 261
Cleethorpes Seafront Bus Services

Appendix Seven — 263
Highway Heavyweights Visit Cleethorpes

Appendix Eight — 267
Wonderland Sunday Market Finale

Appendix Nine — 269
Memories of Wonderland

Appendix Ten — 273
The Wonderland Miniature Railway

Appendix Eleven — 277
A Ghostly Experience

Bibliography & Further Reading — 279
Index — 281

FOREWORD

This book is not a scholarly work; it was never intended to be. It is for the general reader and is based as much as possible on the unwritten first hand memories of those who were there, Wonderland people; in particular the late Doug Best, whose memories of the thirties were still very clear as this work was being prepared. Doug was born on Ward Street, Cleethorpes in 1923 but spent his formative years living in Oliver Street, close to Suggitts Lane railway crossing. After a brief spell as a taxi driver for local firm Fothergill's, he was enlisted into the Royal Armoured Corps on 16th April 1942 becoming a tank driving instructor/mechanic, before being posted overseas with the Grenadier Guards in 1944 as a tank driver, part of the Second Front. He returned from active service in the autumn of 1946. Doug's association with Wonderland had spanned from schoolboy visits to first becoming a Wondersnaps cameraman just after the war, and later, Engineering Manager for the whole site. Added are the first hand memories of others who worked at Wonderland, and from that decreasing band of folk who can remember the post-war heyday of the North Promenade.

Sources are mentioned throughout the text to aid further research. It is inevitable that following a work such as this, additional information (and alas, errors) will come to light which the author would welcome for future correction.

The North Promenade is a quiet place today, but there are exciting plans for its revival. To those who can remember the post-war heyday of Wonderland and the North Promenade, I hope this provides a nostalgic trip back in time that re-awakens happy memories. To those not so old, I hope it provides an insight into the development and glorious history of a traditional British seaside resort. Either way, hold tight and enjoy the ride!

ACKNOWLEDGEMENTS

The genesis for this book started in 2008 after meeting Doug Best again following a break of some 40 years, when we recalled happy days on the Wonderland Miniature Railway. Since then, accumulated scribbled memories gathered over the years have been transformed into a happy voyage of discovery. Foremost thanks must go to Doug himself, without whose long association with Wonderland, combined with his remarkable memory, this book could not have been written and its content lost in the passage of time. Whilst he read and approved this work in preparation, it was with great sadness to learn he passed away in his 99th year, just prior to finally going to press.

I am grateful to local railway historian and author Paul King for the use of the original British Railways auction catalogue relating to the sale of commercial property on the North Promenade and to David Morgan, Senior Route Planner, Network Rail (retired), for his insight into British Rail Management thinking at the time.

Many other good friends have helped along the way, including Armas Best (Son of Doug), Ray Crome & Michael Newbutt (ex Wonderland Miniature Railway), Stuart Blackbourn and members of the Grimsby Cleethorpes Rail Group, Peter Scott, Brian Leonard, School friend David Handy and two much missed dear friends, the late Dennis Parkinson and Roger Bowles.

The history of the North Promenade could not have been written without the aid of contemporary reports which I have acknowledged within the text.

With little to refer to other than Edwardian postcards, a good visual impression of the pre-war North Promenade can be found in the various amateur moving picture records (films) compiled by Phil Sheard of Classic, whose shop is on Grimsby Road, Cleethorpes. He has released these as a series of local history DVD's which enable the reader to gain a broader understanding of the heritage of the North Promenade, together with aspects of the wider history of Cleethorpes as a resort.

Miles of Smiles

I am grateful to Armas Best for permission to use the photographs shot by his late father and those from his extensive photographic collection; also to Patrick McNeill for the use of photographs by his late father Mr H.D.R. McNeill, founder of the Cleethorpes Camera Club.

I am also extremely grateful to friend and fellow museum volunteer, Chris Dibben for his un-ending patience in interpreting and producing the plans of the Wonderland Great Hall & its Rides, the Wondersnaps Dark Room and sketch maps of the North Promenade, from many thumbnail sketches and poor quality images.

Finally to members of the Foxon family without whom this work would never have been possible; to Steve for proof reading and editing; to Mike for his very considerable help with all matters I.T. and to my wife for her patience throughout the whole journey.

Rob Foxon
May 2022

ABBREVIATIONS USED IN THIS BOOK

aka:	also known as
BR:	British Railways
GCR:	Great Central Railway
LNER:	London & North Eastern Railway
MS&LR:	Manchester, Sheffield & Lincolnshire Railway
NELDC:	North East Lincs District Council
SSAFA:	Soldiers, Sailors & Airmen's Families Association.

Prologue

THE CLEETHORPES EXPERIENCE

During a recent visit to Cleethorpes on a fine sunny day, the author watched as a train arrived at the station with families and excited children armed with buckets and spades, heading for the sands. Actually, it was the service train from Barton on Humber and just a single carriage! The promenade and beach were well filled but nonetheless, it was a reminder of those halcyon days when 20 or 30 excursion trains, or 'Trips' as they were known in Cleethorpes, would arrive behind a steam locomotive from a multitude of places in the Midlands and the industrial towns of Yorkshire, each with about 500 happy holidaymakers, all determined to have a good day out!

To gain an impression of the North Promenade during the post-war heyday of the British seaside, let us now turn the clock back to how it was in about 1960 in this fictional (based on fact) account of a family experience of a day trip to Cleethorpes, the like of which would have been familiar to many thousands during a summer season.

"We arrived safely in Cleethorpes station overlooking the promenade on our special train. The sea and sands were already crowded with sun bathers and paddlers. We checked our return train times carefully before leaving the station to ensure we did not miss our train home! We noticed parties of children already had this information tagged to their clothing in case they got lost or separated. We left the station and ventured down the steps, turning left along the North Promenade. After our long journey, we let the children work off some energy on the sands whilst we enjoyed the sandwiches we had prepared before leaving home. Battling through the crowds later, we walked along the promenade past various amusement arcades and the Big Wheel on the sands.

Making our way along, we observed Hawkey's Premier Cafe with its roof top restaurant. Fish & chips we thought; maybe later. There was Brown's seaside rock shop and the Humber Pastimes amusement arcade. Further along was Hawkey's New Capitol Restaurant, more shops and Taddy's public house, though it was a little early in

Miles of Smiles

the day for liquid refreshment, we thought! Next was the brand new Savoy amusement arcade with its bright lights, which looked particularly inviting,

A little further on was the Gayway, a large art-deco style building which reminded us of the Odeon cinema back home. We paused for a few moments to admire the building, the centre of which was a large amusement arcade with slot machines, pinball and one arm bandits. It had two adjoining units; one was the Ritz cartoon cinema for the children, the other, a pair of shops selling ice cream and sea food. Next was the Happidrome amusement arcade and then came the jewel in the crown of the North Promenade, Wonderland itself!

We entered Wonderland off the promenade and were amazed at the size of the great hall and the number and variety of amusements and rides within. It really was a miniature town of fun under one roof. The place was packed with people and we were overwhelmed by the noise from the rides and of folk in high spirits, so we paused to take in the atmosphere, then explore its many attractions. After seeing what was on offer, we rode the Dodgems and the Ghost Train. The more energetic were riding the Waltzer or trying to 'Loop the Loops', but we were looking for family fun and there was plenty of that to be had in Wonderland. The children enjoyed Dearden's junior rides and were thrilled to win a prize on the Hook-a-Duck stall.

From the Big Dipper roller coaster at the far end of the hall, we could hear the sound of a fairground organ drawing us out into the open, but not reaching it before the children had a ride on the Peter Pan Railway. The cars were full with happy families, children in the front furiously ringing the bell and adults on the rear seat, holding tight! Now in full view was the sight of the Wonderland Gallopers, the magnificent golden galloping horse roundabout, complete with its Gavioli fairground organ playing the Radetzky March! We could not help but to pause awhile to admire this Victorian fairground ride. Next were the electric Speedway cars and at the very end of the promenade, the Cafe with magnificent views overlooking the Humber estuary and its shipping. This was all new to our children of course, as we live inland.

Returning along the promenade, we made our way past a large ice cream kiosk serving American whipped ice cream in cornets, a new innovation. The Big Dipper, now in full view, dominated the scene behind the Gallopers and the Speedway cars. Below it was the Lakeside Railway, a delightful steam operated miniature railway taking passengers twice around the boating lake for 6d. We had a ride! Admiring the locomotive were several railway loco drivers and firemen in overalls taking a well earned afternoon break, having brought our seaside special train to Cleethorpes. The miniature locomotive in steam was named 'Grimsby Town', which we were told was built in the Wonderland workshops (the stationmaster may well have been the author!). Sister engine 'Henrietta' was on display beside the station. Everyone was very friendly and after our ride, the driver let one of our boys sit in the engine and blow the whistle, making his day!!

The Cleethorpes Experience

We had to keep a watchful eye on time so as not to have to rush back to the station; for there was still plenty more to see and do. Admiring the various Wonderland side stalls in passing, we remembered a lady carrying a large Noddy (Enid Blyton) soft toy. She was the owner of the Laughing Clowns stall and this was her top prize, though no one was ever likely to actually win it (but see Chapter 12)!

Making our way back along the promenade, our treat for the day was a fish tea at Hawkey's. We called in at some of the amusement arcades in passing to use up our last coppers (Coins) and let the children have a final run on the sands, before returning to the station after a really good day out and a chance to put our feet up on the journey home. Yes! Cleethorpes especially caters for children. Ours have had a great time, so we have too!"

Footnote: It is worth remembering that for many a working class family in those less prosperous times, a day trip to the seaside WAS their summer holiday!

Chapter One

THE RAILWAY COMES TO CLEETHORPES

The first trains to arrive in Grimsby came in March 1848 with the joint opening of lines from Louth to Grimsby by the East Lincolnshire Railway (later Great Northern Railway) and New Holland to Grimsby by the Manchester, Sheffield & Lincolnshire Railway (later Great Central Railway). By the end of that year the MS&L had completed lines from both Lincoln and Sheffield, joining at Wrawby Junction, west of Barnetby and connecting at Habrough with the line from New Holland to Grimsby. By the end of 1848, the Great Northern line from Louth had been extended south to Boston and on to Peterborough and London by 1850, so Grimsby had a direct route to the capital. In 1866, a new line from Scunthorpe, also joining at Wrawby Junction completed the way for industrial South Yorkshire and the Midlands to be connected to the East Coast.

At this time, the Manchester, Sheffield & Lincolnshire Railway was concentrating its efforts on developing commercial traffic to and from Grimsby Docks but was keeping a watchful eye on the potential of the developing seaside resort of Cleethorpes. After much wrangling it constructed a single line branch to Cleethorpes which opened in 1863. The station with its single platform was located close to the promenade, this being platform one today. Although it was the end of the line, there were visions of going further. These were soon discounted however, as any extension would have involved disturbing the High Cliff area which was undeveloped, very fragile, and already being considered as a conservation area. Traffic was developing rapidly.

On Good Friday 1872, five excursion trains brought some two thousand passengers to Cleethorpes from Yorkshire and the Midlands. Cleethorpes was rapidly being transformed from its previous status as a coastal village into a thriving seaside resort!

The line from Grimsby was doubled in 1874 to cope with the increasing traffic and Cleethorpes station was enlarged in 1880. New buildings constructed across the end of the tracks, confirmed its status as a terminus. An elegant refreshment room facing the promenade and a four sided clock tower were the finishing touches. There

1. An early impression of Cleethorpes Station.
Author's Collection

were six platforms, platform six being on the seafront. What more exciting climax to a journey from the industrial towns, than to arrive in Cleethorpes station, beside the sea! Sidings were provided between Suggitts Lane and the station to accommodate the excursion traffic. The original station building on platform one remains, now in use as the 'Number One' pub. The 1880 buildings were largely replaced in 1955/6 by British Railways as part of the modernisation of the Lincolnshire railway network, following the introduction of diesel trains, but happily the elegant station clock tower and Mermaid refreshment rooms were retained and this is how Cleethorpes station remains today.

The Manchester, Sheffield & Lincolnshire Railway changed its name to the Great Central Railway in 1897. Under the dynamic chairmanship of Sir Edward Watkin, the GCR had a dominant interest in not only the holiday traffic, but also in the development of Cleethorpes as a resort. It owned the entire land of the North and Central Promenade's, had an interest in the Pier which opened in 1873, and had invested well over £100,000 in developing and beautifying the seafront. It stabilized the fragile cliffs below Alexandra Road along the Central Promenade and created the Alexandra public gardens for those desirous of a more peaceful visit. For those seeking thrills and excitement, the beginning of the North Promenade between Sea Road and the station was complete with the Victor Colonnade of amusements, shops and bazaars. This transformation by the railway climaxed with the Royal opening by Prince Albert Victor on 2nd July 1885.

Respected Lincolnshire railway historian, Alf Ludlam in his book Trains to the

The Railway Comes to Cleethorpes

Lincolnshire Seaside Volume 3: Cleethorpes, alludes to the Great Central Railway Official Album which said of Cleethorpes: "Beyond Grimsby, the line has been pushed to Cleethorpes, a village once inhabited by a few fishermen, but now changed by a unique effort of railway enterprise into the most crowded watering place in Lincolnshire. It is almost entirely the property of the GCR, who have built a massive sea wall, 65ft wide, the inner side of which is a broad carriageway divided from the promenade by a low wall. A pier, switchback, public gardens and other places of entertainment have been built by the enterprise of the Company, and, in summer, the town is thronged with excursionists from Yorkshire, Lancashire and the Midlands".

In short, the Great Central Railway had transformed a genteel watering hole into a thriving seaside resort by investing very large sums of money and was now going to recoup that investment many times over by providing the resort with thousands of visitors by way of its excursion, or 'trip' trains.

Our interest however, lies in the North Promenade, between the station and its end, on what later became Wonderland. Up to the turn of the 20th century, this had received relatively little attention…

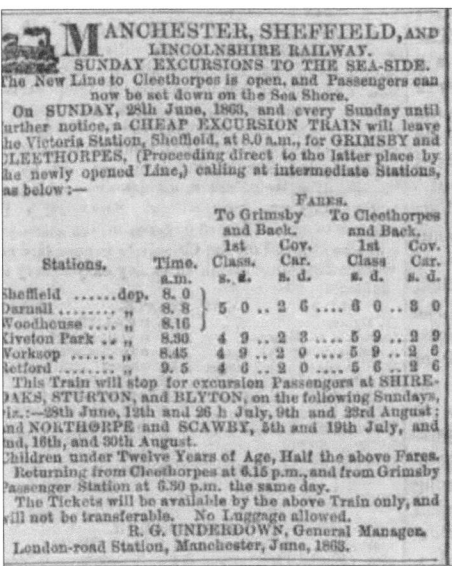

2. Advertised in the Sheffield Daily Telegraph on Friday June 26th 1863 was this early excursion: "MANCHESTER, SHEFFIELD, and LINCOLNSHIRE RAILWAY. SUNDAY EXCURSIONS TO THE SEA-SIDE. The New Line to Cleethorpes is open, and Passengers can now be set down on the Sea Shore. On SUNDAY, 28th June, 1863, and every Sunday until further notice, a CHEAP EXCURSION TRAIN will leave the Victoria Station, Sheffield, at 8.0am, for GRIMSBY and CLEETHORPES, (Proceeding direct to the latter place by the newly opened Line), calling at intermediate Stations".

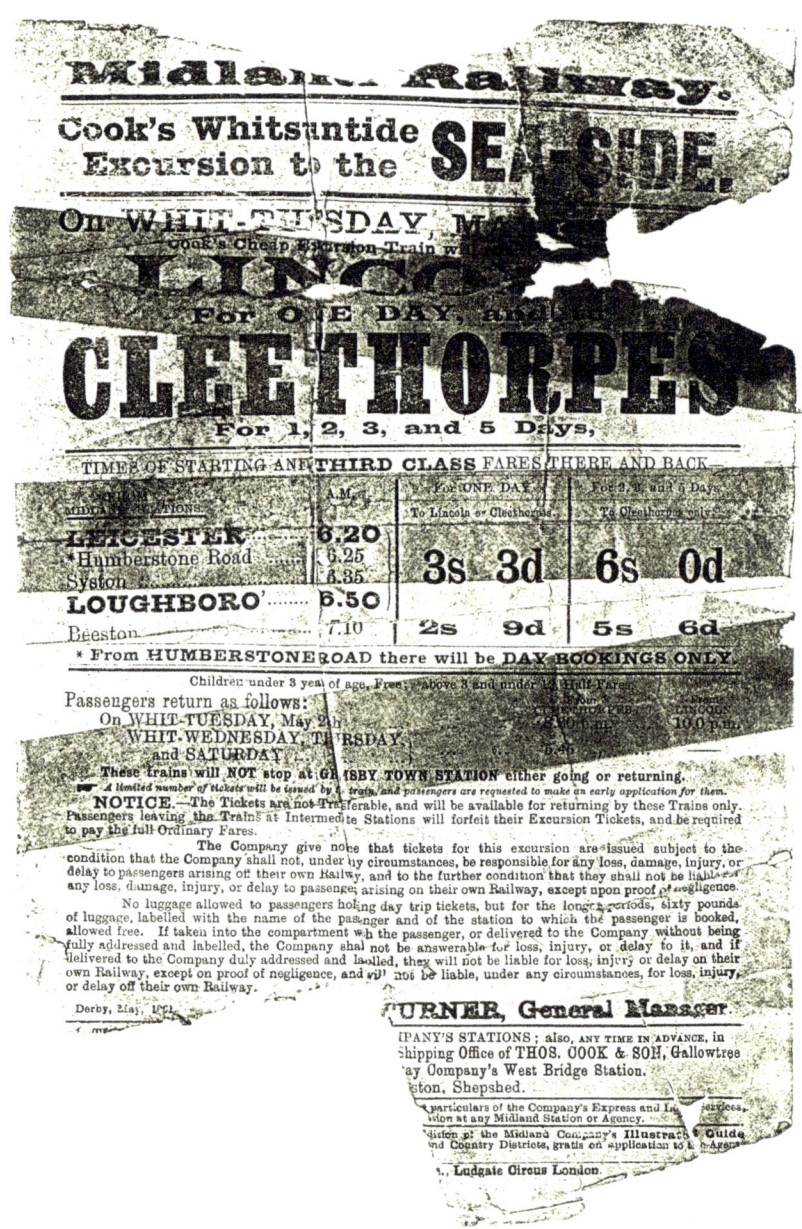

3. Fragmentary Midland Railway Co waybill, dated May 1901, for Cook's Whitsuntide seaside excursion from Leicester (London Road) to Lincoln & Cleethorpes.

Author's Collection

The Railway Comes to Cleethorpes

4. Cleethorpes station in about 1902 from the high viewpoint of the Warwick Tower. Platform One, the original 1863 station, is on the right. Platform Six on the left is adjacent to the North Promenade. The roof of the Auckland Colonnade can be seen bottom centre. Next to the Auckland Colonnade are the roofs of a seaside kiosk, public toilets and Hawkey's Capitol Cafe. There are no promenade developments between Hawkey's and the station. Platform Six was gradually eroded in favour of promenade leisure developments, first with the removal and re-development of the locomotive headshunt, and the remainder being sold for re-development in the 1965 sale.
Author's Collection.

Chapter Two

THE VICTORIAN AND EDWARDIAN NORTH PROMENADE

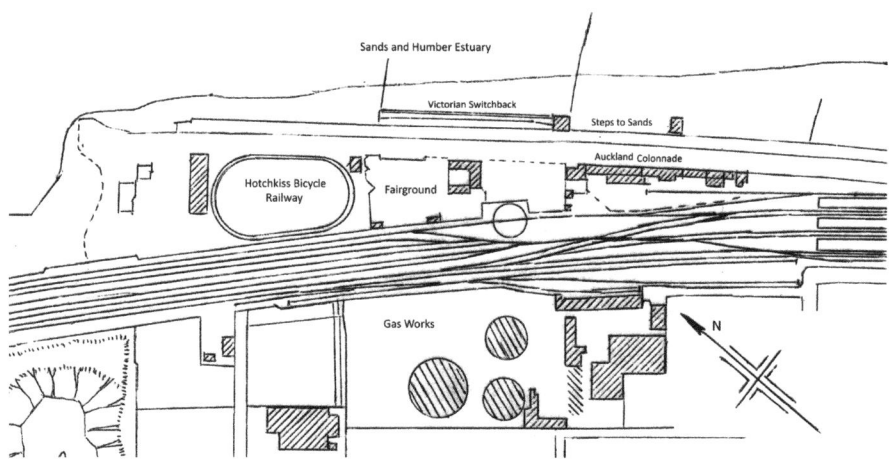

5. Cleethorpes North Promenade c1905

Sketch by Chris Dibben.

A Seething Mass of Happy Humanity

The North Promenade was constructed by the Manchester, Sheffield & Lincolnshire Railway Company (later, the Great Central Railway) in 1885 and consisted of a wide footway and carriage drive, bounded by the Pier Gardens and Colonnades of shops.

The development of Cleethorpes as a resort was well advanced even by the turn of the century. Important features of the North Promenade were its Colonnades; defined in the Oxford Dictionary as 'a row of evenly spaced columns supporting a roof or other structure'. The impressive Victor Colonnade was already complete with its twelve decorated cast iron columns housing a variety of amusements, bazaars and shops between Sea Road and the Railway Station. The other was the Auckland Colonnade which was over 300ft long, of substantial wood and brick construction, standing in splendid isolation mid-way between the station and end of the North Promenade.

The Victorian and Edwardian North Promenade

The Auckland Colonnade was the only permanent structure on that part of the North Promenade for many years. As well as the usual gift shops, it included a pub and restaurant, but Cleethorpes was very strict in its adherence to Sunday drinking laws!

The earliest reference to the Auckland Colonnade comes with the application for an alcohol licence by Mr Robert Jackson in the Grimsby News section of the Hull Daily Mail on 4th September 1889 for his dining rooms in the Auckland Colonnade. Robert Jackson was an established pork butcher and confectioner trading in Freeman Street, Grimsby. He also operated a Grill in the Victor Colonnade. Jackson's Dining Rooms became a well thought of and much respected regular venue for clients such as the annual Police Federation dinner and featured frequently in news reports of functions. He was a very benevolent man and gave much to the community. He welcomed the annual visit of the boys of the Caistor Workhouse, the annual seaside visits of under privileged children from Sheffield, and many other worthy causes. Charles Davis, tobacconist and Arthur Mason, photographer, also had businesses in the Auckland Colonnade in 1894 and Charles Beech, general dealer in fancy goods traded from No's 3 & 4 Auckland Colonnade up until 1901.

The land of the North Promenade was entirely railway owned and restriction signs put up at its junction with Sea Road variously by the Great Central Railway, later London & North Eastern Railway (LNER) and British Railways, declared the North Promenade was a private road and not a public right of way. The Railway Company

6. The start of the North Promenade at its junction with Sea Road in about 1905. On the left are the elegant villas of Victoria Terrace, overlooking the Victor Colonnade. The station clock tower is right centre. Just visible in the right distance is the Warwick Tower.
Author's Collection

invited amusement caterers and entrepreneurs to lease land on the North Promenade to set up visitor attractions, arcades, shops, etc, at their own expense. It was however, a condition of the lease that when it expired, the lessee was obliged not only to vacate the site, but to dismantle any infrastructure they had erected to operate their business! This resulted in the attractive, but sometimes ramshackle, wooden buildings that developed along the North Promenade between the station and the Auckland Colonnade. The larger structures included Hawkey's Premier Cafe & Restaurant, the Empire Colonnade of shops, Brown's Rock Shop, Hawkey's Capitol Restaurant and a substantial block of public conveniences. There were also a number of amusement booths and shops selling fancy goods, etc. Beyond the Auckland Colonnade to the very end of the North Promenade was open land suitable for fairground development. The 25" Ordnance Survey map of 1906 shows only a Bicycle Railway, a look out post and a water tank. It is this area of land that is the main focus of this book.

The Great Central Railway Journal ran a series 'Places of Interest on the Great Central'. In Volume Two (1906) was published 'Places of Interest on the Great Central No3: Cleethorpes'. An extract reads: "If one would frolic and be noisily gay, there is to be found away to the left (from the station) 'All the fun of the fair'. Here there are Merry-go-Rounds, Cokernut-shies, and "Aunt Sallies," which, like old friends, seem to have been with us always. A Switchback is uncoiled for many yards along the sands,

7. *"A Seething Mass of Happy Humanity" 1905.*
The Great Central Railway recouping its massive investment in Cleethorpes.
Author's Collection

The Victorian and Edwardian North Promenade

a Fairy River runs its tortuous course, a Bicycle Railway circles around and there are things to be done and seen for the nimble penny, that no one may lack an exciting moment. From the top of a wooden tower (helter skelter) one may sit upon a little mat and slide gloriously down a spiral way to the sands beneath. What man who has been a boy could resist it?" See Appendix 4 for the full transcript.

In the first years of the 20th century, on the open land at the end of the North Promenade was a series of temporary wooden structures and tents housing minor attractions, together with some early amusements and rides operated by gravity or human endeavour, such as the 'Slipping the Slip' Helter Skelter and the Bicycle Railway that required no external power.

Now the picture postcard was at the peak of its popularity from 1903 until the outbreak of the Great War and many were coloured. Cleethorpes was well covered by the various postcard publishers and some pleasing views provide an excellent visual record of the Edwardian North Promenade. The Switchback Railway on the sands is prominent in some of the views. Later postcards illustrate the development of the North Promenade and its amusements. By 1912, the North Promenade and sands was almost fully developed with rides, arcades, shops, ice cream vendors and the like.

The Switchback Railway on the North Promenade:

The first big ride at Cleethorpes was the Switchback Railway, more commonly known locally as the Tuppenny Switchback. The Switchback Railway opened for August Bank Holiday 1887, but as will be seen, its early history is rather unclear. It was constructed on the sands between the breakwaters opposite what later became Happidrome (today's Indoor Market) and Wonderland. The statement in the Great Central Official Album referred to in the previous chapter claims this being as a result of the Railway: "A Pier, Switchback, Public Gardens and other places of entertainment have been built by the enterprise of the Company. An instant success, it was reported: As many as 4,500 people rode it on Bank Holiday Monday alone!"

A switchback was the earliest form of roller-coaster. There was no access directly from the promenade. Riders climbed the steps from the sands to the upper station and boarded the car, which probably seated four persons. The car was launched from the station by the operator pushing it forward a few yards, when gravity took over and it accelerated in a straight line over three undulations to a mid-station where it stopped and reversed, returning back over two more dips back to the lower station, ending what was in Victorian times, a short but sensational ride. From the lower station the car would be moved forward on to a hand operated lift, to be raised to the upper station to start all over again. There were two cars on the ride. Operators had to be careful not to release the second car too soon, in order to avoid collisions!

Miles of Smiles

The question of safety of these rides was highlighted at the time and the General Manager of the Switchback Railway Company had to defend what we might today call 'fake news' published in the Pall Mall Gazette on Friday 19th October 1888: "THE SAFETY AND SUCCESS OF THE SWITCHBACK". An interview with the General Manager of the Switchback Railway Company: "I call to protest!, said the General Manager of the Switchback Railway Company, when he called in at our office the other day, I call to protest against the assertion made by you in an Occasional Note that we have ever killed anyone on any of our railways. The switchback, Sir, is as innocent of murder as an unborn child. I do not say that we could not kill anyone if we tried; but as a matter of fact we have never killed a human being, and this year we have carried no fewer than 1,600,000 persons. The Switchback, Sir, is one of the greatest institutions of modern times, and I cannot bear to think that it should be wantonly calumniated, as if it were homicidal, even by accident. The switchback is safety itself, and the very essence of the concern, that which gives it its name, is the switch by which the car is switched from one line of rails and run into another. It is quite impossible for such an accident to happen on a switchback railway as that which happened on the roller-coaster at the Crystal Palace. The roller-coaster is an ancient invention by which two cars in rapid succession run rapidly down a curved incline and then ascend about half-way to their original level at the other end of the curve. The brakes did not work, and the ascending car descended, with consequences horrible to contemplate. On the switchback, supposing that a car did run backwards, it would not run into anything; the possibility of risk is minimized".

Nevertheless, the Derby Daily Telegraph for Wednesday 12th June 1889 reported: "SWITCHBACK ACCIDENT AT CLEETHORPES. On Monday night a serious accident occurred on the switchback railway near Alexandra Road, Cleethorpes. One of the cars suddenly left the track, and was precipitated into the road, the whole the occupants being severely shaken and an elderly couple somewhat seriously injured".

Another reference to the Switchback was in an upbeat news item in the Stamford Mercury on Friday 25th May 1894. It read "WORKHOUSE CHILDREN AT CLEETHORPES: The second annual holiday given to the children of the Caistor Workhouse took place at Cleethorpes on Tuesday. There were 50 children, who were brought from the workhouse in waggonettes, forming a procession through the town. They were received at Cleethorpes by several of the Grimsby Guardians and suitably entertained. On the way to Cleethorpes the children were presented with a package of sweets each by Mr Maddison, and upon arrival at the seaside Mr Pell made them a similar present. A good repast was provided for them about noon at Mr Jackson's dining-rooms (in the Auckland Colonnade), where they also partook of tea later on. After dinner they were each provided with a threepenny piece. Mr Lock gave them all free rides on his roundabouts and switchback, which the children heartily enjoyed.

The Victorian and Edwardian North Promenade

Invitations were given by Mr G. Chapman for the children to go to his house, where they were presented with money or small articles, and through the kindness of Mr W. Southworth, vice-chairman of the Grimsby Board Guardians, they were enabled to partake of light refreshments. The party started back for the workhouse about six o'clock, having thoroughly enjoyed the recreation".

The 1889 report of a Switchback Railway near Alexandra Road is puzzling. Could this have been an earlier Switchback to the one that appears in Edwardian postcards? The mystery deepens when nine years later in the Stamford Mercury of Friday 11th February 1898, there appears an announcement by auctioneers Messrs. Dickinson and Riggall of a list of SALE DATES, which include CLEETHORPES: "Messrs. Dickinson and Riggall have been instructed to SELL by AUCTION, on Tuesday, February 15th 1898, on the Promenade, Cleethorpes, aforesaid, about 200 tons of Deals, Baulks, Rails, Fencing, etc, contained in the Switchback adjoining the Promenade, Cleethorpes. The aforesaid, in lots to suit purchasers, contained in the Switchback adjoining the Promenade, and which is now being taken down and lotted. This Sale affords an excellent opportunity for Farmers, Builders and others to secure wood for building, fencing, or other purposes. Sale at 11.30am".

The Bank Holiday revue of Cleethorpes published in the Hull Daily Mail on Tuesday 23rd May 1899 read: "INVINCIBLE TRIPPERS AT CLEETHORPES. Bank Holiday scenes of 30,000 visitors. The atmosphere was both wet and chilly, and Cleethorpes could not have been viewed under more unfavourable conditions:. When the trippers came pouring in during the morning, the sky was of a leaden colour, and the dark clouds were ever threatening the deluge which came later in the day. It went on: The NEW Switchback Railway however had a good test, and the cars always had sufficient complement of hysterical riders of the gentler sex".

Then in the same issue, came a report of another accident: "ON THE SWITCHBACK. An unpleasant incident at Cleethorpes. A most unfortunate collision occurred last evening on the NEW switchback erection just opposite Auckland Colonnade, Cleethorpes. By some mistake, both cars were started down one incline, with the result that when they met the impact was severe. Both cars were laden at the time, and although all the occupants received a shaking, only one, a youth, was injured, and he was badly cut about the hand and head. He was carried away to be medically treated". This undoubtedly refers to the Tuppenny Switchback on the North Promenade that features in many Edwardian postcard views, raising the question. Was this a newly constructed Switchback on the site of the old one, or the replacement of an earlier one on a different site, closer to Alexandra Road?

The Switchback is shown on the 25" Ordnance Survey map revision of 1906, published in 1908. Ahead of its time, it preceded later roller-coasters at Cleethorpes by some twenty years. It is not known how long it lasted, but certainly into the 1920's, when it would have been phased out and rendered obsolete by the new electric rides. The 25" Ordnance Survey map of 1933 shows it only in dotted outline on the sands so it had gone by then, but is useful to identify its former position in relation to later developments. Remarkably, the wooden stumps of the demolished Switchback Railway are still clearly visible in the sands today, revealing its EXACT location, more than a century later!

There are no working Switchbacks left in use anywhere in the world today, but a short film by pioneer cameraman Robert Paul shows one in action in about 1898 which can be viewed on the Huntley Archives website. Film ref: 1011081. It shows passengers alighting at the middle station and reversing the seats, tramway style, for the return ride. This probably did not happen later, the riders returning in reverse for extra thrills!

The Bicycle Railway

A reference to the Bicycle Railway shown as being on the open ground at the end of the North Promenade on the 25" Ordnance Survey map of 1906 comes in an article in the Great Central Journal, published by the Great Central Railway also in 1906. It refers to the Bicycle Railway as 'an attraction at Cleethorpes'. Dr Alan Dowling in his scholarly work Cleethorpes, The Creation of a Seaside Resort throws more light on the mysterious Bicycle Railway when he describes it as being a Hotchkiss Bicycle Railway (see appendix 3) consisting of a single monorail track constructed on stilts about 5 feet above ground on which a sit astride bicycle was ridden. The map shows two ovals of track in the shape of a race course.

8. *The Bicycle Railway in action. Cyclists rode anti-clockwise around the circuit. Behind the tall fence on the left is Suggitts Lane carriage sidings.*
Author's collection.

The Stamford Mercury for 8th June 1900 alluded to new attractions at Cleethorpes. "The NEW Bicycle Railway was operational but the Water Chute was still under completion". The 25" OS map shows the Bicycle Railway occupied a site as large as the later main hall of Wonderland. This can be confirmed by the on-line mapping service of the National Library

The Victorian and Edwardian North Promenade

9. The Hotchkiss Bicycle Railway boarding station at the end of the North Promenade. Suggitts Lane carriage sidings in the background.

Author's collection.

of Scotland where the original 25" OS map of 1906 can be overlaid with a current map of the same area, when it can be seen the Bicycle Railway fits almost perfectly within the Wonderland building footprint! It is not known exactly for how long the Bicycle Railway operated, but it is mentioned in a 1907 newspaper report. Neither is it easily recognisable in Edwardian postcard views, but some do show the raised wooden platform which was the boarding station. There appears to be only a banner across the promenade to draw attention to it and images are scarce.

The Eastern Daily Press for 10th September 2009 included a contemporary account of the Hotchkiss Railway in Great Yarmouth (see Appendix 3), in which it was described as "comprising about a 250ft diameter circle with two rails along which travelled the odd shaped pedal cycles which could carry one or two people". The one at Cleethorpes would have been very similar.

The Stamford Mercury of 10th August 1900 reported: "Twenty two trip trains, each with about 600 passengers, arrived in Cleethorpes that weekend from the Midlands & Lancashire towns including St Helens, but that an accident near Woodhead tunnel had delayed much of the rail traffic. The Switchback and Bicycle Railway's were popular, but the new water chute was quiet". From this and the foregoing report above, we can conclude the Bicycle Railway opened in May 1900 and the Water Chute (near the pier) shortly after, either in July or August.

Miles of Smiles

The Helter Skelter was another popular attraction during those early days, again requiring no power. There was one near the Bicycle Railway and later, two more on the sands which lasted for many years. The one close to the Bicycle Railway was known as Slipping the Slip. It was erected in about 1902, stood about forty feet tall and cost a penny for two slides! Next to Slipping the Slip was a temporary tent like building housing a Mechanical Exhibition, actually an American Bioscope moving picture show. The layout changed each season of course in order to keep up with the times. Other early attractions in the vicinity included swings, a roundabout and Jackson's Restaurant in the Auckland Colonnade.

With electric power available from the generators of steam engines, the scene is now set for the Big Rides and all the fun of the fair!

The Fairy River and Warwick Tower

An early permanent attraction on the North Promenade was THE FAIRY RIVER, opened in 1902. It was a gentle magic 'tunnel of love' water ride in darkness in a flat bottomed wooden boat holding about a dozen people in which various illuminated scenic diorama sets were passed with mirrors used for extra effect. The water was activated by a giant water wheel of between 8 and 10 feet in diameter which was clearly visible behind the boarding platform at the front of the ride. The proprietor of the Fairy River was one Thomas Warwick, of Warwick Revolving Tower fame, of whom we learn more in the following.

A sensational permanent attraction on the open land next to the Auckland Colonnade (now the Network Rail site) was the WARWICK TOWER, erected in 1902, which dominated the whole area. Many postcard views of Edwardian Cleethorpes feature the tower. Originally an American invention, Thomas Warwick took out a British patent in 1894 and formed the Warwick Revolving Tower Company. Warwick Towers are known to have been erected at Great Yarmouth (1897), Scarborough (1898), Morecombe (1898), Southend on Sea, Margate and Douglas Head, Isle of Man. Most were short lived. The Warwick Tower at Douglas Head, was erected in 1899 but destroyed by fire in August 1900. It was rebuilt into a different form and re-opened as a whirligig chain suspended captive aeroplane flight, before finally succumbing in 1906 to yet another fire. The earlier Warwick Towers were electrically operated from steam powered generators.

The Warwick Tower at Morecombe, opened in 1898, was dismantled in 1902 and moved to CLEETHORPES. It was of the standard form being 150ft high with a revolving lift and seating for 200 persons. The electric powered lift had four counterweights, each weighing 5 tons suspended on steel ropes. Entry to the tower was from the Promenade through an Australian style wooden pavilion. The lift revolved as it ascended the

The Victorian and Edwardian North Promenade

10. A view from the end of the North Promenade looking back towards the station in about 1902. On the left is the Switchback Railway and the Slipway. Prominent centre right is the brand new Warwick Revolving Tower and below it on a raised platform, the boarding station of the Bicycle Railway. Its raised monorail track is just visible. To the left of the tower in the centre is the restaurant end of the Auckland Colonnade and in the right distance, the railway station signal box.

Author's Collection

tower and at the top, visitors could step out on to a viewing platform with splendid views over the Humber Estuary and even as far away as the Lincolnshire Wolds on a clear day. It opened on 21st June 1902 and was an instant success, but unfortunately followed the pattern of its predecessors, its popularity lasting in its original form only until 1905. The Australian Pavilion however, with its slot machines was successful and was apparently the only attraction on the Promenade allowed to open on a Sunday! Following the limited success of the tower, Thomas Warwick attached chain suspended boats (similar to those at Douglas, IOM) to the underside of the lift, set it to a mid-position on the tower and using the revolving motion of the lift, turned it into a flying machine with swing boats! In this form, it operated for another three seasons from 1906 to 1909, when it finally closed. The tower was dismantled in 1911 and some of its steelwork used in the construction of the water tower at Healing.

The Warwick Tower's transition to a whirligig was not straightforward however, as Thomas Warwick found himself defending a court action from one of his contractors. The Sheffield Daily Telegraph for Friday 10th May 1907 reported: "THE ATTRACTIONS OF CLEETHORPES. Revolving Tower and Fairy River". "FUN IN

11. A superb postcard impression of the 'Slipping the Slip' helter skelter, constructed in about 1902 on the site of Wonderland, close to the end of the North Promenade.
Author's Collection

The Victorian and Edwardian North Promenade

COURT: Mr. Justice Ridley and a common jury in the King's Bench Division yesterday had before them action by Herbert Clement against Thomas Warwick, the proprietor of a public place of entertainment at Cleethorpes, to recover £143, the balance of an account for work done and goods supplied. The defendant admitted part of the claim, but as to the rest pleaded that the plaintiff was incompetent to do the work, and that the materials supplied were useless for the purpose. Mr Grimswood Mears, for the plaintiff, said the issue of fact was whether the plaintiff had advised the defendant to have two electric motors of 10 and 15hp respectively, or whether the defendant had simply ordered them without asking advice. One of the attractions at the Cleethorpes entertainment grounds was a revolving platform half-way up a tower, on which about 150 people stood and were taken round about twice a minute. Defendant told plaintiff that he had worked it with a little 3hp electric motor, but the people at Cleethorpes were getting a little tired of revolving towers, and he wanted to turn it into a flying machine (laughter) and have boats revolved by some mechanism inside and swung outside from the tower".

It continued "His Lordship: So that the people could become seasick without going to sea (Laughter)? Mr Mears said they could get ail that benefit of a sea voyage with the attendant discomforts (Laughter). The defendant also had a "Fairy River", a trough filled with water that went meandering about the place, possibly underground, driven by a water wheel. People who enjoyed that sort of thing could sit in boats and go along fancying themselves on the "Old Millstream", or whatever the proprietor might call it (Laughter). He wanted a 10hp motor to drive this concern. The plaintiff knows nothing

12. Amusements on the North Promenade in about 1906. Prominent is the Warwick Revolving Tower, now converted to a Whirligig. The Australian Pavilion and entrance to the Fairy River are in the centre, together with the Slipping the Slip Helter Skelter. The Kursaal Bazaar & Café is in the right background.

Author's Collection

about "revolving towers" and "fairy river' but when defendant said the dynamo from which he got the current to drive the motor was 20hp, he told him he could not get more than 20hp out of the 10 and 15hp motors. The defendant, however, replied that he did not want 10hp for the 'Fairy Rive' and it was under these circumstances that plaintiff obtained the motors. The plaintiff gave evidence, and in cross examination, said he had never seen a revolving tower before. Mr Haldenstein (for defendant): What, and you a member of the Institute of Electrical Engineers? (Laughter). His Lordship: I must confess I am in the same boat. I have never seen a revolving round tower. I have been in a boat which went round at Earl's Court (Laughter). Was that a revolving tower? After hearing further evidence, the Judge said it was not a case for a jury and referred it to a referee".

Enter George Wilkie

The introduction to Cleethorpes of showman, George Wilkie, whose name was to become synonymous with the town, was with his aerial rope slide on the sands in 1903. George came from Tynemouth. His father was a rope maker and the origin of his rope slide apparently came about whilst working in a rope factory in Birkenhead. George and his brother fixed a rope from the factory roof down into a hay bale, then used their leather belt to slide down. It was an instant hit with other workers, so the brothers took the idea a stage further by setting up an aerial rope slide at the fairground

13. An Edwardian postcard view of the crowded North Promenade and sands in about 1906. In front of the Tuppeny Switchback boarding station is a Rope Slide, almost certainly that of George Wilkie.

Author's Collection

The Victorian and Edwardian North Promenade

14. A locally published postcard of the brand new Figure 8 Roller Coaster, opened in 1908. It was constructed across the end of the North Promenade. Two cars are in action on the ride. Construction workers are completing finishing touches to the sea wall. Suggitts Lane railway carriage sidings are on the extreme right in front of the chimney. This is not the Big Dipper that older readers may remember!

Author's Collection

at New Brighton. This was the beginning of his career as a showman. A rope slide on the sands at Cleethorpes (probably his), appears in an Edwardian postcard view, close to the Tuppenny Switchback.

The Figure 8 Railway

The Figure 8 Railway was the next major structure to appear. It was a Miller design side friction roller-coaster constructed across the very end of the North Promenade occupying the entire width between the main railway line and the promenade itself. A postcard entitled Cleethorpes 8 Railway by Lee, Grimsby, posted on 24th March 1909 shows the ride clearly brand new and operational, but with finishing work on the foreshore facing Suggitts Lane still in progress. Now in 1909, Good Friday was 9th April, so the summer season had not yet started when the card was posted. We can conclude therefore that the figure 8 opened during the 1908 season, making it one of the very first British examples.

At the top of the incline (lift hill) at the highest point on the ride was a distinctive tower. This has often been mistaken for the similar tower at the top of the later

15. *The Figure 8 lift hill at the start of the ride with a car ready to ascend. It has no passengers, so was probably a test run during the commissioning trials of the ride.*
Author's Collection.

The Victorian and Edwardian North Promenade

16. A rare picture postcard view of the entrance to the Figure 8 Railway at the end of the North Promenade, soon after it opened in 1908.

Author's Collection

Wonderland New Dips, which was demolished in 1974. The entrance to the Figure 8 faced Suggitts Lane. Large warning signs declared "WARNING: Do not stand up in the CARS" and "WARNING: Keep your seats in the CARS" were prominent. The single cars seating four passengers were hauled up the lift hill to the highest point on the ride, after which they were released from the haulage rope and gravity took over, sending them over a series of dips in a figure of eight formation until they arrived back at the base station, creating a thrilling ride. Surviving postcards show three cars in action on the ride at once. It is not known exactly how long the Figure 8 ride remained in use, but a cine film record from about 1920 shows it to be still in place. It is likely therefore that it survived until the major re-modelling of the Wonderland site which took place during the winter of 1925/6.

Alongside the Figure 8 and parallel to it was a Bazaar & Cafe housed in a long building set at right angles to the promenade; its frontage being the end of the building facing the Promenade. It was known as the KURSAAL and housed events at various times. A postcard view shows the building there at the same time as the Warwick Tower with swing boats (1906-09) but not the Figure 8 railway, so the Bazaar & Cafe must have appeared in 1906 or 1907. A notice in the Nottingham Evening Post on Friday 22nd July 1910 invites Sunday School and Choir parties to the Kursaal Arcade Cafe (adjoining the Figure 8); enquiries to Mr W. Watson, Proprietor.

Miles of Smiles

Constructed on the foreshore beyond the Switchback, opposite the Bicycle Railway was the CAPTIVE AEROPLANE FLIGHT. The fairground 'Captive Aeroplane' is generally described as a roundabout with large 'aeroplane' type swing boats, similar to the Warwick Tower whirligig mentioned earlier. The Captive Aeroplane at Cleethorpes however, was a large timber structure which resembled a roller coaster and about the same size as the Figure 8. Very little is known about it, but when providing additional information about an Edwardian postcard image published on a website, local historian David Grimstead drew attention to a notice in the Lincolnshire Chronicle dated 29th July 1910,. It read: "Cleethorpes Proposed Captive Aeroplane or Aeroplane Flight on the foreshore. Application received by Board of Trade from Captive Aeroplane Ltd for permission to erect on the foreshore of the River Humber, on a site about 100ft north of the Switchback Railway at Cleethorpes, an Aeroplane Flight or Captive Aeroplane consisting of an open timber structure about 200ft long, 145 feet wide and 42 feet in height… T H Pelham, Assistant Secretary to the B.O.T., Harbour Department". A postcard entitled North Promenade from N. Cleethorpes, shows a view from the very end of the promenade looking back towards the railway station. On the left is the

17. A fascinating picture postcard view of the North Promenade looking towards the station in about 1911. On the left is rare visual evidence of the elusive Captive Aeroplane Flight, mentioned in the 1910 notice, which appears to take the form of a roller coaster ride. Behind it on the sands is the Switchback Railway. In the centre distance is the Slipping the Slip helter skelter. On the right is the impressive frontage of the Kursaal Bazaar & Cafe and in the foreground by the Slipway on the promenade are a set of weighing scales with lady attendant.

Author's Collection

The Victorian and Edwardian North Promenade

slipway leading down to the sands and on the right the Kursaal Bazaar & Cafe referred to previously. Most importantly, prominent on the left is the structure mentioned in the 1910 notice, so 'Captive Aeroplanes', as the ride became known, did materialise. It appears to take the form of a roller coaster, presumably with cars mimicking aeroplanes, but little else is known. It is not shown on any map and the only further brief reference to it appeared in the Sheffield Daily Telegraph on Tuesday 6th June 1911: "CLEETHORPES. Cleethorpes was crowded yesterday by holiday makers from the West Riding and the Midlands. Twenty-six excursions were scheduled, but so great were the crowds from Sheffield, Nottingham and Leicester that the trains had to be run in duplicate, and close upon 30.000 trippers were estimated as having arrived by noon. Large numbers crossed over from Hull, and as there had been a big influx of visitors for the week-end, the town was crowded. The amusements at the west end of the promenade, the Figure Eight Railway, the Joy Wheel, the Captive Aeroplanes, etc., were well patronised. The Pier Dancing Hall and the Pavilion concerts were also thronged". There are no further references and no known photographs. It had probably gone by the outbreak of war.

On the beach next to the Switchback were children's swings and then the Shooting Range (with moving targets) in a large timber structure. Next to it was the Lighthouse Helter Skelter and the Joy Wheel. Swings, Slides and Kiosks on the seaward side of the Promenade included Hancock's Electric Fish Pond and Hancock's Sea Foam Candy (Candy Floss). Edwardian postcard views show flags were used extensively to draw attention to the attractions.

Of the JOY WHEEL, records in the National Archives show that permission to construct a Joy Wheel on the beach at Cleethorpes by the Joy Wheel Syndicate was granted in 1911. This impressive open sided structure features in many of the Edwardian postcards. It consisted of a conical polished disc in the centre of the enclosure which revolved with increasing speed, centrifugal force gradually throwing the riders off! Although popular with visitors at the time of its opening, it was short lived and by 1920 the structure had become the new Hancock's Palace of Pleasure (see later chapter).

A really splendid postcard published by Harrison, Lincoln posted on 5th July 1911 shows a mass of attractions on the sands by the station, including an American Bioscope in a wooden shed like building. Moving pictures had hitherto, been mainly a fairground attraction. Cinema's (buildings designed to show films) did not come into being until around 1909, so this may have been one of the earliest screenings of movies in Cleethorpes. The Bioscope on the beach would certainly have attracted the attention of Health & Safety officials today; inflammable nitrate film projected by limelight in a wooden building!! The programme of silent films would have consisted of short Actualities, News & Travel films, and Melodrama's, using a hand cranked 35mm projector.

18. The beach stage opposite the station with a Pierrot Act in progress in the years just prior to the Great War. The White Star Pierrots advertised three performances a day. In the background are the Pier Head Tea Rooms that replaced the original Pavilion destroyed in the 1903 fire.

Author's Collection

19. Locally published postcard by Hardy's of the Pierrots.

Author's Collection

The Victorian and Edwardian North Promenade

A popular form of live seaside entertainment before the Great War was the Pierrot Troupe. Alf Wilson's White Star Pierrot's performed on a stage on the sands opposite Cleethorpes station, daily at 11.15, 3.00pm and 6.45pm. A contemporary postcard shows the Troupe in 1907. This may have been their introductory season. The origin of the Pierrot was that of a sad clown dressed in white with white make up. It was later adapted as a pantomime mime act. A Pierrot was attracted to anything white and pure; snow, lilies, etc. The White Star Troupe usually consisted of six members. There is evidence of them still performing in 1913.

By 1911, the Warwick Tower had gone and a big ride driven by a steam engine, possibly a gyrating Cake Walk (named after the dance popular at the time), had replaced it on the open site. This area of open land was now becoming known as Pleasureland. By the outbreak of the Great War, structures on the promenade included the Auckland Colonnade and a mass of attractive frontages of side shows, bazaars and arcades leading towards the station. A postcard view from about 1905 shows the last but one building before the railway station to be John Hawkey's Photographic shop. This may have been his studio or a shop selling film. John Hawkey was much better known for his cafe and restaurant business next door, later his Premier fish & chip restaurant.

In 1912, the East Coast Amusement Company Limited was formed by Anthony Hill, James Thomas MP and Matthew Dowse. On the area of open land at the end of

20. 'Hoop-La' on the vacant open air fairground site of the former Bicycle Railway in 1912. On the left is a Venetian Gondola 'Ark' ride. These are temporary attractions for at the end of the season the giant 'Dip-the-Dips Roller Coaster (1913-1925) would be constructed, taking over the entire area. Note the new water tower and the locomotive & carriages of the Great Central Railway in the background. This later became the site of Wonderland.

Edward Trevitt Collection

Miles of Smiles

21. Amusements on the North Promenade in 1913. On the left is the former Australian Pavilion, the Warwick Tower having gone. Next to it is the ornate entrance of the Fairy River, the Slipping the Slip helter skelter and the new East Coast Amusement Company Dipping the Dips roller coaster. Further along the promenade is the Kursaal Bazaar & Cafe. Behind it can just be seen the structure of the Figure 8 Railway.

Author's Collection

the North Promenade, now known as Pleasureland, no time was lost in constructing a giant roller coaster taking up the whole width of the site to the railway. This was known as DIP-THE-DIPS (or Dipping the Dips). Visual evidence from old photographs suggests it opened in 1913. It was a Miller design side friction roller coaster using flanged wheels to guide the cars and side rollers to keep it central on the track. The lift hill was prominent to the crowds on the promenade walking past, who could see the cars climbing to the tower, the highest point on the ride. The entrance was directly from the promenade and an East Coast Amusement Co flag flew above it. Dip-the-Dips took up the footprint of the former Bicycle Railway, slotting in nicely between the Slipping the Slip helter skelter and the Kursaal Bazaar & Cafe, yet still leaving room for a set of children's swings, the Bowl Slide and other large outdoor attractions in between.

Robert Jackson of Jackson's Dining Rooms in the Auckland Colonnade died in 1912, his catering business being taken over by Mrs Margaret Smalley, who ran it as Smalley's Restaurant until at least 1930.

The Victorian and Edwardian North Promenade

22. The North Promenade and sands just prior to the Great War. On the extreme left, the half timbered style building on the promenade is public toilets. The long building is the Auckland Colonnade. Beyond on the promenade can be seen the Slipping the Slip helter skelter, the Dip the Dips roller coaster and in the far distance the Kursaal Bazaar & Cafe. In the foreground on the sands is the Joy Wheel and behind it, the Lighthouse helter skelter. The Joy Wheel was new in 1912.

Author's Collection

By the time of the Great War, the North Promenade was almost fully developed, the beach was packed with attractions, both large and small and there were three roller coasters to choose from, the Switchback, Figure 8 and Dipping the Dips. Cleethorpes was a thriving seaside resort!

23. A busy Platform 4 at Cleethorpes station in about 1912 with the arrival of an excursion train crammed with happy holidaymakers.

Author's Collection

24. A delightful Edwardian view of the North Promenade in about 1912 with amusement arcades and the Auckland Colonnade on the left. On the sands is the Switchback Railway, Rifle Range, Lighthouse helter skelter and the Joy Wheel.

Author's Collection

The Victorian and Edwardian North Promenade

25. Attractions on the beach in 1912 included this children's roundabout and swings. Mineral waters and drinks are on sale from the stalls. The top of the Rope Slide can be seen is just behind. The pier pavilion is visible in the centre distance.
Edward Trevitt Collection

26. 'Chair-O-Plane' on the beach in 1912. This 'Flying Chairs' ride was probably of US origin as it rotates in an anti-clockwise direction, unlike British convention. It was almost certainly the property of George Wilkie as it also appears in a view of Pleasureland on the North Promenade in the 1930's (plate 54) and in a newspaper advertisement for Wonderland in 1938 (plate 93). Rifle Range and dome of Hawkey's Lighthouse Helter Skelter are on the right.
Edward Trevitt Collection

Miles of Smiles

Some Impressions of Edwardian Cleethorpes

Sheffield Independent Tues 28th May 1901

GRIMSBY AND CLEETHORPES: *"Whitsuntide commences the season at Cleethorpes and the attractions this year have increased. Visitors are tempted with a magnificent pier and gardens, capital concert room (for musical selections and dancing), a capacious promenade, switchback, water chute and aerial railway. There are of course, the usual sand attractions. Twenty one special excursions arrived up to noon, and these were what the officials described as "heavy". For Grimbarians, the Horse and Dog show proved a great attraction".*

Hull Daily Mail Tuesday 1st April 1902

"Trippers were not inclined to be extravagant, and the cheaper their pleasures were, the more they enjoyed them. There was a good crowd on the Pier, but the great centre of attraction was the north end of the Promenade, where for few pence the pleasure seeker might enjoy the thrilling of the switchback, the cycle railway, the electric fish pond, the rifle gallery, or the coconut shy. What a selection! Meanwhile the children could swarm, without let or hindrance, up and down the idle water chute at the risk of breaking their little necks; though not the risk of falling in the lake, seeing that the latter was entirely filled with sand".

Hull Daily Mail Wednesday 7th June 1905

"In the general attractions at Cleethorpes, all the FAMILIAR SIGHTS will be evidenced, but there are practically no additions. Our old friends, the Switchback, House of Many Troubles, Ariel Railway, Old Mill Stream, Revolving Tower, Bicycle Railway, etc, have all been overhauled. Cleethorpes has risen to the occasion and with the cheap bookings and the admirable facilities offered to Hull patrons, they can count upon a most delightful holiday at this go-ahead spot on the Humber".

Hull Daily Mail Tuesday 13th March 1906

A TALE OF FLOOD. *Great Damage at Cleethorpes: "The tail end of the gale that has raged along the East Coast during the past two days spent itself out at Cleethorpes on Monday night, resulting in enormous damage amid a grandeur of nature. For several hours the immense stretch of Promenade, a portion of the railway, and the entire length of Poplar-road, reaching as far as Grimsby Road, was submerged, where the waves were dashed hither and thither. As most people know, there are a number of iron seats on the Promenade adjacent to the broad footpath near to the shore. The whole of these seats were driven and hurled across the promenade against the iron palings that fence off the railway. Many of them were twisted up like tin. Every shop situated upon both Colonnades was flooded, and the stock extensively damaged. At the Auckland Colonnade end, the sea flooded the railway, and poured torrents down the slight incline reaching to Poplar-road, rushing along into the houses, to the alarm of the occupants and the destruction of their furniture. The continual washing the waves tore up the Promenade roadway, and this morning it presented itself a mass of dislodged stones intermingled with mud and sand. The water that had still remained on the railway line was converted into ice. Naturally the flood caused some inconvenience to the railway officials, but they managed to avoid any delay in the traffic. Two baths, green houses, stoke-hole, etc., belonging to the G.C.R. Co., were flooded several inches, and here again the damage considerable. A little, damage was done to the switchback. Altogether, although the havoc does not appear at first glance to be gigantic, it is nevertheless most extensive, owing to the hundred and one small things that have suffered. Fortunately, though the gale was blowing right ashore, no vessels were driven out of their course".*

Hull Daily Mail Wednesday 15th August 1906

"If the Cleethorpes Urban District Council will speedily realise the need for erecting a commodious shelter on the Promenade somewhere the vicinity of the Switchback? On wet days hundreds of trippers are drenched for lack of this essential provision".

Sheffield Daily Telegraph Thursday 22nd August 1907

CROFT'S CHILDREN AT CLEETHORPES. *"Tuesday was a red-letter day for a happy crowd of Croft's children (from Sheffield) who were enabled to spend a day at Cleethorpes. Assembling early in the morning at the Victoria Station, they were met by Councillor and Mrs Crowther, accompanied by Mr Hobson, headmaster of the Crofts School, Mr W. H. Bennet, M.A., of Burton Street School, and Messrs. Coop and Spittle, and Miss Cowell. At Cleethorpes they found splendid weather awaiting them. After lunch and cocoa, the children adjourned to the sands, where two happy hours were spent in paddling and digging. The great treat of the day was when Mr W. Bolland, the genial manager of the Pier, took the children to the helter skelter, the switchback, the roundabouts, the cycle railway, and finally for a voyage on the mysterious fairy river. A stick of Cleethorpes rock was a much appreciated parting gift. The children were then taken to the Pier Gardens for the White Star Pierrot Troupe concert, and tea* at the Dolphin Restaurant followed. Here also the children were very kindly treated by Mr Pratt and Miss Stevens, the manageress. Among the visitors during tea were Canon Webb and Mr Pratt. Later the children had a walk on the Promenade, and then returned to the railway station, where, after the roll call, they entrained en-route for home, after one of the happiest holidays known in the history of the Crofts School outings".

Hull Daily Mail Wednesday 5th August 1908

GRIMSBY 'MAIL' ITEMS: *"Despite the enormous crowd at Cleethorpes on Bank Holiday, with the exception the "Figure 8" and the Switchback, every one of the remaining amusement caterers describes the takings as wretched. This has been the general cry during the season, and when it ends, as it will in about another fortnight, the sum total will not be a pleasant prospect for the winter months. The fact is, that with the general depression in trade, most of the day trippers come out for the day with little or nothing left for fads and fancies, and in many cases they bring their food with them".*

Sheffield Daily Telegraph Friday 28th May 1909

CLEETHORPES. *"The season which opens at Cleethorpes for Whitsuntide promises to be a record one, providing the weather is kind. The trips booked by schools, clubs, and other seekers after fresh air and relaxation are far in excess of any previous year. Sheffield and Rotherham are particularly well catered for with regard to cheap trains during the holiday. Dancing on the pier, pavilion, pier-head, and gardens is a great attraction at Cleethorpes, and special bands have been engaged for this purpose. An excellent vaudeville troupe, including several artists who have been on the Moss and Stoll tour, have been engaged for the Pier Gardens. There is a sacred concert on the Pier Sunday the Northern Concert Troupe, which includes some well known artists, and they will give concerts every following day during their engagement. A wise arrangement is that the boisterous part of the attractions do not interfere with those who go for rest and quiet, for the figure eight railway and other novelties beloved by a section of holidaymakers are separated by a mile or two of promenade from the golf links and other restful spots. The new American Skating Rink, one of the largest and best the country, situated near the Station, should be a great Origin attraction. The docks at Grimsby and the ever-changing panorama of shipping in the Humber make Cleethorpes and Grimsby exceptionally interesting to town dwellers".*

Chapter Three

Wish You Were Here

An Edwardian Picture Postcard Album of Cleethorpes

All images from the Author's Collection

Dating postcard views can be a little tricky. If posted, the view cannot be later than the postmark date. If not posted, it may be possible to identify the publication date, so the actual photograph will be older by at least a year, maybe more to allow for colorization, production and distribution, hence a 1905 set would probably have utilised 1904 photographs. Add other factors into the mix, such as background detail and you arrive at an educated best guess!

This selection of Edwardian picture postcards portrays a delightful impression of the earliest days of the North Promenade.

27. The classic postcard view of the North Promenade from the pier in about 1905. The Central Slipway is in the foreground with the Station clock and Warwick Revolving Tower in the distance. The sands are crowded with holidaymakers and day trippers.

Miles of Smiles

Thursday 11th August 1910: *"My Dear May, Just a line to say Baby Ida and I are at Cleethorpes for a week. We are spending a glorious time the weather is all that can be desired and we already feel better for the change. Kenneth does not make mud pies but goes and knocks over those other children have made he does seem to be happy and can say lots of words you will see a difference when you come. Don't be long before you write if only a postcard. It is quite a place for children here and there are many here and love the sands. Love from Elsie".*

c1908: *"Dear Elsie, I hope you are enjoying yourself as I am doing the same. We have had a lot of wet but it is fine now. I have had a postcard from Stella. I have had a ride on the donkeys. I must now close. Yours, Hilda".*

28. Shops and bazaars in the Victor Colonnade in about 1905

29. An early view of the North Promenade near the station. Amusement developments have yet to reach this part of the promenade. The full length of Platform 6 is clearly visible.

Wish You Were Here

30. Looking down on the North Promenade from the Warwick Tower in about 1902. The roof of the Auckland Colonnade is foremost in the centre of the view. The white building on the sands is the Rifle Range. Other attractions on the sands are limited to seaside vendors. Amusements on the promenade between the Auckland Colonnade and the station are few. Platform 6 of the station with its short lived locomotive headshunt remain as built, before promenade amusement developments encroached upon it.

31. Another very early view of the end of the North Promenade. The Victorian switchback railway was well established by the time of this view in about 1902. The Bicycle Railway is in the left background, albeit not very prominent, on account of it being a ground level attraction.

Miles of Smiles

Tuesday 15th August 1911: *"Dear Friend, Arrived here quite safe having glorious weather & enjoying ourselves immensely. We thing it a lovely place. We have also nice apartments. Hope everything all right. Yours, Mr & Mrs Robinson".*

32. A delightful impression of the North Promenade and sands opposite the Auckland Colonnade in about 1910.

33. The North Promenade looking back towards the station in about 1912. On the left is the end of the Switchback Railway where the cars reversed for the return run. The Castle like structure on the right is thought to be part of the Fairy River. Behind is the Slipping the Slip helter skelter and in the distance the Australian Pavilion, former entrance to the Warwick Tower, now gone.

Wish You Were Here

Wednesday 10th August 1910: *"Dear Dora, We are having some splendid weather I have had to get some cream for my face but we hope it will keep up. Eunice & Harry".*

34. A very early view c1903 of the end of the North Promenade with the Switchback Railway and George Wilkie's Rope Slide on the sands in the foreground. The building with chimney on the left is the kitchen of Jackson's Dining Rooms, the Auckland Colonnade. The Warwick Tower is new.

35. A similar view, this time in about 1910 of the end of the North Promenade showing what would later be the site of Wonderland. The Switchback Railway is opposite what is now the Cleethorpes Indoor Market. In the background is the Slipping the Slip helter skelter, the Kursaal Bazaar & Café and behind it, the Figure 8 Railway.

Miles of Smiles

Monday 1st August 1910: *"Just a line as promised arrived safely. Plenty of people, lovely weather, am having a fine time hope you are doing the same".*

Monday 18th August 1919: *"Dear Mrs Mitchell, Just a line to tell you we have been on the Figure 8 and we have had some fun you could have heard me laughing when we was going down the dip there is thousands of people it is nice by the seaside. Love to both, E".*

36. The North Promenade and Sands looking towards the Station in about 1905. The Lighthouse helter skelter is on the sands. Newly constructed promenade buildings on the right stretch from the Auckland Colonnade (just out of view on the right), to the Railway Station. They include Hawkey's Capitol Café, the Empire Colonnade, Brown's Rock shop, various Amusements and Hawkey's Premier Café.

37. The much favored picture postcard view of Cleethorpes from the Pier, showing the Slipway, Victoria Hotel, Victoria Terrace, Victor Colonnade, Station and sands, in about 1905.

Wish You Were Here

38. The crowded sands and promenade near the station in about 1905. One of the attractions on the sands is the American Bioscope, which would have been one of the earliest screenings of moving pictures in the town. Other attractions include roundabouts, Punch & Judy shows and more, in this delightful view of the Edwardian seaside in full swing!

39. The North Promenade in about 1912. Buildings on the left include the Empire Colonnade, various Amusement Booth's, the Humber Mechanical Exhibition and Hawkey's Capitol Café. The chimney in the distance is that of Jackson's Dining Rooms at the far end of the Auckland Colonnade. In the centre distance can just be discerned the Rifle Range. Nearer on the sands is the Lighthouse helter skelter and the brand new Joy Wheel.

CHAPTER FOUR

CLEETHORPES AND THE GREAT WAR 1914 – 1918

Noted Cleethorpes historian and author, Dr Alan Dowling, in his writings of Cleethorpes during the First World War, said that in early August 1914, the 3rd Battalion of the Manchester Regiment arrived in Cleethorpes by rail, where they were to be stationed throughout the period of hostilities. The 3rd Battalion was a Training and Recovery Unit, training raw recruits and rehabilitating injured servicemen. They set up pickets at strategic points along the coastline to warn of any possibility of enemy invasion. In 1915, in order to protect the River Humber from penetration by the enemy, construction of two forts at the mouth of the Humber began. On the Yorkshire bank was the Bull Sands Fort and on the Lincolnshire coast, Haile Sands Fort. An anti submarine boom stretched between the forts to prevent incursions by enemy submarines into the river. In 1916, the 3rd Battalion presence in Cleethorpes was said to be about 4000 strong. In the same year, a Machine Gun School was established at Cleethorpes, so the movement of service personnel to and from the resort throughout the war was considerable.

The North Promenade and amusements however, remained open throughout but understandably, visitor numbers were much reduced. Newspaper reports highlighted the plight of boarding house keepers, many of whom relied entirely on visitor income for a living. Potential holiday-makers from Sheffield during the early part of the war would have been particularly depressed by the report in the Sheffield Daily Telegraph on Saturday 27th February 1915: "CLEETHORPES. That lively little neighbour of Grimsby, would not be recognised by its Sheffield devotees, who certainly would not find it a very gay spot at night just now. For the Cleethorpes lodging-house keepers at any rate the winter is depressing, for the outbreak of war ruined the holiday season, the profits from which is all they have to live upon in many cases for the rest of the year. Despite its spell of adversity, Cleethorpes is making the best of things, and the attractions of the popular pleasure resort are to be advertised as usual. Still, a song of thanksgiving will go up from the heart of many a harassed widow if the July sun shines upon a world at peace". This was of course a winter time projected view of the forthcoming season.

With many men folk away, it was obvious that visitor numbers would be reduced, but at least Cleethorpes was open to those who were able to take a break. There were no newspaper advertisements by amusement caterers; ad's during the period of hostilities being limited to the availability of hotel and boarding house accommodation.

Nevertheless, the 1915 summer season went ahead, but less busy than usual. The Sheffield Daily Telegraph on Tuesday 3rd August 1915 reported of the Bank Holiday: "QUIET HOLIDAY AT CLEETHORPES. Despite the absence of excursion facilities, there was a good influx of holiday-makers at Cleethorpes yesterday, though the crowds were much below the normal for this holiday. Hull and district were responsible for many arrivals, and there were large contingents from Manchester, Sheffield, Leeds, Leicester and Nottingham districts. Generally, however, there was a restrained air about the festivities, and fewer amusements and attractions were offered than usual. The weather was gloriously fine".

Further writings by Dr Alan Dowling describe the most serious atrocity inflicted on the resort. Enemy bombing raids by Zeppelin airships were causing havoc to both shipping and land targets along the East Coast of England and unfortunately, Cleethorpes was the victim of such a raid during the early hours of 1st April 1916, when a Zeppelin dropped three bombs on the resort. One caused damage to the Town Hall, another damaged property in Sea View Street, but the third was a direct hit on the Cleethorpes Methodist Chapel on Alexandra Road where about 70 recruits were billeted, resulting in 31 dead and many more injured. This was to be by far the most serious enemy action Cleethorpes sustained during the war.

It seems there were brief highlights to the wartime pattern of life however, as the Hull Daily Mail reported on Saturday 11th August 1917: "CONGESTED CLEETHORPES. Boarding-house keepers had a pleasant surprise on Saturday. From noon visitors began to arrive by hundreds, and at night the town was congested with holiday folk. Every incoming train was crowded, passengers being packed in the guards vans like sardines. As a result of an inrush which had never been anticipated, the food supply in the shops was soon exhausted, but fortunately Cleethorpes has Grimsby adjacent, and this relieved what would otherwise have been a famine. The visitors, most whom are staying several days, are munitions workers, with plenty of money, and they are spending it freely. All the incoming trains to-day were similarly crowded as on Saturday, amusements were in full swing as early as 8am, and as high water was at breakfast-time hundreds of people of both sexes were bathing". (The imagination runs wild!).

Miles of Smiles

Whitsuntide 1918 was reported a busy time on the Promenade with a considerable influx of visitors, followed by a satisfactory summer season.

The floats of an anti-submarine boom stretching into the river from the pier are clearly visible in a film record of Cleethorpes in views from the Kingsway promenade shot in about 1920. Today, the most visible reminders of the First World War in Cleethorpes are the Bull Sands and Haile Sands Forts, neither of which saw active service.

So Cleethorpes survived the Great War relatively unscathed and the immediate post-war years into the twenties were a time of consolidation and recovery, before pressing ahead with further resort developments. Visitor numbers did not recover to pre-war levels until the early twenties, after which it was EXCITING TIMES AHEAD!

Cleethorpes and the Great War 1914 – 1918

Some Impressions of Cleethorpes during the Great War:

Pall Mall Gazette Saturday 7th August 1915

> SWEET MACHINES PLUNDERED. *"During the hearing of a charge against two respectably dressed boys, at Grimsby, of stealing chocolate from an automatic machine, the manager of the company owning the machines said there had been a systematic raid this season on the machine on Cleethorpes promenade. Over two thousand packets of sweetmeats had been stolen, said the witness, who produced a large bagful of metal discs and wire found in the machines. The lads were each fined five shillings".*

Sheffield Daily Telegraph Tuesday 25th April 1916

> CLEETHORPES. *"Cleethorpes yesterday experienced the quietest Bank Holiday within memory. There were no excursions, and practically the only visitors to the town were relatives of soldiers quartered in the district, or folk from Grimsby. The weather was dull, cold, and showery, and the only outdoor entertainment was the football match, Grimsby Town v. Lincoln City, at Blundell Park".*

Sunday Mirror Sunday 13th August 1916:

> CAPTURE IN TUCK SHOP (From Our Own Correspondent): Grimsby, Saturday. *"A sentry on duty at Cleethorpes at midnight noticed a light on the promenade and heard the sound of splintering wood. He turned out the guard, who doubled to a small confectionery kiosk on the Kingsway. This they surrounded, and the corporal of the guard, entering, found James Birchall, a private of the Manchester's, within. He had broken the door open and ransacked the shop. Charged today with shop breaking, Birchall was committed for trial".*

Sheffield Daily Telegraph Tuesday 6th August 1918

> *"Cleethorpes had the satisfaction, yesterday, of entertaining more visitors than at any holiday since the early days of the war. Sheffield, Nottingham, Leicester, Derby and Hull, all sent big contingents, and there were numerous arrivals from Lancashire. The beach and promenade the most animated aspect, and though there were fewer attractions than in the days of peace, the visitors appeared to find plenty to entertain them. The weather was dull and close, with threats of rain".*

Chapter Five
EXCITING TIMES AHEAD!

Pleasureland or Wonderland?

The East Coast Amusement Company, established in 1911, operated the entire land area from the Auckland Colonnade to the very end of the North Promenade itself. The Company was aquired by George Wilkie in 1921 from Anthony Hill and Mr J.H. Thomas MP (later, the Lord Privy Seal). In partnership with Cleethorpes businessman, Matthew Dowse, George Wilkie re-modelled the site at the end of the North Promenade during the winter of 1925/6 into what was to be known as Wonderland and ran it with his sister in law Elizabeth (Ma) Wilkie. Over the years, this has been the site of many and various amusements and rides, the area becoming known as Pleasureland, so it will be seen that historical accounts and descriptions of rides are closely intertwined with those of Wondcrland, which became the major attraction at the end of the North Promenade.

One of the final East Coast Amusement Co display adverts prior to the remodelling of the site, was carried by the Sheffield Daily Telegraph on Thursday 9th July 1925. It read "For Health & Pleasure visit Pleasureland (Promenade) Cleethorpes". It included an image of the Dip the Dips roller coaster. Attractions mentioned were: "The Giant Mountain Dip the Dips, Famous Bowl Slide, Whirl-a-Ball, Flying Chairs, Over the Falls, Electric Scenic Railway and a Host of Other Attractions. East Coast Amusements Co., Ltd". The accompanying editorial read: "DIP THE DIPS. Amongst the many amusements at Cleethorpes probably the most popular and certainly the one holding the most thrills is the Dip-the-Dips, or Aerial Scenic Railway. The car is caught by projection on an endless chain and borne up a long incline, over 100 feet, high. An ingenious arrangement locks to ensure that in case of mechanical breakdown during the ascent, the car is automatically fastened in position, and there is no element of danger. Upon reaching the summit a fine view of Cleethorpes and the sea is obtained,

Exciting Times Ahead!

**The Giant Mountain DIP-THE-DIPS,
The Famous Bowl Slide,
Whirl-a-Ball, Flying Chairs,
Over the Falls,
Electric Scenic Railway,
And Host of other Attractions.**

**EAST COAST
AMUSEMENTS Co., Ltd.**
G. WILKIE, Managing Director.

*40. This East Coast Amusement Co. advert was the final one before the major re-modelling of the North Promenade site and the construction of the Wonderland building.
Hull Daily Mail 16th July 1925.*

and the car glides round, a warning to "Mind your Hat" is noticed. This is appreciated as a few seconds later the car commences to gain speed, and everyone holds tight whilst it performs series of dives earthwards and swoops upwards. There is no bumping, and one has the sensation of stunting in an aeroplane. A final dive, and then comes a straight run along the braking platform. The smartly uniformed attendants are kept busy booking encores. It goes on: Mr Wilkie has spent very many years catering for public amusements and believing Cleethorpes to have great future, has drawn up some elaborate plans for additions next year to the present buildings owned by the Company on the North Promenade" (the 'New' Wonderland!).

The major remodelling of the three and a half acre site on the North Promenade involved the removal of the Figure 8, the dismantling of the Dip the Dips roller coaster and its re-building in a new place close to and parallel with the railway at the very end of the site. At the summit of the lift hill was constructed a distinctive tower pronouncing it to be New Dips which overlooked the Humber estuary and Suggitts Lane. This is the one older readers may remember. Officially New Dips, it was more usually known thereafter as the Big Dipper and remained a thrilling ride for the next 48 years!

On the site vacated by the Dip the Dips (originally the footprint of the Bicycle Railway on the 1906 OS map) was erected a large hanger like building, measuring some 400ft by 140ft. Construction work started in November 1925. It provided work for a team of 100 men. The building is believed to have been a former First World War submarine shed from Barton (or Barrow). This became the Great Hall of the new Wonderland complex which still stands today.

The Great Hall partly opened, without ceremony, at Easter 1926. The Grimsby News for Friday 21st May 1926 noted in its Cleethorpes preparations for Whitsuntide: The new Wonderland is in a much more complete state than it was at Easter, a floor has been laid, there are more amusements under its capacious roof and the boating lake is ready.

Miles of Smiles

41. Looking over the town and railway to the North Promenade from the construction site of the Theatre Royal, at the top of station approach, in 1920, gives a good impression of the layout of rides at the end of the North Promenade before Wonderland was constructed. The original 'Dip-the-Dips' roller coaster (1913-1925) is prominent in the centre, whilst the older Figure 8 Railway (1908-1925) at the very end of the Promenade is on the left. In the right distance can just be seen the domed top of Hawkey's Lighthouse Helter Skelter, on the sands.

Edward Trevitt Collection

42. Looking over the railway station to the North Promenade from the construction site of the Theatre Royal in 1920. The decorated dome of Hawkey's Lighthouse Helter Skelter on the sands is on the left. The round building in the centre is the former 'Joy Wheel', now Hancock's 'Palace of Pleasure' with 'Jolly Boats' banner around the dome. The buildings in the foreground are those of the original Manchester, Sheffield & Lincolnshire Railway station, now Platform One, which date back to 1863.

Edward Trevitt Collection

Exciting Times Ahead!

The Hull Daily Mail for Thursday 8th July 1926 noted in its holiday revue: THE NEW DIPS AND LAKELAND. "One person at least has enormous faith in Cleethorpes becoming the pleasure resort of the East coast, and this is Mr Wilkie, Managing Director of the East Coast Amusements Limited. For several years, Mr Wilkie has been working on plans for a huge pleasure ground, with everything under cover. During the last winter a start has been made and an army of workmen employed, racing against time, to complete the undertaking. The result is a real transformation of the north end of the promenade. The old Dip the Dips has been reconstructed, and in its stead there is the New Dips with more thrills in one ride than a whole day on any other amusement, The structure is built round the Children's Lakeland, where the youngsters can go boating in perfect safety as, even if it were possible to upset the boats, the depth of water is only a few inches, and the attendants are on the spot. Such an occurrence is practically impossible. The hall adjoining, styled 'Wonderland', is where all the latest novelties in the amusement world are housed. Flying Chairs, Dodgem, the Wembley Slide, Scenic Railway, and a host of other attractions have been provided and in case of unsettled weather, over 20,000 people could spend a full day in this magnificent building, enjoying all the latest novelties. A quick lunch buffet has been provided and light meals are served at reasonable rates. Along the Promenade, the very latest thrill styled The New Whip is also the property of the Company".

43. Hull Daily Mail 8th July 1926. The first East Coast Amusement Co advert following the re-modelling of the site. Note the caption heading 'New Dips and Lakeland'. The Wonderland name was not fully adopted until 1928.

Fairground development in Britain was heavily influenced by that in America, in particular New York's Coney Island where many new technological developments were demonstrated on rides. Anthony Hill was a Welsh American and it is likely that following a visit by him to Coney Island, this influenced the forward thinking of the East Coast Amusement Company. George Wilkie was in tune with this, so the rides in Wonderland were very much American influenced.

The template or layout, of the great hall remained unchanged throughout its life as an indoor amusement centre. There were three big rides along the centre of the hall, plus New Dips, now known as the Big Dipper. Additional rides were added progressively such as the Ghost Train. There was a maze to get lost in and a large number of supporting side stalls and free standing attractions such as the Wonderland Monkeys, Darts Academy, Mancho Tables, Hoo-Pla, Swings and Roundabouts. The juvenile attractions of J. Dearden's were an early feature of Wonderland.

Two of the big rides in the Great Hall from the opening, or shortly after in 1926, were the DODGEMS and the ELECTRIC SCENIC RAILWAY (Scenic Ark). There was also of course, The Big Dipper. The third big ride, Midget Motors (Custer Cars) appeared in the great hall the following year. Mention is also made of the New Circus. This was probably a small animal house type attraction in the corner of the great hall.

The Wonderland Dodgems would have been amongst the first, if not actually the very first to operate in the UK. They were one of the original big rides advertised from the opening of the Great Hall in 1926. The dodgem cars were small half barrel shaped and clearly of US design. The track was 60ft x 50ft with probably, twenty bumper cars. These were electrically powered from an overhead mesh, contact being made via a pole attached to the rear of the car with a skate making contact with the overhead powered mesh.

A most unfortunate accident occurred early in the operation of the Dodgems when a rider sustained serious head injuries after the skate became detached from the electric pole attached to the rear of the car landing on the rider's head; the East Coast Amusement Company having to pay substantial damages.

Power was probably at 100 volts DC, the return path being through the metallised track surface. It is not known how long the original cars were in use. Dodgem car development was very rapid and British manufacturers including Robert Lakin, Orton & Spooner and Supercars of Coventry had all entered the scene by the early thirties, so it seems likely the original cars would have been replaced well before the war but no photographic evidence has been found to confirm this.

Supporting side stalls included the MANCHO TABLES. Mancho was a British Games Manufacturer, well known in the twenties for games like Table Top Bowls. The Mancho fairground attraction was a Roll-A-Ball game in a cabinet resembling an early pinball machine. Launch the ball from the wood slide and it rolled around the top of the table and (hopefully) dropped into one of a series of numbered holes on its descent. It cost 2d for 3 balls and a score of 21 or more was required to win. There was Turner's MODERN DARTS ACADEMY situated close to the Dips steps. In the centre of the hall by the first aid post was The WONDERLAND MONKEYS. There were ten poles with a (toy) monkey attached, each connected by a cable to the players operating handle on the counter. Players turned the handle and the monkey climbed the pole. The first monkey to reach the top was the winner. Players needed to turn the handle as quickly and as smoothly, as possible to achieve the desired result and win the game. This required a certain amount of skill as there was a slipping clutch in the

Exciting Times Ahead!

44 & 45. The Mancho Tables and Wonderland Monkeys were two early side stall attractions in the Great Hall of Wonderland c1926.

Both: Author's Collection.

Miles of Smiles

mechanism and vigorous action resulted in the monkey falling to the bottom again. If Your Monkey Drops Down, Stop and Try Again! ROLL-A-PENNY was a self standing side stall just inside the Dock entrance to Wonderland. Players rolled a coin down a wooden chute on to a table with printed lines and squares. Land the coin within a designated pair of lines or a square to win. The circular stall had slides for up to eight players at once. Doug Best remembers the rather stout man who ran it had a kiss curl (fashionable at the time) on his forehead and was one of the characters of Wonderland. Alas, his name has been lost in the passage of time.

Another attraction from day one was a bowling alley version of the Skee Ball. The player bowled a wooden ball to the end of the alley whereupon it was launched into the air and landed in a circular target with numbered rings. The closer it landed to the centre, the greater the score and bigger the prize. It was worth remembering however, that the excitement was always greater than the reward! Another sign in the hall near the Big Dipper read MONA BALL and ELECTRIC DISC, but it is not known exactly what these were.

46. Inside the Great Hall of Wonderland shortly after its opening in 1926, looking towards the Big Dipper boarding station. The banners in the background read 'Mona-Ball' and 'Electric Disc', though it is not clear what these attractions actually are.
Sam Barnes screenshot / Classic Collection.

Exciting Times Ahead!

Also advertised for 1926 were the Flying Chairs (Chair-O-Plane), the 'New Whip' and 'Famous Bowl Slide' on the promenade. The Whip was headlined in advertising between 1926 and 1929, but may have been at Wonderland for much longer. Doug Best remembers it being in the great hall in about 1936, where it replaced the Custer Cars. The Whip (or Skid) was a ride originally designed and built by the W.F. Mangels Company of Coney Island. William F. Mangels took out a patent in 1914 and it soon became an extremely popular fairground ride. The Whip was a flat ride enclosed in a surround measuring about 60ft x 40ft. It consisted of two circular turntable platforms on opposite ends of a rectangular centre platform. Electric motors drove a cable running along the platform edge linking the turntables. Attached to the cable at regular intervals were cars, typically eight, each seating two or three persons, which ran on a laminated wooden track. The cars followed the track as the cable moved. When it reached one of the turn-table platforms, the speed picked up forcing riders to one side as the car 'whips' around to the opposite side of the platform, creating a thrilling ride.

The Hull Daily Mail for Thursday 16th June 1927 noted in its holiday revue: THE HOLIDAY SPIRIT. "Before coming to Cleethorpes many years ago, Mr Wilkie, the Managing Director of the East Coast Amusements Co., had put in several years at various prominent seaside resorts all around the coast. Upon his arrival here he made the assertion that properly advertised and by go-ahead methods on the part of the inhabitants, Cleethorpes would eventually rival the great Blackpool as a pleasure resort. From small beginnings Wilkie has become the principal of the largest firm of amusement caterers in Cleethorpes. The huge building known as "Wonderland," at the north end of the Promenade, has been brought up-to date with the latest side-shows and accommodates over 20,000 people. The "New Whip," which proved the great thrill at Wembley (the British Empire Exhibition), is situated close by; also is the latest novelty in the form of "Miniature Motors' on a miniature Brooklands. The great "Dips" with their half mile ride round Lakeland, continue to draw crowds, and on the lake dozens of youngsters can always be seen "paddling their own canoes" in perfect safety. Mr Wilkie has been prominent in the latest 'big push' to advertise Cleethorpes, and his early prophecy seems to be in a great measure coming to pass".

The above mentioned Midget Motors (sometimes referred to as Miniature Motors) were the CUSTER CARS on a miniature Brooklands race track. The Custer Electric Speedway was a smaller version of the later Speedway cars. It was the product of the Custer Speciality Company of Dayton, Ohio, and developed by American inventor and entrepreneur Levitt Luzern Custer. In about 1925, he produced a tiny car called the Cootie. It was a small battery operated two-seater, which in appearance was a miniature road car of the day, but only the size of a go-kart. A version of the Cootie fitted with spring steel bumpers and wheel surrounds was marketed as an amusement bumper car. It had instant appeal to amusement park operators because it was fitted with balloon (pneumatic) tyres, so did not require a specially prepared track. In Wonderland the Custer Cars were situated at the foot of the steps leading up to the Big Dipper. There were 20 cars. Charging the batteries was a continuous process! The ride was accompanied by a small Gavioli organ. Although not mentioned in advertising after 1930, it is likely the Custer Cars operated until the mid-thirties. When they were eventually discontinued, the organ was retained and stored in the joiners shop.

Already being known as 'Wonderland', but it was still officially THE NEW DIPS AND LAKELAND in East Coast Amusement Co advertising; the Wonderland title not coming into general use until 1928. The first mention of 'Wonderland' in advertising appeared in a small display ad' by Dearden's in the Hull Daily Mail for Wednesday 13th June 1928. "When in Wonderland, visit J. DEARDENS AMUSEMENTS: Juvenile Roundabouts, Coconut Gardens, Dart Saloon and Derby Races". Above this modest advert on the same page was the official East Coast Amusement Co. display advert, still headed THE NEW DIPS AND LAKELAND!

The Hull Daily Mail for Wednesday 13th June 1928 was lavish in its praise for Cleethorpes in its Holiday revue: "CAREFREE CLEETHORPES FOR SUN AND HEALTH. MORE ATTRACTIONS THAN EVER FOR SUMMER 1928! HOLIDAYMAKERS FINE START IN JUNE SUNSHINE. A RESORT WHERE THE VISITOR IS NOT PESTERED". The accompanying editorial read: THE ATTRACTION. "Cleethorpes is unique, in that it caters for any and every type of visitor. To enumerate, but a few of its attractions there is for those who seek downright enjoyment a wonderful choice. At the north end of the mile and half long promenade stands what is claimed to be the largest covered in amusement park the country. The Great World's Fair Exhibition at Olympia (actually, the 1924/5 British Empire Exhibition at Wembley) was combed out by Cleethorpes amusement caterers, and as ever, one can see this year mechanical novelties that have not yet been seen at any other seaside resort".

From the Hull Daily Mail 13th June 1928: "NEW DIPS AND LAKELAND: Although this is the official title of the great amusement park at the north end of the promenade, it is more popularly known as "Wonderland". The park is owned by the East Coast Amusements Co. and Mr George Wilkie, the managing director, is without doubt a man who thoroughly understands and caters for the needs and requirements of pleasure seekers".

The editorial goes on: "The latest addition to the great number of novelties owned by the company is the "Atlantic Flyer". This is the only one of its kind in the country and is the original machine exhibited at the World's Fair at Olympia (actually the British Empire Exhibition). A trip in this will well satisfy the thirst for a thrill. The "Dips" continue their popularity, and the children's boating lake is still as great attraction

Exciting Times Ahead!

as ever. In Wonderland Mr Wilkie gathers the best and latest amusements and having got them believes in letting people know all about it. Publicity pays, says he, and no one has done more for Cleethorpes in this direction than the Great Little Man".

Wonderland was the largest covered amusement centre on the East Coast and could shelter up to 20,000 people; perfect for unpredictable East Coast weather! There were three entrances off the Promenade, the centre one being the Main Entrance. A curved sign over the main entrance read "WONDERLAND Accommodation for 20.000 people under cover. Prop: G. Wilkie". This still left a large outdoor area beyond the great hall, dominated of course by New Dips. Inside the Big Dipper was the Boating Lake (Lakeland) measuring some 300ft x 80ft with a centre island. The long shed housing the Kursaal Arcade and Cafe at the end of the Promenade, dating back to about 1906 was retained, but cut back to about half its original length to make room for the re-sited Big Dipper. The other shed alongside was removed. This still leaving plenty of space for more big rides!

47. NEW DIPS AND LAKELAND: Although this is the official title of the great amusement park at the north end of the promenade, it is more popularly known as "Wonderland". Hull Daily Mail 13th June 1928. The top image shows the Atlantic Flyer from the British Empire Exhibition at Wembley, which was in Cleethorpes for the 1928 season.

East Coast Amusement Company advertising gives a good impression of the early development of Wonderland. Care however, needs to be applied in the precise interpretation of the rides as many are described as 'new' but perhaps with a subtle name change, thus appearing to be new! A list of alternative names is included in Appendix 1.

July 1926: NEW DIPS AND LAKELAND. The Famous Bowl Slide, The New Dodgems, Flying Chairs, The New Whip, Electric Scenic Railway, New Circus.

June 1927: NEW DIPS AND LAKELAND. The New Dodgems, New Whip, Famous Bowl Slide, New Midget Motors, Flying Chairs, Electric Scenic Railway.

June 1928: NEW DIPS AND LAKELAND. The New Dodgems, New Atlantic Flyer, Famous Bowl Slide, New Midget Motors, New Radio Cars, Electric Scenic Railway.

Miles of Smiles

48 & 49. The exterior of Wonderland when new with its extended canopy and traders beneath was quite different to its post-war appearance. The upper image shows the main entrance in the centre of the building shortly after opening in 1926. The lower image, the main entrance with overhead banner which read 'Wonderland. Room for 20,000 people'.
Albert Parker screenshot/Classic Collection.

Exciting Times Ahead!

June 1929: WONDERLAND. New Dips, Grand New Open Air Skating Rink, Radio Cars, New Dodgems, New Rapids, Midget Motors, Electric Scenic Railway, New Whip, New Caterpillar.

Ride notes:

1926: The New Dodgems were the electric dodgems first pioneered in the US and as such would have been amongst the first, if not actually the first, introduced to the UK. They were located at the Station end of the Great Hall. The Electric Scenic Railway would have been the big ride in the centre of the hall. It was probably a Savages fairground scenic ride, manufactured in Kings Lynn. Doug Best remembers a scenic ride being in the centre of the hall in the thirties.

1927: The New Midget Motors were probably the battery operated Custer Cars, again from the US and described elsewhere. The New Whip was located at first outside on the promenade, later moved into the Great Hall. The Famous Bowl Slide and the Flying Chairs were outside on the promenade.

1928: The Atlantic Flyer was a giant Flying Chairs roundabout previously in the funfair of the British Empire Exhibition at Wembley. It was in Cleethorpes for the 1928 season only, located outside on Pleasureland.

1929: The Grand New Open Air Skating Rink was located in the former lake which had been drained for the purpose. The New Rapids and the New Caterpillar were probably located in Pleasureland on the promenade.

The Grimsby Canine Society's Show at Cleethorpes was an interesting departure during the close season, Doug Best remembers a dog show in which his family's Collie was entered. It was held in Wonderland and staged around the dodgem track in the late twenties. The Hull Daily Mail for Friday 24th February 1928 reported: OVER FIVE HUNDRED ENTRIES. "Owing to unsuccessful efforts to secure a hall sufficiently large in Grimsby in which to hold the show, the Grimsby and District Canine Society were obliged to go to Cleethorpes. Through the courtesy of Mr Wilkie, they were able to house the dogs in "Wonderland" on the Promenade. The total entries numbered 531, and the exhibits were close upon 170. Some excellent quality exhibits were seen in all sections, particularly the Alsatians, wire-haired Fox Terriers, Pekingese and most of the variety classes. The Great Dane class was an outstanding feature and although the competition was limited to fewer entries, the quality was as good as seen in most open shows".

Perhaps the Children's Lakeland with its tiny paddle boats was not as successful as had been hoped, for the lake was converted to 'OPEN AIR ROLLER SKATING!' The Hull Daily Mail for Wednesday 19th June 1929 in its Sunny Coast Resort review writes of Councillor George Wilkie, Managing Director of the East Coast Amusements Company at Cleethorpes. "He has, as usual, games that are novel this season. It is very seldom that "Wonderland" opens for the season without something original being introduced. Visitors will find complete transformation this year in that the Lake has

> **MIKADO CAFE, Wonderland, CLEETHORPES.**
>
> VISIT THE QUICK LUNCH BUFFET.
> LARGE OR SMALL PARTIES CATERED FOR.
>
> TAKE TRIPS ON THE SPEED BOATS & SEA CARS

50. The Mikado Cafe. Sheffield Evening Telegraph 28th June 1930

been converted into a huge open air roller skating rink which is claimed to be the largest of its kind in the country, a special composition floor has been laid at great cost and is said to be equal to ice".

"Other novelties have been introduced in this enormous encased amusement park which will accommodate 20,000 people. The 'Dips' with its half-mile of thrills is acknowledged to be one of the finest rides in the country and it is commonly heard that only the original "Wembley" ride could equal it (a reference to the giant roller coaster at the British Empire Exhibition fun fair of 1924/5). Since Mr Wilkie's return to Cleethorpes just over six years ago, the amusement park has changed beyond recognition. He is a great advocate of newspaper publicity and was one of the founders of the Cleethorpes Advancement Association and its first President, an office which he holds at the present time".

The Boston Guardian for Saturday 10th August 1929 carried a short piece, typical of its time:

20.000 EXCURSIONISTS AT CLEETHORPES. "Over twelve thousand visitors arrived at Cleethorpes at the weekend and over twenty thousand excursionists took advantage of the Bank Holiday trips. Conditions on Saturday were depressing, for the day was cold and showery and at night there was a persistent downpour. Sunday was brighter, but the weather could not be described as genial. There was a heavy run on all indoor amusements, and the Wonderland covered amusement park was refuge for hundreds of holiday-makers on Saturday. On Monday the weather opened badly, but conditions later were much better".

In an advert dated 28th June 1930, the Wonderland quick lunch buffet referred to previously, was named as the Mikado Cafe, situated within the great hall of Wonderland where both large and small parties are catered for. It also suggested holiday makers take trips on the Speed Boats and Sea Cars.

The scene was now set for all the fun of the fair!

Exciting Times Ahead!

CLEETHORPES
THE IDEAL SEASIDE HOLIDAY RESORT.

Some Impressions of Cleethorpes in the Twenties:

Without doubt, the best impression of Cleethorpes in the Twenties comes from 'Babette', lady reporter of the Hull Daily Mail who wrote in glowing terms of her visit to Cleethorpes in the Friday 9th August 1929 edition, reproduced here in full.

Babette: Round the Resorts

"Babette, lady reporter for the Hull Daily Mail makes her annual summer visit to East Coast resorts in high season and visits Cleethorpes. Much of what she describes is outside the scope of this book, but it provides a refreshing impression of Cleethorpes in the summer of 1929, so is reproduced here in full. Her journey starts at Corporation Pier in Hull where she boards the Humber ferry to New Holland. Her train is waiting for the journey to Cleethorpes. The Humber ferry service between New Holland and Hull was established by the Manchester, Sheffield & Lincolnshire Railway in 1848. It would appear she travelled by normal service train, rather than a seaside special, hence the change of train at Grimsby.

Hull Daily Mail Friday 9th August 1929

> *AROUND THE RESORTS: "BABETTE" PAYS HER SUMMER VISITS. CLEETHORPES AND ITS MANY ATTRACTIONS. If you have never been to Cleethorpes, the seaside resort where it does not matter if it rains, then you ought to go, because you will find a great many things to amuse. In fact, I think if you have not been, your education has been sadly neglected. The journey there is not a difficult one, although it is certainly a little crowded. Still at holiday times, we don't mind crowds, do we? I went over on Thursday morning and found quite a crowd at the Pier awaiting their turn on the boats and as it was a most delightful morning with fresh breeze blowing across the river, had an excellent trip on the ferry and landed well in time on the opposite side, New Holland. As they have got the bridge finished now, the train was waiting to take us along, and before we could get in a carriage the people were getting into the first class carriages and*

where else they could. We had to stand until we reached Grimsby, and then got out to change on to the Cleethorpes train. The platform was crowded and kiddies have a habit of going near the edge of the platform, which makes my blood run cold. I was very relieved when one young mother with four little ones caught the one child who was rather too venturesome, and brought him back to safety by the scruff of his neck, saying, "Albert, I'll clip you," she did! The train steamed and we jostled into carriages about twenty at time, kiddies had to be nursed and the rest had to stand if they did not procure seats quickly.

ORDERLY CROWDS. I was rather surprised that the people did not bring tuck baskets out as soon as we had started. My experience of excursions generally, is that as soon as the train starts, it is a signal that every child in the carriage is hungry, and then for the rest of the journey one dodges crumbs and sticky lemonade bottles. No, there was nothing of that. It was a most respectable trip. One does not have to go far in Cleethorpes to see the fun. The sands can be viewed as you arrive into the station, and then out you step and you are practically on the beach. The sea front must be miles long, and the pavement, and roads are both wide, with a huge kerb stone, which people sit on. The sea was right out; in fact, it looked at first as it had disappeared altogether. It goes nearly a mile out. The sand from the promenade to the water is very gently sloping and that is why kiddies can play there all day with absolute safety. It is one of the ideal spots for children, and the sand, as I remarked once before when I went over, stays where is put. I can recommend it for kiddies who are anxious to make sand pies, castles, or dugouts.

THE FUN OF THE FAIR. Along the front or the one side you will find ample amusement. It is like a fair ground, with every description of game, side show and joy ride you can think of. As it happened, it was a gorgeous day with the sun shining up in the sky and no wind, but had it been otherwise, the place they call Wonderland is aptly named, because it affords both shelter and amusement. All along front the people were wearing paper hats. Most of them were shaped after the style of Captain's aboard ship and very smart they looked on those whom they fitted. Some of the young men though, who had just left school were wearing them, and was a case 'Come out, can see our feet!' They certainly came well over their ears. Still, they all enjoyed themselves immensely, and there is no end of fun in watching the crowds pass without actually participating yourself.

THE PRICE OF A MEAL. Each side you look, on the North Side there is amusements and after I had taken lunch I found that I had been extravagant, because there are such a lot of eating-houses along the front, where you can get a real "spread" at giving away prices. For instance, I could have bad a plate of peas and chips for 4d and finished with two penny worth of sea foam candy for

Exciting Times Ahead!

a sweet. I ought to have thought of this sooner. I would have saved money. In the town, as I wandered through, leaving the fun fair for a while, I noticed that every taste is catered for, and there are rows and rows of shops where almost anything can be purchased. Let us start on a row of them. Here is an oyster shop. They are selling bags of shrimps, too and I believe, winkles. Next to it they are buying paper hats of every hue, buckets and spades. A cafe takes precedence next, and a man outside shouts that you can have beef or lamb, chicken or duck, with green peas and new potatoes Walk right in, there's plenty of room! He points invitingly to a blackboard upon which a menu is indicated. Everything looks good and the crowds break up, some going in whilst others go further down the road. Next comes a sparkle from a jewellers shop window where you buy all sorts of knick-knacks to take home. A rock stall with bars of huge dimensions comes next, whilst ornaments of every hue can be bought next door, each bearing the inscription 'A Present from Cleethorpes'.

THE BATHING POOL. There is, of course, an excellent tram and bus service and Grimsby is soon reached. The farther you go to the south end, of course, the prettier the surroundings become. We reached the bathing lake in time for the pantomime of the afternoon, and I don't think I have laughed so much for ages. This bathing pool, one of the largest in England is excellently equipped. There is ample room for spectators, both to sit comfortably and to promenade. A band plays from alcove and dainty afternoon teas are served. Costumes can be hired of course and fun begins. There is a shallow end of six inches for children, whilst a deep end offers facilities for the swimmer.

Further along the boating lake is a great attraction, and a very pretty one it is. By it there is children's corner, where they can sail boats and bathe and have really a good time. The lake is to be enlarged, and when finished will make a tremendous trip whereon many a pleasant hour may be enjoyed.

INFORMATION AT ONCE. Cleethorpes possesses an Information Bureau, which is situated in Grant Street, and is of untold help to visitors and residents alike. Mr Leonard Atkinson, the manager and secretary, has staff who like himself are most obliging answer questions of every description with civility and patience. You can book here for anywhere, including London. Mr Atkinson took me round and we were in time to see the London bus which had just come in, depositing its load of passengers. It would surprise many people to know just how many visitors arrive daily from London and the South coast. I had a chat with Councillor G. Wilkie and his wife. I found them by the switchback (New Dips), which they own. This by the way, is one of the finest switchbacks in England and I can guarantee a thrill for whoever tries it. I went on. I had been once before and screamed almost from the start the finish. It is lovely and almost takes your breath. I am sure Councillor Wilkie had never had one so noisy on it before. I went into several shows and thoroughly enjoyed myself. Cleethorpes is improving every year and one thing I noticed in particular was the clear Market Place. It used be crowded with buses taking people round the town. Now the market people can trade with comfort.

THE SEA CAR. One of the sights Cleethorpes, which is not seen in many places, is the sea car. These are like boats on wheels. They pick passengers up in the town and take them round, then go down to the sands and driving out to the sea, take to the water like a duck takes to it and by some mechanical device the mechanism is taken from the wheels to another part of the boat, and you go for a sail. When the allotted time is up, it just goes on land again and deposits people in the town. They are really great and your visit will not be complete without a turn on these sea-cars.

THE PIER. The pier holds a concert hall and dance place and young people take every chance of these amusements.

I am just wondering if I have left anything out which I wanted to tell you. I must thank Mr L. Atkinson for his kindness and information. After finding a nice little cafe for tea it was nearly time to get home and was advisable to get to the station in good time, because of the crowds in Cleethorpes. We were fairly comfortable and then a large family entered. Two of the children must have known that I have a prize corn, for they scored a bull's eye every time! I really didn't like to say what I was thinking, but my advice is if you have feet blessed with corns tuck them under the seat, by far the safest way. When we eventually got to the boat we found that a train had been in before us and practically filled it. Still, they did eventually pack us all together, with cars and motor bikes and heaps of buckets and spades and tired little mites. There was a cry on the slope down to the boat 'Where's our 'Erb?' Erb was eventually unearthed from between two ladies with an overweight of avoirdupois, between whom he had got wedged. The ladies concerned glared at each other, and the crowd proceeded. One chap fell down, and several other children being dragged along by irate parents couldn't stop and they fell over him, which did not help matters. As he picked himself up he bumped his head on a portable gramophone a man was carrying – don't people enjoy a trip out? For a real good, jolly time, or holiday for the kiddies, this place on the East Coast takes a lot of beating. It has ample indoor amusements, as well as the open air. Cleethorpes is jolly place and one which is easy to remember!"

Chapter Six

THE NORTH PROMENADE BETWEEN THE WARS

The 1920's:

By the early twenties holiday traffic had returned to pre-war levels but the country was still in difficult times, and the great depression had yet to come. Nevertheless, developments and improvements to the resort were ongoing and prosperous times lay ahead.

On the North Promenade came the transition from the first generation of rides and attractions that were state of the art at the turn of the century, into a more dynamic mechanical and automatic age. George Wilkie had transformed the open land at the end of the North Promenade into Wonderland during the winter of 1925/6 and the conversion of the Joy Wheel into Hancock's Palace of Pleasure had radically developed amusements on the foreshore around the same time. Still operational on the sands in the early twenties was the Victorian Switchback Railway, but the Figure 8 at the end of the promenade (which dated back to 1908) had been dismantled as a result of the new Wonderland development and the relocating of the Dip the Dips roller coaster, now New Dips.

The Switchback (probably) again made the news for all the wrong reasons when both the Nottingham Evening Post and the Sheffield Daily Telegraph on Tuesday 2nd June 1925 reported an accident on the Switchback at Cleethorpes: "SWITCHBACK COLLISION. Seven holiday-makers from Leicester had an alarming experience on a pleasure railway of the switchback type yesterday at Cleethorpes. Seven holiday makers were injured, one seriously, when the car in which they were riding was descending the incline with a rush and an empty car, failing to mount the hill in front, ran backwards. The two cars crashed in the hollow and were wrecked. Several of the passengers were flung out on to the track".

Hancock's Pleasure Palace,
NORTH PROMENADE.
(PROPRIETORS: J. R. HANCOCK & SON, LTD.)
Amusement Caterers & Manufacturing Confectioners.

JOLLY BOATS, SWINGS, FISH PONDS, RACING CYCLES, GAMES, Etc. :: REFRESHMENTS, ICES. ACCOMMODATION FOR LARGE OR SMALL PARTIES. COVERED-IN PORTION OF SANDS FOR WET WEATHER. AN IDEAL PLAYGROUND FOR CHILDREN.

When you come out of the Station look for the White Dome.

51. Sheffield Daily Telegraph 26th June 1930

Judging by the reference to 'descending the incline with a rush' and of a car in front, it is not entirely clear whether this was actually on the Victorian Switchback Railway, believed still operational at the time, or the Dip the Dips roller coaster opposite. Neither is it clear when the Switchback Railway was actually taken out of use as there are no further references to it. The above incident, if it was indeed the Switchback (it most likely was, as the injuries reported appear not to be serious enough to be from the faster Dip the Dips), then it would have been its death knell as by 1925 it had become outdated and superseded by more thrilling rides. The Switchback was however, the first big ride at Cleethorpes and much loved by holidaymakers for more than 30 years.

Along the entire promenade facade of the new Wonderland building was a canopy extension of the vaulted roof providing shelter, beneath which was a variety of fancy goods traders, ice cream vendors, rock sellers and the like. The canopy was there throughout the thirties but not after the war, so was probably removed as part of the wartime scrap metal recovery drive.

The open promenade frontage extending to about 320ft between Wonderland and the Auckland Colonnade had already become known as Pleasureland. It was a very dynamic area of fairground rides and attractions managed by the East Coast Amusement Company (Wonderland). Changing frequently, there is still much to

The North Promenade between the Wars

52. Hull Daily Mail 18th June 1930

discover about the rides and attractions on this part of the promenade, many of which were owned by independent fairground operators and present for short periods only.

Next to Wonderland on the Pleasureland site was the Fairy River, mentioned in the Great Central Railway Journal in 1906. This was an open fronted attraction, the oldest on the promenade. A display advertisement in the Thursday 9th July 1925 edition of the Hull Daily Mail read "DON'T FAIL TO TAKE A CRUISE ON THE ORIGINAL FAIRY RIVER (Cleethorpes Promenade): Half-a-mile trip amid Beautiful Scenery, Wonderful Dells and Mystic Caverns. The River has been running for the past 23 years. NO DANGER WHATEVER". The accompanying editorial continued: "It is claimed of the Fairy River at Cleethorpes that it was the first of its kind, and this is quite possible, for it has been running for 23 years. The entrance is very pretty". The advertisement included an image of its very elaborate promenade frontage. Doug Best recalls, as a youngster with his friend in about 1933, exploring the Fairy River with torches during the winter close season. The water had been drained and they discovered numerous large rats!

Close to the Fairy River in the late twenties was the Sunrise Cafe and a Chair-O-Plane (Flying Chairs) roundabout. Next was Lawrence Wright's music booth with live music being played throughout the day. Blackpool based Lawrence Wright was perhaps the most popular song writer, publisher and music entrepreneur of his day. He created song booths at seaside resorts as a way of marketing his work. Each booth had a full time pianist and a compere to encourage people to enter, sing along and purchase his latest song book or song sheets. Doug remembers they sold song sheets for 6d! The New Rapids, next to Lawrence Wright was advertised for the first time in 1929.

By the early thirties in a dynamic and rapidly changing situation, the Flying Chairs had been replaced by a Big Eli Wheel (mentioned in East Coast Amusement

Miles of Smiles

DON'T FAIL TO TAKE A CRUISE ON THE ORIGINAL FAIRY RIVER
(Cleethorpes Promenade),
Half-a-mile Trip Amid Beautiful Scenery, Wonderful Dells and Mystic Caverns.
The River has been running for the past 25 years.
NO DANGER WHATEVER.

53. The Fairy River. Hull Daily Mail Thursday 9th July 1925

54. Pleasureland. This superb postcard image of the North Promenade in the thirties shows on the left, the kitchen end of the Auckland Colonnade. The white kiosk next is Lawrence Wright's music booth, then a Flying Chairs roundabout, the Sunrise Cafe and the Fairy River. The full proportions of the giant Wonderland building become very apparent in this view, which clearly shows the canopy extension on the promenade side of the building. On the beach to the right, the former Switchback Railway boarding station has been converted into toilets.

Author's collection.

The North Promenade between the Wars

55. *The North Promenade in the early thirties with the Skee Roll arcade, Big Eli-Wheel, Sunrise Cafe and Fairy River. Wonderland is in the extreme right.*

Author's Collection

Co advertisements), together with other big rides and amusements. There was a Skee Roll arcade. The Skee Ball was another variation of the Roll-A-Ball similar to the one inside Wonderland mentioned earlier. Patented in 1909 in the US, it was a ramp that could be set up in arcades and amusement parks, a kind of primitive bowling alley that allowed players to bowl a wooden ball up a ramp and into a hole with a pre-assigned point value. It was dubbed Skee-Ball after the Skee (Ski) Hills.

Smalley's Restaurant, occupying most of the Auckland Colonnade, was a long established feature of the North Promenade. The following is an edited extract from the Hull Daily Mail Holiday Review, dated Thursday 8th July 1926:

"SMALLY'S RESTAURANT. The name of "Smalley" conveys much to the regular visitor to Cleethorpes. The establishment occupies a frontage of 200 feet and abuts the Promenade at the north end. So far as liquid refreshment is concerned, only the finest beers and wines are served, also mineral waters. Without doubt, more people are catered for at the "Colonnade" than any other establishment. Parties of 100 to 1,500 are served with equal dispatch, the new tea room alone seating 600. The whole of the staff are under the personal supervision of Mrs Margaret Smalley and nothing is left

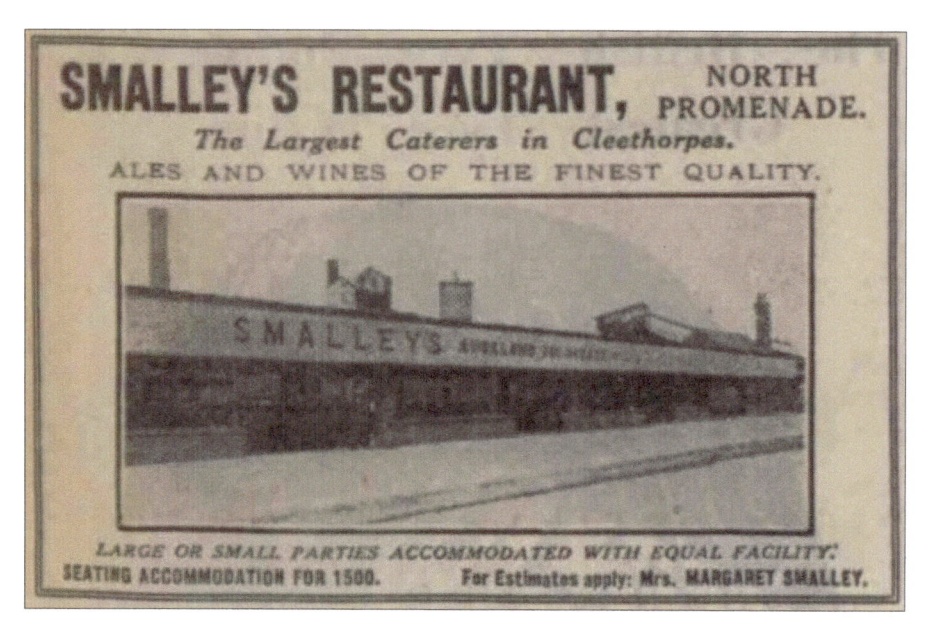

SMALLEY'S RESTAURANT, NORTH PROMENADE.
The Largest Caterers in Cleethorpes.
ALES AND WINES OF THE FINEST QUALITY.

LARGE OR SMALL PARTIES ACCOMMODATED WITH EQUAL FACILITY.
SEATING ACCOMMODATION FOR 1500.   For Estimates apply: Mrs. MARGARET SMALLEY.

56. Smalley's Restaurant. Sheffield Daily Telegraph 26th June 1930

undone that might add to the comfort of visitors. Meals are served at any hour of the day and prices are most reasonable. Intending parties should write for terms and other information to Mrs Margaret Smalley, The Colonnade, Cleethorpes". The Auckland Colonnade extended for over 300ft along the Promenade.

Back to the promenade, and on the beach opposite was the site of the former Switchback Railway, now demolished, but with the station building on the sands still intact converted to public conveniences. A short distance further on is the Rifle Range (with moving targets). This later became the Monkey House, a big green shed on stilts on the sands. Next to it was the Lighthouse Helter Skelter; there were swings, slides and kiosks on the seaward side of the Promenade including Tommy Atkins Hard Rock stall, Hancock's Electric Fish Pond and Hancock's Sea Foam Candy (candy floss). The Joy Wheel attraction had been short lived and by 1920 this massive pier like structure, extending a short distance from the promenade over the sands to almost the high tide line had been converted to form Hancock's Palace of Pleasure.

Hancock's Beach Amusements & Palace of Pleasure c1920 – 1939:

HANCOCK'S PALACE OF PLEASURE was the transformation of the former Joy Wheel situated on the foreshore and was a long standing feature of the North Promenade. Its exact opening date is obscure, but a photograph taken from the construction site of the Theatre Royal in 1920 overlooking the North Promenade shows quite clearly the former

The North Promenade between the Wars

Joy Wheel structure with 'Jolly Boats' in large letters emblazed around the roof line. It was later enlarged and extended with a cafe facing the Humber estuary. The Palace of Pleasure was first mentioned in newspaper advertising in 1925.

The following description is an amalgam of pre-war Holiday Reviews published in the Hull Daily Mail:

"HANCOCK S PLEASURE PALACE. There's Hancock's! It was a cry often heard as the trains steam into Cleethorpes and visitors have good cause to remember the happy hours they have spent in the Palace of Pleasure. The Jolly Boats are always a popular amusement, and the electric fish ponds and various automatic games also are

57. The sands looking towards the station in the 1930's. The Monkey House on the right was the former Rifle Range on the promenade. It had live animals which would have been a rare opportunity for the folk of the day to see. By the early thirties, a second Helter Skelter had appeared on the beach. This was known as 'Hawkey's Lighthouse Helter Skelter'. It had two tracks so riders could race each other down from the top! Behind the Helter Skelters is Hancock's Palace of Pleasure (the former Joy Wheel), seen in the distance.
Author's Collection

HANCOCK'S

THE ORIGINAL SEA FOAM CANDY MAN

SPECIAL 1936 OFFER

To all our patrons, born in 1936 and previously.
GREAT " COME-TO-CLEETHORPES " OFFER

1/- LUNCHES   1/- TEAS

The only Real 1/- Meal on the Promenade. Covered Accommodation on the sands for over 1,000 children. All the latest games and beach amusements.

THE PALACE OF PLEASURE CAFE

HANCOCK'S for Value, Service and Civility

58. Hancock's. Hull Daily Mail 22nd May 1936

well patronised. The Promenade Cafe, which directly overlooks the sea, is situated on the far side, and underneath the building is the "Kiddies' Paradise," where hundreds of youngsters are to be seen digging and frolicking whilst their parents enjoy themselves in the Palace. The old original "Palace of Pleasure" stands on the foreshore at the north end of the front and is easily picked out from anywhere along the beach by reason of its white dome. Every season Hancock's amusements are brought up to date. The famous "jolly boats" again occupy the centre of the palace, whilst a host of new mechanical novelties have been introduced. The promenade cafe, which runs round the building on the east side overlooking the sea, has been extended and improved during the winter (1927) and no more pleasant a spot can be found to enjoy an afternoon cup of tea. In the cafe which surrounds the building, one can enjoy refreshment whilst obtaining an uninterrupted view of the river with its ever-changing panorama of shipping. It has seating for 120 persons. Music is provided by means of loud speakers situated in various parts of the cafe. Children are especially catered for and miniature aerial flyers, etc., have been erected. Underneath the palace over 1,000 kiddies may find amusement and shelter should the weather prove showery. It is seldom that the children care to leave the Palace once they have seen the fine array amusements provided. The family of Hancock (J.R. Hancock & Son Ltd) has been in the same business for a great many years and none understand the visitors' requirements more than they". Advertisements'

The North Promenade between the Wars

HANCOCK'S
FAMOUS
BEACH AMUSEMENTS
NORTH PROMENADE

The "Palace of Pleasure"
is situate on the Sands nearly opposite the Station

Extensive COVERED-IN AREA provides an ideal Playground for the Children in inclement weather

•

CAFÉ OVERLOOKING SEA   **SPECIAL 1/- FISH TEAS**

PARTIES CATERED FOR

CLEANLINESS, CIVILITY, SERVICE—**OUR MOTTO**

•

Proprietors - - **J. R. HANCOCK & SON, LTD.**

Regd. Office : "Kandylea," Elm Road, Cleethorpes

59. Fish Teas for a shilling! Hancock's Palace of Pleasure 1939.
Author's Collection.

Miles of Smiles

also reminded visitors that Mr J.R. Hancock was the original Sea Foam Candy (candy floss) man and sea front ice cream seller.

Attractions at Hancock's included the Jolly Boats, Swing Boats, Racing Cycles (Bicycle Railway Roundabout), Fish Ponds and various Juvenile rides: Yachts, Chair-O-Planes, Aeroplanes and Flying Fish, most of these being on the sands adjacent. The covered portion of sands for wet weather was largely that underneath the Palace of Pleasure itself. In 1936, the Balcony Cafe was offering Luncheons and Teas for one shilling (5p). In 1937, 1938 & 1939, the offering was Fish Tea's, again for a shilling.

Located at many spots along the seafront and sands were the kiosks and stalls of BROWN'S SEASIDE ROCK. They advertised regularly from 1926. The Hull Daily Mail for Thursday 8th July 1926 included in its Holiday Review: "CLEETHORPES ROCK. The favourite sweet-meat at the seaside is undoubtedly 'rock' and at Cleethorpes, with very few exceptions, the retailers are supplied by H. B. Brown and Son. Messrs Brown's factory is situated in Victor-street, Grimsby, and it is a model of hygiene and cleanliness. Each boiling of sugar is poured on the cooling plates and as soon as firm enough to handle is pulled by special machinery until white as snow. A portion of this is coloured with pure vegetable colouring and used for the outer cover and letters. As the years roll on so does the reputation of the oldest established firm who specialise in Cleethorpes Rock improve. Visitors are always assured of a clean, wholesome and newly made sweet-meat when purchasing at Brown's. From early morning to late at night the model factory is turning out thousand after thousand sticks of rock in sizes from the kiddies' soother to the giant family stick. This is often rushed down to the promenade on exceptionally busy days and is on its way home in somebody's pocket before it has had time to cool. The management of the business is still in the hands of Mr Fred Brown, and other members of the family superintend in various departments. If you must have rock, be sure it is Brown's".

On 19th June 1929, the Hull Daily Mail announced: "BROWN'S MODEL ROCK FACTORY. A novelty that is to be introduced in Cleethorpes this year is a model 'Rock' factory. This scheme has long been in the mind of Mr Fred Brown, who is general manager of B. Brown & Son. There is no secret in the making, none is claimed, and visitors will be able to witness the entire process of conversion from sacks of sugar into various sized sticks of sweet-meat. Demonstrations at Frequent Intervals Daily". Brown's Model Rock Factory was located in a long narrow building next to the railway tracks behind the Empire Colonnade. Access to it was through a narrow passageway between the Empire Colonnade and Brown's Seaside Rock shop on the Promenade. When in full operation, it was staffed by about a dozen women and four men making the traditional seaside delight. Visitors could see the whole process of rolling both large and small sticks and one of the men explained how 'Cleethorpes' was made to read through the length of the rock!

ROCK! ROCK! ROCK!
BUY FROM THE MAKERS,
H. B. BROWN AND SON,
Established 1881.   Prop.: F. C. BROWN.

The Only Firm in Cleethorpes that Can Supply Any Quantity at Any Time.

ONLY THE FINEST INGREDIENTS USED.   GUARANTEED PURE.

BE SURE AND VISIT THE WORKING EXHIBITION ON THE PROMENADE.

Works: **98, VICTOR STREET,**
TEL. 3501 GRIMSBY; 143 CLEETHORPES.

60. Rock! Rock! Rock! Sheffield Independent 1st June 1933

There was a SEAFRONT BUS SERVICE operating from 1925. An account by Norman Drewry, reproduced in Cleethorpes & District Remembered by Brian Leonard reads: "In 1925 the Provincial Tramway Company started a seafront bus service along the promenade at Cleethorpes. It started at the northern end of the promenade (Wonderland) and ran along the promenade until it reached the Brighton Street slipway, then joined the Kingsway and terminated at the Bathing Pool. It operated at Easter, Whit Bank Holiday and then week-ends until the summer season began, when it ran daily". See appendix 6 for the full account.

RIDE THE SEA CARS: Another transport feature of pre-war Cleethorpes was the use of amphibious vehicles to take holidaymakers for a ride along the sands and into the sea for a short trip. This was particularly appealing at low tide when the sea could be some distance out from the promenade.

Norman Drewry continued: "What really caught my eye were four motor boats mounted on wheels. When they were fully laden they drove into the sea and when the water was deep enough, the propeller took over propulsion from the wheels. These amphibious vehicles usually plied for trade on the sands opposite the railway station. When the tide was out people had a long ride on the sands and a much shorter sea trip. They were built on a Ford lorry chassis and were called Floating Charabancs. Cleethorpes was the first resort to use them. The oldest one dated from 1925. As far as I know, none survived the war".

Miles of Smiles

The Floating Charabancs were, in appearance, large rowing boats on road wheels holding about a dozen passengers. Film footage of them in action shows the rear axle to have been modified with an extra shaft emerging from the rear with a propeller attached to it. When in the water, this could be engaged as an 'extra' gear. The radiator always seemed to boiling, the appearance at first glance giving the impression it was steam powered!

The 1930's:

A new attraction at Cleethorpes for the 1930 & 1931 seasons was Cripsey's motor cycle Wall of Death. It was included in Wonderland newspaper advertising as Death Riders in 1930 and Drome of Death in 1931. The Cripsey family were local to Cleethorpes, so this may have been a joint promotion between Roy Cripsey and George Wilkie. The Wall of Death was situated on the Pleasureland site of open ground, close to the Wonderland building.

The Cripsey wall was 32ft diameter and about 20ft high. There was seating for 150 to 200 people provided at the top of the wall so the audience could look down into the ring. Outside the wall was a platform with rollers, on which the riders demonstrated their machines as a way to draw folk in. "HELL RIDERS! They Defy Gravity And Death!" The motor cycles were Indian Scout 600cc V-twin machines manufactured by the Indian Motor Cycle Company in the USA from 1920-1927. The Wall of Death model had a seat mounted on the handlebars, with leg supports on either side of the front

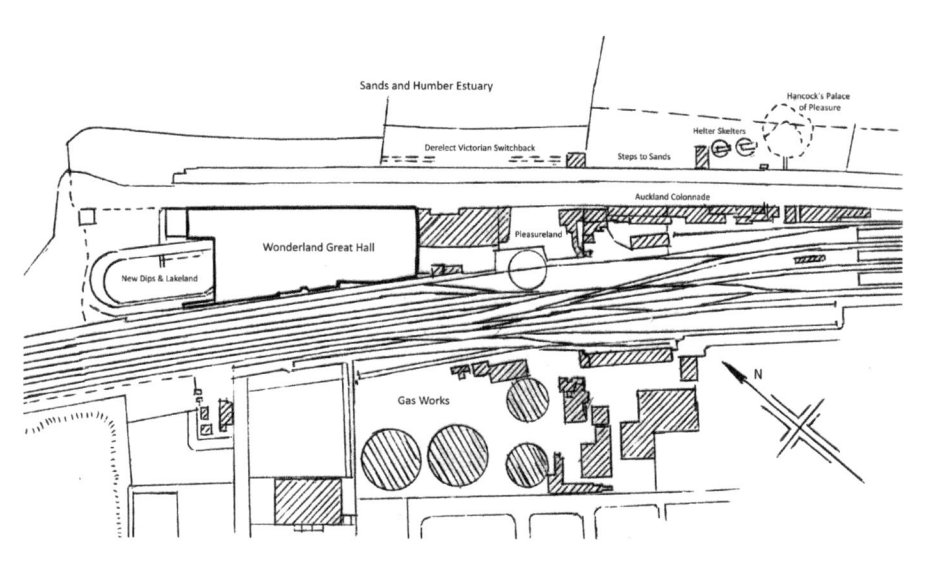

61. Cleethorpes North Promenade c1933.

Sketch by Chris Dibben.

The North Promenade between the Wars

wheel, for a daredevil passenger. A typical programme would be of around 30 minutes duration with about five acts demonstrating horizontal riding on a near vertical wall.

Accidents were remarkably few, but the Hull Daily Mail on Wednesday 11th June 1930 reported: "WALL OF DEATH CRASH. RIDER'S ATTEMPT TO AVOID WOMAN'S HAND. Two of the riders in the Wall of Death (in which motor-cyclists ride round the perpendicular walls of a deep pit) were injured at Cleethorpes on Tuesday. Their announcer, Ellis Williams, and a Mrs Warrington, a visitor from Leeds, were also hurt. Arthur Towers, one of the riders, swerved in his course to avoid Mrs Warrington's hand, which was hanging over the lip of the pit, and crashed to the bottom, on top of George Pollard, the second rider, and the announcer. Towers received wrist injuries, bruises, and concussion, Pollard a lacerated elbow, Williams injuries to head and back, and Mrs Warrington a torn hand".

The Sheffield Daily Telegraph on Thursday 26th June 1930 said of Cleethorpes: "ATTRACTIONS AT CLEETHORPES. There are few seaside resorts that cater more adequately for visitors than Cleethorpes, and the attractions that are provided appeal to all classes of the community. To both old and young the north end of the Promenade and foreshore makes a decided appeal because of the countless forms of amusement that are provided. At this point stands what is claimed to be one of the largest covered-in amusement parks in the country, known to visitors as "Wonderland". Accommodation is provided for upwards of 20,000 people, and one can spend a whole day among the latest mechanical novelties including Switchbacks, Dodgems, Mystic Caves, etc. On the foreshore, at the north end there is erected a huge Palace of Pleasure, where again both youngsters and up grown people can enjoy the exhilarating joy rides, aerial railways and innumerable other devices that provide thrills and enjoyment".

In the 1930's fairground, the big rides such as the Cake Walk, Gallopers and Scenic Rides, were either steam driven or powered by electricity generated from a steam engine. Doug Best remembers a pair of Steam Yachts operating for a while at the very end of the North Promenade.

He also remembers a couple of redundant steam engines being dumped out of use and stored under the Wonderland Big Dipper close to the railway at about the same time. These were the factual basis of Barney's Tale (see chapter 15).

The 1932 season came to a close on Sunday 18th September, but during the early hours of the following morning, a fire was discovered which completely destroyed the historic Golden Dragons scenic Ark ride which dated back to 1913, together with its organ. It had been operating on the open air Pleasureland fairground site on the North Promenade, between the Auckland Colonnade and Wonderland. The Sheffield Daily Telegraph reported the incident in its Tuesday 20th September 1932 issue: "CLEETHORPES FIRE. Steam Roundabout Destroyed in Amusement Park. Early yesterday a steam roundabout was destroyed by fire in the amusement park on the

Miles of Smiles

Cleethorpes Promenade. The roundabout was owned by Mrs Harniess, the wife of the well known travelling showman, and with its destruction went an electrically-driven organ which cost £2,000. The fire was discovered by Police-constable Hill, who was patrolling the promenade. The Cleethorpes Fire Brigade, who were quickly on the scene, had a difficult task which lasted some three hours. There was little chance of saving the structure and the firemen concentrated their efforts in preventing the fire from spreading to adjoining stands. Fortunately, there was little wind, otherwise the outbreak might have been serious, for the firemen were handicapped by a shortage of water. Mrs Harniess, who was in Doncaster, was yesterday summoned to Cleethorpes". It seems a cruel irony that the efforts of the fire fighters should be hampered by a lack of water on the promenade seafront!

The 1933 OS Map shows two Helter Skelters on the beach. The second one was known as Hawkey's Lighthouse Helter Skelter. It had two tracks so riders could race each other down from the top! Next to the Helter Skelters was Hancock's Palace of Pleasure (admission free!).

One of the characters of the North Promenade was 'Two Stick Charlie'. Charlie

62. Hawkey's Capitol Cafe with Walter West's Humber Automatic Exhibition on the left. In between is the railway access passage. On the right are the promenade toilets.
Albert Parker screenshot/Classic Collection.

The North Promenade between the Wars

Holmes lived near St Aiden's Church in Cleethorpes and frequented the North Promenade and Wonderland, dancing with his sticks, entertaining the crowds of holiday-makers. He wore a flat cap and plus fours, and was well known in Wonderland for dancing on the steps of the electric scenic, and for throwing his sticks at boys who tormented him!

The Hull Daily Mail, always a champion of Cleethorpes, in its Thursday 30th May 1935 Holiday Review wrote: "FUN CENTRES. Even if you have a sour disposition, a visit to Hancock's Amusements will cure you. You are sure to leave troubles behind and emerge with a smiling face and sweet contentment of mind. Have a trip on the Jolly Boats, or dash round on the Racing Cycles, and forget your little worries. Hancock's is a good place for the children, too, and there is covered accommodation on the sands for about a thousand youngsters. A feature on the North Promenade, which attracts the attention of sportsmen, young and old, is J. Dearden's amusement centre (in Wonderland). There, there is something to suit everybody. All along the promenade the Humber automatic machines are to be seen, and cause endless fun and amusement to visitors. The latest game, Varsity Hockey, is quite new to the East Coast".

Continuing towards the station, next to the Auckland Colonnade were the promenade public toilets and next to them, Hawkey's Capitol Cafe & Restaurant. Between the Capitol Cafe and Walter West's Humber Automatic Exhibition was the railway access passage off the promenade. West's Humber Automatic Arcade was first mentioned in the advertisement accompanying the editorial in the Hull Daily Mail above, "Come and try your skill on the latest pin tables and automatic machines. New Varsity Hockey game is proving very popular".

A film record shot by Albert Parker (local Chemist and Photographic Dealer) of the North Promenade in the thirties shows crowds on the sands and a Punch & Judy show in progress opposite the station. An Escapologist performs for the crowds untangling himself from being tied up in chains whilst hanging upside down! Ice cream, seaside rock and fish & chips are clearly big business! Opposite, on the Promenade is the impressive Brown's Rock Shop. Along its roof line is painted 'H.B. Brown & Son. The Largest Rock Manufacturer on the East Coast'. Above the Empire Colonnade is 'Useful Presents' and 'Sweets & Chocolates'. The Empire Colonnade of shops was a large wooden structure but by the thirties, was no longer a Colonnade as its original frontage had been replaced with a canopy. Hawkey's Premier Cafe & Restaurant is close by together with the 'SPOT. EM' amusement booth. Painted on its gable uprights is 'The Most Interesting Game on the Promenade'. SPOT.EM was probably a game where the aim was to land a token completely over a square. At that time there were various other Gifts & Fancy Goods shops and Brown's Model Rock Factory behind the promenade buildings. Closer to the station was Hardy's Ice Cream stall. "You scream and I scream; we all scream for Hardy's ice cream!" Their factory was in Hamilton Street, Grimsby.

Miles of Smiles

The North Promenade between the Wars

63 to 72. Impressions of the North Promenade in the Thirties.
Albert Parker screenshots /Classic Collection.

63. The Empire Colonnade near the station with Spot 'Em amusement booth.
64. Sea Cars operating from the sands opposite Hawkey's Premier Cafe.
65. 'Two Stick Charlie' making his way past the Empire Colonnade towards Wonderland.
66. The North Promenade with Brown's Rock Shop, Humber Automatic Exhibition, Hawkey's Capitol Café, Promenade Toilets and the Auckland Colonnade.
67. The two Helter Skelters on the sands and Hancock's Palace of Pleasure.
68. Lounging on the sands by one of the breakwaters.
69. Landing on the sands from the twin tracks of Hawkey's Lighthouse Helter Skelter.
70. The Rifle Range on the promenade. This later became the Animal House.
71. The crowded North Promenade. Auckland Colonnade on the left.
72. Wonderland with girl performers taking a break.

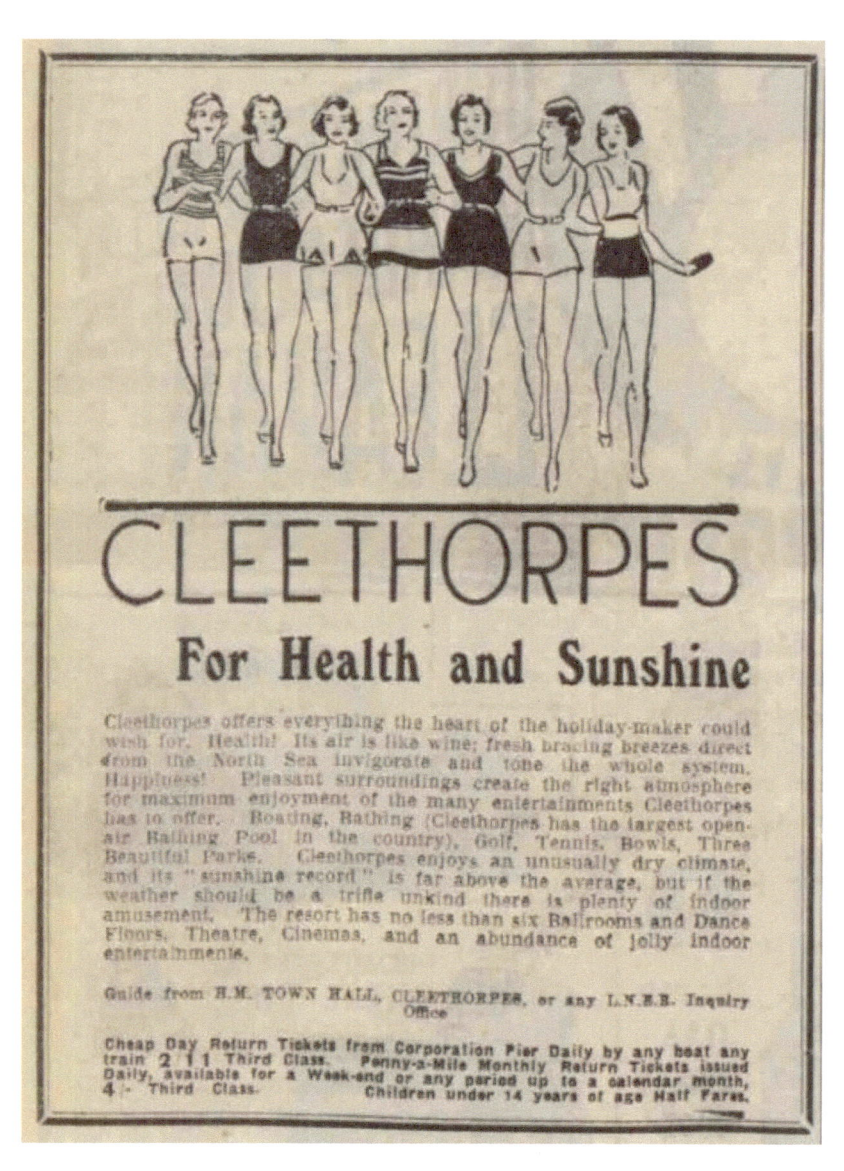

73. Cleethorpes, For Health & Sunshine. Hull Daily Mail 22nd May 1936

The North Promenade between the Wars

The GLOBE OF DEATH, present for the 1936 and 1937 seasons was probably not an East Coast Amusement Co. venture, but was located on Pleasureland, close to the Wonderland building. The Globe of Death was patented in the US by Arthur Rosenthal in 1904. It was a fairground and Carnival attraction where stunt riders rode motor cycles inside a mesh sphere ball, similar to the Wall of Death but in this act, the riders can loop vertically as well as horizontally. Unlike the Wall of Death, the globe can contain several motor cycle riders at once. Doug Best remembers a Miss Elizabeth Schmitt as being one of the daredevil riders.

Considerable excitement and interest was aroused when the German airship Hindenburg flew low over Cleethorpes on a Trans-Atlantic flight from Lakehurst Naval Air Station, New Jersey, to Frankfurt in Germany. Folk who witnessed it said its sheer size led one to believe it was floating across the roof tops. The Hindenburg was the largest dirigible ever built and made its maiden flight on 5th March 1936. It was luxury travel for 50 to 70 passengers with almost as many cabin staff and crew. Cruising speed was a modest 85mph, reducing to as little as 45mph with a strong head wind! Dependant on weather conditions, a westbound flight from Germany to America would take between 53 and 78 hours. During that year it made 17 trans-Atlantic crossings with return flights from Germany to America and Brazil. These were considered more as demonstrating the potential of airship travel, rather than scheduled services. During May & June of 1936, it crossed the UK several times, displaying its menacing giant Nazi Swastika, prompting questions to the Air Ministry as to whether it had the right authority and as to whether it may have been spying. Contemporary news reports document sightings over South Wales on 14th May, Bradford on 22nd May, the West Country on 28th May, Lincoln on 26th June and the Kent coast on 5th July. On or about 22nd May on a return flight from America to Germany, the Hindenburg veered from its usual course and hovered very low over Keighley in West Yorkshire to drop a bouquet of flowers with a request from a German priest that they be placed on a relative's grave. Two schoolboys found the package and the request was duly honoured. The Hindenburg then continued its journey flying over Bradford, Leeds and Hull, before passing over Cleethorpes. The image of it above Hancock's Palace of Pleasure is dated May 1936, so was probably that occasion. A few weeks later on 30th June, it flew over Cleethorpes again on a west bound flight to America, this time escorted by aircraft of the RAF. It flew over Grimsby yet again on 12th October 1936 on its final trans-Atlantic return flight of the 1936 season from America. This was the Hindenburg's only full season of operation for it was spectacularly destroyed in an explosion and fire the following year whilst docking at Lakehurst on 6th May 1937 with considerable loss of life, thus ending any future vision of widespread airship travel.

Miles of Smiles

74. *The giant Hindenburg Zeppelin airship passing low over the North Promenade on its way from Lakehurst Naval Air Station in New Jersey, returning to its base at Frankfurt in May 1936.*

Author's collection.

The North Promenade between the Wars

75. Your Health Comes First. Sheffield Daily Telegraph 18th May 1939

The Sheffield Daily Independent newspaper announced it was running its own special train to Cleethorpes on Thursday 18th August 1938. "The Special LNER train will start from Sheffield at about 11AM, calling at Rotherham, Mexborough and Doncaster. On the return journey, the train will leave Cleethorpes at about 8 p.m. Fares include tickets for the following: One ride on a Corporation runabout bus between the Station and Bathing Pool, one admittance to Pier and Pier Pavilion, one ride on the Boating Lake or one admittance to Bathing Pool, or Wonderland one ride".

Exciting new developments along the North Promenade during the thirties included Hawkey's New Capitol Cafe, situated by the railway passage off the promenade. In May 1939, their advertisement proclaimed that Hawkey's had been established for over 45 years. They already operated the Premier Cafe & Restaurant further along the promenade. Hawkey's started originally with a cafe in Riby Square, Grimsby. The New Capitol Cafe had seating for 450 diners. In 1939, Hot Dinners were one and threepence, 1/3d (7p) and Special Fish Teas cost a shilling 1/– (5p)!

On the beach stage opposite the station for the 1939 season was Jimmy Slater's Super Follies, a seaside performing troupe. As well as female impersonator, Jimmy Slater, it starred Grimsby born comedian Freddie Frinton, a rising star at the time who

76. Good Food & Good Service. Grimsby Daily Telegraph 14th June 1939

went on to great success on television with Meet The Wife, playing opposite Thora Hird. The Super Follies performed at venues throughout the UK during the thirties, forties and fifties.

The prospect of war however, was clearly on the horizon and notice of Black Out and ARP ground exercises appeared in the Grimsby Evening Telegraph on Friday 19th May 1939: "Saturday Midnight to Sunday 2.00am. All lights should be extinguished or screened between these hours in Grimsby and Cleethorpes".

Details of a large new Leisure Complex on the North Promenade were unveiled in the Scunthorpe Evening Telegraph for Friday 19th May 1939: "NEW HALL OF ENTERTAINMENT. PROGRESS IN SCHEME FOR A BETTER CLEETHORPES. INCREASED FACILITIES ON THE PROMENADE. The first part of an ambitious project to make Cleethorpes 'the Blackpool of the East Coast' so far as seaside amusements are concerned, will be opened at Whitsun. It is the new hall of amusements being constructed adjacent to "Wonderland" by Mr Whilma Wilkie, and it will be the most modern building in Cleethorpes. Pale peach coloured terra-cotta, and black stay-bright steel with a 50 feet glass and terra cotta tower dominating it, will be among the main features of its construction.. It will cost over £4000. But it will be the beginning, probably, of a much larger and infinitely more enterprising scheme to modernise that part of the front at Cleethorpes and to immensely enhance its attractiveness for holidaymakers from the big centres of the North and Midlands, recapturing patronage. In the opinion of Mr Whilma Wilkie and his Uncle Mr George Wilkie, who are among the leading amusement caterers in the North, Cleethorpes must be brought up-to-date if it is to

77. Cleethorpes most popular Concert Party. Open Air Music Hall on the beach stage opposite the station in 1939.
Author's collection.

78. Black Out. Grimsby Daily Telegraph 19th May 1939

The North Promenade between the Wars

recapture some of the many visitors who once flocked to it, but have now transferred their patronage to places like Skegness. The Wilkie's are prepared to lead the way; spend money to do so. It is their hope that the Corporation will support them by continuing their programme of improvements to the old front and that resident's generally will realise the importance of modernising the amenities of the town and keeping abreast of the times. I have spent more money in this particular building than I intended to do, but I wanted it to be thoroughly modern in every respect, Mr Whilma Wilkie told a Telegraph reporter It will, I have no hesitation in saying, be far and away the most striking building in Cleethorpes; and it is only the beginning of what we really have in mind. It is our hope and intention another year to construct a similar frontage for the whole length of Wonderland, and thus assist in improving the appearance of the Promenade.

We have had quite enough of the old fashioned looking wooden structures.

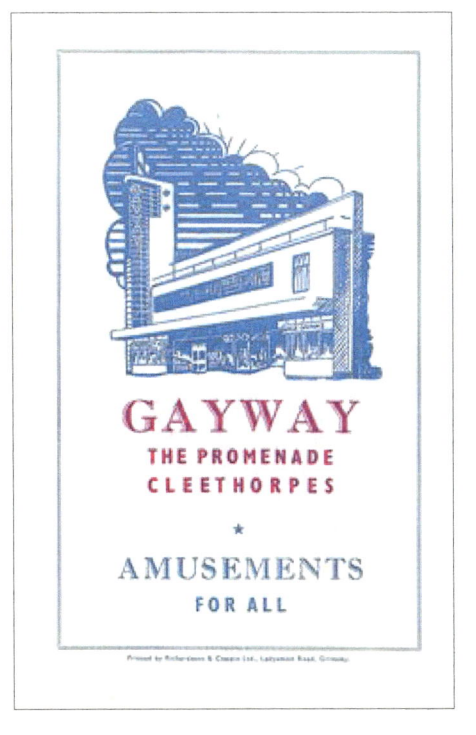

79. *The new Gayway entertainment complex opened at Whitsuntide 1939. It was a Wilkie family enterprise and part of the 'Better Cleethorpes' scheme of the time. After the war, the Gayway was flanked by the Ritz Cinema and Shops, built in the same Art-Deco style.*
Author's collection.

The Town Council at Cleethorpes is spending some money now on improvements. We feel in the construction of this new building and with the eventual fruition of our other plans, we shall be doing something to help them. So long as we get the support of the Town, we will go right ahead". Mr. Wilkie continued, "Amusements play a tremendous part in the public life; especially among holiday crowds".

The report continued: "LEAD TO OTHERS: Amusements made Blackpool what it is to-day. There is nothing stopping Cleethorpes' progress, and now that we have made a big start in the right direction, I hope others will follow. The new building has been designed by Mr George Provis of Park Lane, London, one of the foremost scenic architects in the Elstree Film Studios and the designer of Mr. Wilkie's great new Palace of Amusements at New Brighton. Its 80 feet frontage will, in fact, bear a strong resemblance to a modern cinema. The maximum depth will be 90 feet and the tower

Miles of Smiles

80. The brand new Gayway Amusement Complex in 1939 close to the Auckland Colonnade. Jimmy Slater's Super Follies were playing on the beach stage.
Author's Collection.

will be an imposing column of curved glass. The building will house two shops, one at each end of the front, and inside will be installed all the very latest forms of automatic amusements. Some delay in construction has been occasioned by shortage of steel and other building commodities, but Whitsun will definitely see the opening of the new and brighter Cleethorpes' amusement palace".

Every day is a happy day at the Gayway! Interestingly, it was not known as the Gayway until shortly after its opening at Whitsuntide 1939. The Gayway was indeed a major new North Promenade development. It was constructed on the site of the old Warwick Tower (today the Network Rail site) next to the former restaurant end of the Auckland Colonnade. The prospect of a similar Art-Deco frontage across the entire Wonderland building was certainly appetising, but momentum was lost with the outbreak of war and the passing of that champion of Cleethorpes, George Wilkie, in 1944.

Cleethorpes however, was not going to war without a bumper Summer Season, as was reported in the Grimsby Daily Telegraph on Friday 14th July 1939: "KEEPING UP TO DATE. For Cleethorpes itself is taking active steps to keep abreast of the times and to provide for its visitors all the means to enjoyment and relaxation they seek during the short respite when they come to greet the sun on the East Coast! EFFORTS FOR A BETTER AND BRIGHTER CLEETHORPES: The new refreshment rooms near the Pier and the new amusement hall on the North Shore (Gayway) are examples of this. Rain or shine, there's always something to do at Cleethorpes during the holiday season. Cleethorpes can justly claim to have something of everything that goes to the making of a real all round holiday resort. It has, one of its chief assets, an invigorating climate with an abundance of that tonic air for which it is now becoming far famed. For the open-air enthusiasts there are the sands and the sand dunes and excellent and safe bathing when the tide is in. Thousands of children from many distant towns find days of happiness and delight on the long stretches of beach".

CLEETHORPES

MANY IMPROVEMENTS IN SHEFFIELD'S NEAREST RESORT

Miles of Smiles

Impressions of Cleethorpes in the Thirties

Hull Daily Mail Friday 12th September 1930

"Looking Back On The Summer: HOW LOCAL SEASIDE RESORTS HAVE FARED, REVIEW OF 1930 SEASON. "Seaside resorts on the East Coast are looking back on the season of 1930 with mixed feelings. Cleethorpes: The season at Cleethorpes will be remembered as one of the worst for many years. The weather was entirely to blame. Those hardest hit have been the amusement caterers, particularly those on the beach. August Rank Holiday week, the one week of the season when amusement caterers usually make a harvest, this year was ruined. The amusement caterer Wonderland, although has had a pretty bad season, has a measure had to thank the weather for business that had been done. Long period visitors have been fewer than in previous years, but the fact that the season shows signs of stretching out longer than usual, might help to compensate many. The Naval visit in July was responsible for a great influx of visitors. Motor traffic has also not been so heavy, although some long-distance motor coaches from London and the Midlands have carried large numbers. Day excursions by train have been light. The situation might be sized up by the statement of the manager of the Cleethorpes Advancement Association. Last year, he said, we had two hundred inquiries about apartments. This year we have only had three."

Hull Daily Mail Thursday 30th May 1935

"CLEETHORPES SUNSHINE. SANDS & EVERY HOLIDAY DELIGHT. CLEETHORPES: The place where the sun opens wide its welcoming arms to holiday-makers. A health resort, possessing unique geographical advantages, it requires no introduction to the majority Hull people. Cleethorpes open to the bracing North Sea breezes, blessed with a record sunshine average, a place of broad, safe sands for happy children, and with facilities within its bounds for every modern sport and pastime. In these days when economy has to exercised, Cleethorpes makes a bold and almost unchallenged claim. The railway fare is low, accommodation, another very important item, is exceptionally reasonable, yet extremely good. It would, of course, be foolish to say that it never rains during the summer at Cleethorpes, but just consider for a moment that last year it enjoyed nearly 200 hours more sunshine than the average for the country, thus making it one of the sunniest spots on the English coast".

"ULTRA-VIOLET RAYS: Medical science has declared that the true way to health lies in the absorption into the body of the ultra-violet rays which are present in sunshine. The measurements taken in different centres, the Sunlight

The North Promenade between the Wars

League of Great Britain proved that Cleethorpes held the record daily average of ultraviolet rays". (Thought: with changes in the environment, this statement would be vigorously challenged today!)

Hull Daily Mail – Wednesday 27th July 1938

"Make it CLEETHORPES this year. CARNIVAL WEEK. Despite demands for staggered holidays, August is still inevitably the favourite month for vacations. August is the children's month and Cleethorpes is the children's paradise. Firm sands, safe bathing, a thousand and-one amusements, rock that is a famous childhood memory; these things make it the ideal spot for the family holiday. But Cleethorpes has a near-universal appeal. It has become the Blackpool of the East Coast. Why is it that Sheffield and Leeds swear by Cleethorpes; why hundreds of trips are sent to this spot on the coast from the industrial inland, from the steel and smoke of Scunthorpe, from the pleasant pastures, the peaceful agricultural areas of North Lincolnshire, whose folk want a whiff of the sea and the stimulation that Cleethorpes gives . . .
SOMETHING FOR EVERYBODY!

It is because Cleethorpes has sought to please everybody; whatever your taste. Cleethorpes is your cup of tea. And the advantages of Cleethorpes are specific; boating, bathing, angling, tours including camping, golf, cinema and theatre, plus a vast amusement park. There are the parks and recreation grounds, bowling greens, putting greens, tennis courts (hard and grass), model yachting lake, paddling pool. Cleethorpes can get lit up too! Its illuminations are on in September.

HANCOCKS: Hancock's have provided a magnificent eating house overlooking the sea, making it unnecessary to trek back to the hotel or the boarding house. What could be a more inviting prospect? And Hancock's is another name for value, service, and civility. Hancock's provide teas, lunches, snacks, and food,

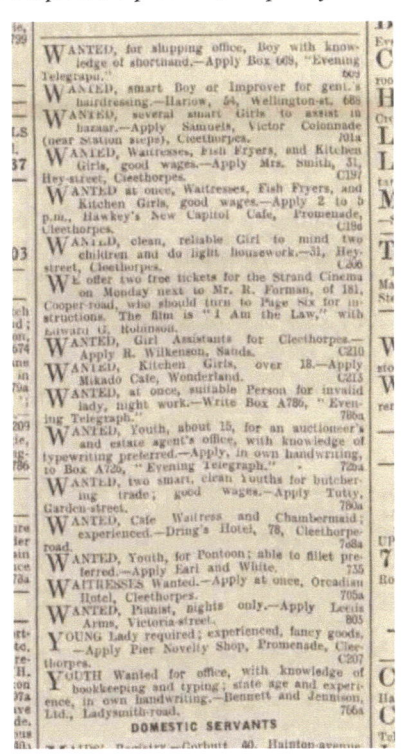

81. Lineage ad's for seasonal staff. Grimsby Evening Telegraph 25th May 1939. None of these would be acceptable today!

par excellence in the Cafe over the Sea. Hancock's, who claim to be the original Cleethorpes sea foam candy men, also have the Palace of Pleasure cafe on the sands, and offer their speciality fish teas.

BROWN'S ROCK: It's not just because it's sweet. There's something that makes you think of pleasant times by the sea, of romps on the sand. I've seen through this sort of experience, because it is part of the atmosphere of Cleethorpes. Messrs H. B. Brown and Sons have shops and stalls all along the sea front, where there are special holiday bargain parcels for all who present the advertisement that Messrs Brown's have on this page".

Grimsby Daily Telegraph Friday 14th July 1939

"SOMETHING OF EVERYTHING AT CLEETHORPES Lincolnshire's Health Gift to Britain: That's the title by which Cleethorpes is becoming wider and wider known. Every year, greater crowds come to Cleethorpes. Every year, its popularity with the people from some of the great industrial centres of the North and places much farther afield expands, both as a place for day excursions and as a residential resort for those who are able to get away to the seaside for a spell each summer. And now that the call for holidays with pay has become increasingly insistent and more generally complied with, there is no doubt that Cleethorpes' measure of popularity will continue to grow.

KEEPING UP TO DATE. For Cleethorpes itself is taking active steps to keep abreast of the times and to provide for its visitors all the means to enjoyment and relaxation they seek during the short respite when they come to greet the sun on the East Coast!

EFFORTS FOR A BETTER AND BRIGHTER CLEETHORPES. The new refreshment rooms near the Pier and the new amusement hall on the North Shore are examples of this. Rain or shine, there's always something to do at Cleethorpes during the holiday season. Cleethorpes can justly claim to have something of everything that goes to the making of a real all round holiday resort. It has, as one of its chief assets, an invigorating climate with an abundance of that tonic air for which it is now becoming far famed. For the open-air enthusiasts there are the sands and the sand dunes and excellent and safe bathing when the tide is in. Thousands of children from many distant towns find days of happiness and delight on the long stretches of beach".

Chapter Seven

WONDERLAND IN THE THIRTIES

A Miniature Town of Wholesome Fun

Using contemporary reporting as a guide, one gains a good impression of the development of Wonderland before the war. As well as the headline rides and attractions mentioned, all the usual side-stalls and smaller rides were present in the great hall in supporting roles.

The HIGH DIVER was an attraction advertised in 1930. Doug Best remembers an unusual outdoor attraction in the thirties was that of a one legged diver who jumped from a platform on the Big Dipper into a tank containing about six feet of water. He did this several times a day!

There was a serious accident on the Wonderland Big Dipper on Tuesday 10th June 1930, ironically on the very same day as the Wall of Death incident mentioned earlier. The Hull Daily Mail for Wednesday 11th June reported: "On a switchback at Cleethorpes on Tuesday, Joseph Ward, 17, an excursionist from Sheffield, who was stated to have stood up in the car while it was descending the steepest dip, was thrown out and received a broken thigh and arm. His condition is serious". Clearly, the 10th June was not a good day on the North Promenade!

Once again extolling the virtues of Cleethorpes to the holidaymaker, the Hull Daily Mail for Thursday 18th June 1931 carried a feature: "ALL

82. Wonderland. Hull Daily Mail 18th June 1930

Miles of Smiles

TYPES CATERED FOR. So far as attractions are concerned, Cleethorpes caters for all types of individuals, for young and old, for the lively tripper, and for the more sober-minded, rest-seeking holiday-maker. The visitor who desires fun can find it at the north end of the Promenade, where stands Wonderland, capable accommodating 20,000 people, and claimed to be the largest covered-in amusement park in the country. Within its confines he can enjoy all fun of the fair. New diversions this year are a GHOST TRAIN, and a MINIATURE RAILWAY. Nearby are other mechanical novelties and amusements. Along the front of the Promenade extends the beach, which makes a happy playground for children, and justifies the title of the Children's Paradise, for there is ample room for large numbers of kiddies to disport themselves and build castles, forts and other things so dear to the heart of the young".

Spring 1931 advertising by Fairdom Ltd proclaimed: "FUN AND THRILLS GALORE! SCOOTER SUPREME on the Promenade, the Speed Car with the Forward and Reverse Movement. For the kiddies, the MINIATURE RAILWAY in Wonderland, the Smallest Engine in the Country". There was also: "When in Wonderland visit J. DEARDEN'S AMUSEMENTS Juvenile Roundabouts, Coconut Garden, Dart Saloon and Derby Races. The Best in Wonderland".

Each season was one of progression. In 1931, the Ghost Train was new, the boating lake was restored and roller skating moved closer to the promenade under an extension of the main hall roof. Local adverts announced the GHOST TRAIN and SPEEDBOATS as new attractions. A contemporary postcard shows rowing boats and a larger passenger boat in operation on the boating lake. An island accessed by a bridge, at various times boasted a water chute and even a miniature golf course. Between the wars there were rowing boats, motor boats (water dodgems) and a passenger carrying boat which could seat up to 24 passengers.

THE GHOST TRAIN had an attractive frontage. The cars were basically a travelling bench seat for up to three adults which disappeared into the Lost World haunted cavern. Ghostly noises and screams emanated from within before the car emerged again through two sets of doors back into the main hall with Spooked pale faced passengers! Folk would gather by the exit doors as the cars emerged to observe the ghostly faced riders exiting along a short guided walkway. The experience was not yet over however, as a powerful fan under the walkway blew air upwards, lifting the dresses of unsuspecting females; more screams!

There were two short lived miniature railways in Wonderland in the thirties. The first miniature railway in Wonderland (indeed, the first in Cleethorpes) was the Cagney Railway. It ran from the joiners shop in the corner of the great hall by the dodgems, out in a straight line behind the adjacent Pleasureland amusements for about 60 yards, terminating close to the main line LNER locomotive turntable (now the Network Rail site). Doug Best recalls it was a US Cagney style steam 4-4-0

Wonderland in the Thirties

tender locomotive with several sit in coaches. He thought the track was probably two feet gauge (recent research reveals it was actually 12 5/8") and the ride cost 2d. The loco faced outwards and hauled its carriages a short distance out into the open, before propelling them back again. He recalled riding it several times. Little more is known, other than it only operated for the 1931 and 1932 seasons. See appendix 5 for an overview of the Cagney Railroad system. The Cagney miniature railway was mentioned in a display advertisement by Fairdom Ltd in the Hull Daily Mail on Thursday 18th June 1931 (see above), along with their SCOOTER SUPREME on the Promenade. The second miniature railway in Wonderland was Webb's Miniature Railway in 1933, of which nothing more is known.

83. Grimsby Telegraph Monday 28th March 1932. 'A Holiday Ride on the Miniature Railway at Cleethorpes'. The only known image of the short lived Cagney Miniature Railway that operated in Wonderland during the 1931 and 1932 seasons..

A most unfortunate incident was reported in the Hull Daily Mail on Saturday 1st August 1931. "CLEETHORPES TRAGEDY. Man Killed On Big Dips: The "Big Dips" at Wonderland, Cleethorpes, were the scene of a terrible accident last night, as a result of which one man lost his life and another man is in hospital suffering from head injuries. There is some mystery as to how exactly the accident happened. Four men, all believed to be seamen from the SS Orford, went up in the dips, and when the car returned it contained only two men. The missing two were found lying on the floor underneath the tracks, both apparently unconscious, and bleeding from the head. The inquest verdict was accidental death".

The big ride in the centre of the hall was an ELECTRIC SCENIC RAILWAY. A Fairground Scenic or 'Ark', was a lavishly decorated circular ride with undulating platforms over a number of 'hills' and a well established fairground attraction. The earliest Ark's had a Noah's Ark theme with animals set on the platforms two by two, hence the generic name. A Noah's Ark was mentioned in 1931 Wonderland advertising, but editorial in the Sheffield Daily Independent on 1st June 1933 suggests this may actually have been a juvenile roundabout. Doug Best remembers the big ride in the centre of the hall in the thirties as being a Scenic with Gondolas.

An image showing 'Wilkie's Grand Royal Gondolas From Venice' fairground scenic operating at the Great Grimsby Mop (Statute) Fair in about 1920 shows

Miles of Smiles

84. Wilkie's Grand Royal Gondolas in action at the Mop Fair in Grimsby in about 1920. This was probably the centre ride attraction in the new Wonderland in 1926.
Author's Collection

that far from having Venetian Golden Gondolas, it actually had toast rack type charabanc's, each seating about twelve riders on the platforms! As part of George Wilkie's travelling fair, it seems likely that this ride may have spent time as the centre attraction in the Great Hall of Wonderland when it first opened in 1926, but this is pure speculation.

If however the scenic Ark that Doug remembered in the Wonderland Great Hall in the thirties was indeed a Savage's ride, then the Gondola's represented those of the Doge's of Venice in the Grand Procession. The Doge was the title of the most senior elected official of the Republic of Venice. One of the ceremonial duties of the Doge was to celebrate the symbolic marriage of Venice with the Sea. This was done by casting a ring from the State Barge, the Bucentaur, into the Adriatic. The Gondola's on the ride included a representation of the State Barge. Scenic rides were a much loved feature of fairground and amusement parks, best remembered by their theme.

Doug Best remembers another big ride in the Great Hall in the thirties was a giant swing boat roundabout. About twenty suspended boats seating up to three adults each, swung out by the effects of centrifugal force in proportion to the speed of the roundabout, thus giving the sensation of 'flying'. The name of the ride and exactly when and for how long it operated is not known for there is no mention of it in Wonderland advertising.

Wonderland in the Thirties

The early thirties were clearly difficult times. No new rides were advertised for the 1932 season however a review in the Hull Daily Mail on Tuesday 21st June 1932 draws clarity on New Dips and the Scenic Railway (or Scenic Coaster) as being the same ride! The editorial reads: "AMUSEMENT PARK. What would Cleethorpes be without its magnificent (Wonderland) amusement park? To many people the mere mention of this popular seaside resort conjures up visions of the many breathless and delightful times they passed in this miniature town of fun. Foremost among the many amusements in the amusement park is the scenic railway, where, after one is conveyed to the full height of the erection, the train makes its descent in thrilling manner, accompanied by a series of shrieks and bursts of laughter from the occupants. The park is open every day of the week from 9 a.m. until 11 p.m. Without exaggeration, it would not be difficult to pass a whole day in the park's precincts without time dragging. The rail fares from Hull are extremely reasonable, day tickets being available at 2/11d" (15p today)!

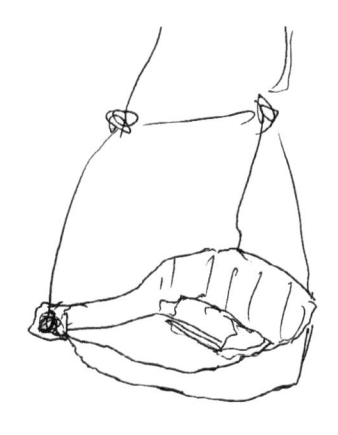

85. Impression of Swing Boats. A centre ride attraction in the Wonderland Great Hall in the thirties. Sketch by Doug Best

The Sheffield Daily Independent Tuesday 1st June 1933 reported in its Cleethorpes revue: "WONDERLAND PARK. There is one part of Cleethorpes which is sure to have a large percentage of the visitors at some time of the day or night, and that is the Wonderland Amusement Park, where the managing director (Mr G. Wilkie) can be relied on to have the latest pleasure devices in operation. This conglomeration of amusements covers a space of seven acres, where 20,000 people can be entertained at one time. Since it was originally constructed seven years ago, many additions have been made, both to the building and the side shows, so that those who knew it years ago would scarcely recognise it now, and considerable time can be spent in inspecting it. One of the popular features is the Big Dipper, in which the cars make three circular trips before coming to the final big dip. Among the new attractions this season will be the Dickens' Art Gallery, in which there are 250 pictures of Dickens' characters. Other attractions include a favourite with the juveniles, the Noah's Ark, the Dodgems and the Water Dodgems, the Auto-Car Ride, the Ghost Train, the Miniature Railway, together with amusement stalls with their various devices. There is also a cafe within the grounds to cater for different tastes. Adjoining Wonderland is a Boxing Hall, at which displays will be staged weekly (The Kursaal). Another attractive restaurant is the

Miles of Smiles

WONDERLAND AMUSEMENT PARK.
LATEST ATTRACTIONS INCLUDE

Giant Dipper.   Dickens' Art Gallery.
Scenic Coaster.   Water Dodgem.

COVERED BUILDING TO HOLD 20,000 PEOPLE
Open Daily (including Sundays), 9 a.m. to 11 p.m.
Managing Director : G. WILKIE.

PICK O' DANCES
AT
THE CAFE DANSANT,
KINGSWAY.
DANCING EVERY AFTERNOON at 3, Every Evening at 8.
COFFEE DANCE Every Saturday Morning at 11.
CAFE OPEN FROM 10 A.M. ALSO SUNDAYS 10 A.M. TO 10 P.M.

MEET YOUR FRIEND AT THE
SUNRISE CAFE,
NORTH PROMENADE.
THE SMARTEST LITTLE CAFE IN CLEETHORPES.
AFTERNOON TEAS, GRILLS, ICES, SODA FOUNTAIN.
SMARTNESS.   EFFICIENT SERVICE.   QUALITY.
For Terms and Specimen Menu apply the Manageress.

86. Wonderland Amusement Park. Sheffield Independent 1st June 1933

Sunrise Cafe which is on the North Promenade. It lays claim to being 'The Smartest Little Cafe in Cleethorpes', noted for its afternoon teas and grills and its efficient service".

For 1933, the WATER DODGEMS were advertised as 'new', however for Water Dodgems, read either Speedboats (from 1931) or perhaps more accurately, Motor Boats! The Water Dodgems referred to should not to be confused with the later post-war electric water dodgems on the promenade. The little two seat motor boats powered by two stroke (pop-pop) petrol engines shown in the 1933 display advert were to become a feature of the boating lake until well into the sixties. Another new attraction for 1933 was the Dickens' Art Gallery. Also mentioned as 'new' was the Scenic Coaster (see above). The Dickens' Art Gallery is not mentioned again after the 1933 season. Perhaps the majority of Cleethorpes visitors were looking more for thrills, than artistic stimulation, alluded to in a later chapter!

It was near the end of a poor season when an East Coast Amusement Co display advertisement for the WONDERLAND AMUSEMENT PARK appeared in the Hull Daily Mail on Monday 11th September 1933. It read: "Latest attractions include Giant Dipper, Scenic Coaster, Water Dodgems, Dickens' Art Gallery. Half price on all amusements. Interesting that the Giant Dipper and the Scenic Coaster are actually the same ride (see above), but appear together in the same advert! Promoting a Special Event, it continued: BOXING. Cheap excursion from Hull Pier, Wednesday 13th September; depart Hull Pier 6.35pm; depart Cleethorpes 10.55pm. Price 1/-. BOXING at 7.45pm (Licensed under B.B.B.C.) Wednesday next, 13th September in the PREMIER STADIUM, WONDERLAND. Events include a very special eight round contest, Harry Cross (Hull) v Kid Lawton (Goole); also a special four round juvenile contest, Billy Hewitt (Hull) v Cliff Wardale (Grimsby). Don't miss these events!"

The headline new attraction for 1934, destined to become a Wonderland long term favourite, was LOOPING THE LOOP. Looping-the-Loop (Over the Top in a Swing), also known as the 'Loops' or 'Cages', was a Wonderland creation, constructed in-house and patented by Mr George Wilkie, the Managing Director. A circular wire cage holding two people was attached to six pivot arms with counterweights. There

Wonderland in the Thirties

87. One of the sturdy little motor boats in action on the Wonderland Boating Lake in the thirties. The wooden structure of the Big Dipper which surrounds the lake is clearly visible.
Author's Collection

were six cages in the set. The action was that of a playground swing, swinging back and forth, gradually gaining momentum, then with super-human effort, the cage could swing over the top through a full 360 degrees (Over the Top in a Swing), hence it 'looped'. The ride duration was at the discretion of the operating staff but a brake was fitted which could be applied if it was deemed a rider had had his allotted time! It was described subsequently in thirties advertising as Wilkie's Latest Thriller, Looping the Loop, or Over the Top In a Swing!

A brief visiting attraction in Wonderland during the thirties was AL CAPONE'S BULLET PROOF CAR (See Appendix 7), which was displayed in the Blacksmith shop during its UK tour. Following the Chicago gangster's arrest in 1931, Al Capone's armoured car went on an extensive tour of the US, before arriving in the UK a couple of years later in 1933. It went on display at the Kursaal in Southend on Sea initially where it was photographed for a special souvenir postcard, before setting out on an extensive tour of the UK. The postcard was published and sold at the various venues where it was displayed. Researchers beware however, as the photograph is of the car on display at the Kursaal in Southend on Sea,

88. Hull Daily Mail 16th May 1934

Miles of Smiles

89. Souvenir postcard of the visit of Al Capone's bullet proof car to Wonderland. This is misleading because the actual image shows it on display at its base, the Kursaal in Southend-on-Sea! The cards were over-printed with the local venue.
Author's Collection.

but overprinted with the guest venue; the illustration being overprinted 'Wonderland, Cleethorpes'. Details of the actual UK tour itinerary appear to have been lost in the passage of time, but it is known to have visited and been displayed at a large number of venues throughout the country including Manchester and Blackpool.

No new rides were announced for 1935, but all the old favourites, Big Dipper, Dodgems, Ghost Train, etc, were still there. The Hull Daily Mail on Thursday 30th May 1935 reported: "What would Cleethorpes be without its magnificent Wonderland Amusement Park. Here we have a covered building to hold 20,000 people, and every possible form of amusement that makes it a truly miniature town of wholesome fun. To many people the mere mention of Cleethorpes conjures up visions of where is maintained, the most modern machinery known to sanitary science".

New attractions for 1936 included the BROOKLANDS RACE TRACK, the MIRRORED MAZE and the KIDDIES SPEEDWAY. The Mirrored Maze, a new attraction in the great hall was operated by George Blyth. Find your way out! A trick of his was him cleaning a (non-existent) window at the final exit, thus confusing visitors who would turn back into the maze again!

In the Hull Daily Mail for Wednesday 24th June 1936 in its 'Cleethorpes for Happy Holidays' revue appeared: "WONDERS OF WONDERLAND. Now for more precise details of some of the high-spots of Cleethorpes. Wonderland – Wonderland

Wonderland in the Thirties

indeed! Every conceivable passport to fun is here in a vast space that has covered accommodation for 20,000. It is open throughout the week, Sundays included, from 9am to 11pm. Latest attractions include the Giant Dipper; Brooklands' Racing Track. For moments of palpitating pleasure, the Scenic Coaster; the Mirrored Maze that mazzles; Water Dodgem; a Loop-the-Loop which is a Prince of thrillers; and the Children's Speedway. Mr G. Wilkie, the managing director, has patented a new Loop-the-Loop which is at Newcastle this week and then it goes on to Morecambe. It also wrote: While you are in Wonderland you should make sure of visiting the amusements offered by Mr J. Dearden. A particular delight for youngsters will be the roundabouts, designed especially for juveniles. Then there are the Darts Saloon, Derby Races, and the Coconut Garden. Make a day-or days, of it!"

The Sheffield Independent for Saturday 16th May 1936 includes the first mention of the GLOBE OF DEATH motor cycle stunt riding attraction where the riders speed around a full 360 degrees in a wire mesh globe. "Adjoining the Park is the Automatic Arcade in which the thrilling motor cycle ride called the GLOBE OF DEATH can also be seen. A visit to Brooklands Racer Track gives one an unusual experience. The Water Dodgems and a host other attractions are provided".

The Sheffield Daily Independent for Saturday 1st May 1937 reported: "Visitors to Cleethorpes will find delightful diversions from the north to the south side of the town. One of the outstanding attractions is the Wonderland Amusement Park at the north end of the promenade. It is controlled by Mr George Wilkie, who has very wide experience as an amusement caterer all over the country. Wonderland draws large crowds throughout the season. All the amusements are under cover and there is accommodation for no fewer than 20,000 people. The Park is open daily (including Sundays) from 9.00am to 11.00pm. It goes on: During the close season the Park has undergone a scheme of redecoration and the stalls have also been remodelled on most attractive lines. Amongst the attractions there can be found the 'Big Dipper', which provides thrilling rides. New attractions include the PETROL SCOOTER on one of the largest tracks in the country, the newest type of Looping the Loop, the Mirror Maze, ELI WHEEL, MONA RAILWAY and a specially constructed track for the "Dodgem" cars. The Water Dodgems and a host of other attractions are provided for those desirous of spending a happy day".

The Big Eli Wheel was a standard fairground or seaside big wheel similar to the one still in use today on the sands opposite the railway station. In 1938, it was located outdoors at the end of the promenade just beyond the Great Hall, close to the Dips along with the Chair-O-Plane (Flying Chairs) and the Brooklands Racing Track. The Mona Railway was Dearden's kiddies train roundabout. Not mentioned in the above report were two other new attractions at Wonderland, the LOOP-O-PLANE and the CYCLEDROME.

> **WHEN IN "WONDERLAND"**
> **LOOK FOR**
> # J. DEARDEN'S AMUSEMENTS
> :: JUVENILE ROUNDABOUTS ::
> COCONUT GARDEN, MONO RAILWAY
> DART SALOON and DERBY RACES.
> **THE BEST IN "WONDERLAND."**

90. Grimsby Daily Telegraph 14th June 1939

The Cycledrome Scenic platform ride mentioned in 1937/8 advertising, probably replaced an earlier big ride in the centre of the hall. This had motor cycles on the platforms but should not be confused with the brand new Robert Lakin post-war Cycledrome that older readers may remember, which we come to later.

The Hull Daily Mail for Tuesday 20th July 1937 reported: "Wonderland Folk who have visited Cleethorpes know the happy time that can be spent in the famous Wonderland Amusement Park, but there are many people in different parts of the country who have had the good word passed on to them by holiday-makers on their return from Cleethorpes. For this season the Wonderland Amusement Park has secured

*91. Dearden's new Mona-Rail juvenile roundabout in Wonderland.
Hull Daily Mail 27th July 1938.*

Wonderland in the Thirties

a contrivance which is calculated to give the greatest thrill ever. Emanating from America, it is known as the Loop-o-Plane, and consists of an immensely strong steel pillar at the top of which are hung two long arms, one at either side. At the lower end of each arm is the 'Plane', in which the joy-riders are accommodated. The thrills come when the planes begin to loop. The sensation experienced by the riders (it is claimed) is similar to that of 40ft fall, the looping of an aeroplane, or power dive, yet it does not shake up the passengers".

The Loop-O-Plane operating at Wonderland during the 1937-1939 seasons should not be confused with a later similar machine which worked for one season only in about 1960. As well as highlighting the Loop-O-Plane, Wonderland advertising in 1938 included the Cycledrome, Big Eli Wheel, Water Shute, Ghost Train and 'Come and Learn How to Drive a Car' on the New Brooklands Speedway!

The Hull Daily Mail for Wednesday 27th July 1938 described Cleethorpes in rather more creative and emotional terms:

92. Hull Daily Mail 27th July 1938

"WONDERLAND. Cleethorpes and the Wonderland Amusement Park are as necessary to each other as were Tweedledum and Tweedledee. When you want to add to the thrill of just being alive, just walk into Wonderland and you'll get gingered no end. They have the latest mechanical devices for increasing the blood pressure, for giving you the excuse to sail with your girl into less prominent places, for fetching your heart into your mouth and for making the world seem crazier than it is. Try the Loop-o-Plane. It's good! It continued: DEARDENS: Dearden's, on the Promenade (in Wonderland), offer to amuse without a muse. They take you from the routine sameness of existence and transport you to delight that dazzles and literally takes away your breath. For the children there is the Mona Railway, the Juvenile Roundabouts, contraptions that will make Cleethorpes an even brighter memory. For those who wing a wicked arrow, there are classic darts. If you are horsey, try the Kentucky Derby. The Coconut Gardens will make you think of the southern seas". The imagination runs wild!

93. A rather poor quality image showing the outdoor amusements at the very end of the promenade looking back towards the Wonderland Great Hall. The Brooklands Racing Cars are in the foreground with the Big Eli-Wheel just beyond. Behind the wheel is a Chair-O-Plane. Dominating the scene on the right is the lift hill of the Big Dipper.
Sheffield Independent 28th May 1938.

94. Postcard view of the Boating Lake in the thirties. Dominating the scene is the Big Dipper. The high level structure to the right is the Dips Car Shed. The Boating Lake was further developed by the construction of a Water Shute and Miniature Golf Course on the centre island, for the 1938 and 1939 seasons.
Author's Collection.

> **WONDERLAND AMUSEMENT PARK**
>
> OFFERS HOURS OF JOY WITH ONLY THE LATEST ATTRACTIONS.
>
> **THE FINEST COVERED-IN AMUSEMENT PARK in the COUNTRY.**
>
> ACCOMMODATION FOR OVER 20,000 PEOPLE.
>
> GHOST TRAIN—AEROPLANE RIDES—DODGEM CARS—PETROL SCOOTERS—SCENIC COASTER—ZOO—MIRROR MAZE—GIANT DIPPER.
>
> AND A HOST OF
>
> **SPLENDID NEW 1939 ATTRACTIONS.**

95. Sheffield Daily Telegraph 18th May 1939

Ever the champion of Cleethorpes, in a final pre-war holiday push, the Hull Daily Mail on Tuesday 23rd May 1939 wrote: "WONDERLAND AMUSEMENT PARK There was never a holiday-maker yet who could resist an amusement park. It is half the joy of a vacation to go all gay and hilarious for a time, to give oneself up to the round of gaiety and thrills on the latest amusement machines. And what place could be better than the Wonderland Amusement Park, at Cleethorpes. It is stacked with the very latest stunts, gadgets and thrilling contraptions to satisfy the excitement of youth or the pleasure of grandma. Everything, however, is constructed and operated with every regard for the safety of the patrons. Take a trip on the Loop-o-Plane and have the biggest thrill of the year, the Big Eli Wheel, see the Cycledrome, and cascade down the Water Shute, laugh in the Ghost Train, or learn how to drive a car on the new Brookland Speedway. Mr G. Wilkie is the Fun King, and his efficient staff will see that you enjoy yourself!"

Then in the Scunthorpe Evening Telegraph for Friday 14th July 1939 came some sad news:

"PROMINENT IN LIFE OF CLEETHORPES. Death of Mr George Smith, Wonderland's Secretary. Cleethorpes has lost a well-known and highly-respected resident with the death yesterday of Mr. George Smith, aged 74, of Brooklands, 17 Cromwell Road. A native of Eastrick, Yorkshire, where the funeral will take place tomorrow, Mr Smith had lived in Cleethorpes since 1918, and had taken a keen interest in the business and social life of the town. On coming to Cleethorpes he was the proprietor of a drapery store in the Market Place. For the last five years Mr Smith had been secretary of the East Coast Amusement Company, the owners of the Wonderland Amusement Park, Cleethorpes. He was secretary of the Cleethorpes Plate Glass Protection Society, member of the Chamber of Trade, and was chairman of the now defunct Cleethorpes Advancement Association. Ever since he had lived in Cleethorpes he had been a member of the Elm-Road Bowling Club. Mr Smith had been ill for some 14 weeks. He leaves a widow and one daughter, Mrs D. Wilkie".

Darker times had already arrived, but the pre-war golden age of Wonderland ended on a high with the annual close of season local charity fund raising event on Sunday 17th September 1939. The country was now at war and this time, the North Promenade would be closed for the duration.

Wonderland in the Thirties

Some Impressions of Wonderland in the Thirties:

Hull Daily Mail Thursday 30th May 1935

"WONDERLAND: What would Cleethorpes be without its magnificent Wonderland Amusement Park. Here we have a covered building to hold 20,000 people, and every possible form of amusement that makes it a truly miniature town of wholesome fun. To many people the mere mention of Cleethorpes conjures up visions of where is maintained, the most modern machinery known to sanitary science".

Hull Daily Mail Friday 22nd May 1936

"WONDERLAND: There is sufficient covered accommodation to hold 20,000 people, and it is open throughout the week (including Sundays) from 9am to 11pm. Mr G. Wilkie, the managing director, has secured all the latest attractions, which include the Giant Dipper, the Brooklands Racing Track, the Scenic Coaster, the Mirror Maze, the Water Dodgems and, the prince of thrillers, Looping the Loop. Then there is the Cafe Dansant, in which George and his Aristocratic Band play, while there is dancing at 3pm and 8pm daily. The cafe itself is open daily, including Sunday. While you are in Wonderland you should make certain of a visit to the amusements of Mr J. Dearden. The youngsters will appreciate a run on the roundabouts specially made for juveniles. In addition there is the Dart Saloon, Derby Races and the Coconut Garden".

Hull Daily Mail Wednesday 24th June 1936

"WONDERS OF WONDERLAND. Now for more precise details of some of the high-spots of Cleethorpes: Wonderland – Wonderland indeed! Every conceivable passport to fun is here in a vast space that has covered accommodation for 20,000. It is open throughout the week, Sundays included, from 9am to 11pm. Latest attractions include the Giant Dipper, Brooklands Racing Track, for moments of palpitating pleasure; the Scenic Coaster; the Mirrored Maze that mazzles; Water Dodgem; a Loop-the-Loop which is a Prince of thrillers; and the Children's Speedway. Mr G. Wilkie, the managing director, has patented a new Loop-the-Loop which is at Newcastle this week and then it goes on to Morecombe".

Hull Daily Mail Tuesday 11th May 1937

CLEETHORPES: "Thought: Although boats pass Cleethorpes every minute of the day; Wonderland Amusement Park gives you Thrills Every Second!"

Miles of Smiles

```
month.—C. Lane, Baker, Ramsgate, Louth.
                                        393
WANTED, 2 smart Girls, aged 18 or over, to
  assist at stalls.—Apply Dearden, Wonderland.
                                        C341
WANTED, Girl assist in house and shop.—53.
```

96. Wanted: '2 Smart Girls'. Lineage ad' for seasonal staff.
Grimsby Daily Telegraph Friday 14th July 1939.

Hull Daily Mail – Wednesday 27th July 1938

DEARDENS: "Dearden's, on the Promenade (in Wonderland), offer to amuse without a muse. They take you from the routine sameness of existence and transport you to delight that dazzles and literally takes away your breath. For the children there is the Mona Railway, the Juvenile Roundabouts, contraptions that will make Cleethorpes an even brighter memory. For those who wing a wicked arrow, there are classic darts. If you are horsey, try the Kentucky Derby. The Coconut Gardens will make you think of the southern seas.

VARIETY OF INTERESTS. At Wonderland, it's all the fun of the fair from early morning until late at night. Here an infinite variety of amusements are to be found. Sea, sand and sunshine, with all the accompanying pleasures that go to make a seaside holiday a truly enjoyable and health giving one. Cleethorpes has all this! "

Chapter Eight

THE NORTH PROMENADE AND THE SECOND WORLD WAR

During the summer of 1940 the North Promenade was closed to the public and barbed wire erected along the whole length of the North and Central Promenades. Hawkey's Cafe was requisitioned by the War Department. Wonderland was requisitioned by the Army and used first for military vehicle maintenance and the storage of ammunition, then in 1943 it was taken over by the Ministry Of Supply and used for the assembly of American military vehicles that had been supplied in kit form through the ports of Grimsby and Immingham.

Other wartime changes included the full re-commissioning of both the WWI Forts at the mouth of the Humber for the period of hostilities. Haile Sands Fort (on the Lincolnshire side) and Bull Sands Fort (on the Yorkshire side) of the Humber estuary remained in use after the war until 1956. Cleethorpes pier was breached during the summer of 1940 to prevent enemy invasion, making what was left, the shortest pier in the country. Funds were available post-war to re-instate the pier but the local authority decided not to restore it and use the money elsewhere. The breached isolated stretch of the pier was eventually demolished in the spring of 1949. At the Suggitts Lane end of Wonderland, substantial concrete tank traps were constructed on the sands below the Big Dipper to prevent invasion. After the war, children would play on them and they became a feature of that part of the sands, but you had to be tall to be able to jump from one to another! They were still there after the 1953 floods when the sea wall to Suggitts Lane was strengthened and not finally removed until the radical rebuilding of the sea defences between the North Promenade, Fuller Street and the Docks following the floods of 1976 and 1978.

Unconnected with the war but nonetheless notable, was the announcement of the passing of George Wilkie, that champion of Cleethorpes and founder of Wonderland, at his home in Wallasey in 1944.

Miles of Smiles

The North Promenade was reopened in the spring of 1946. Wonderland was returned to civilian use at Easter and re-opened for the first post-war summer season at Whitsuntide, marking the beginning of a new golden 20 year post-war era for the largest covered amusement centre on the East Coast (Pleasure the Weather can't Spoil!) and indeed, for the whole of the Cleethorpes North Promenade. The sight of visitors, the screams from the Big Dipper and the smell of candy floss and doughnuts had returned at last!

Chapter Nine

THE POST-WAR NORTH PROMENADE

A major change came when the Skegness Standard on Wednesday 17th December 1947 gave notice of the formation of a new Company, Arcadia Amusements (Cleethorpes) Limited, with a nominal capital of £7000 in shares. The Directors were Mr H. Wilkinson (Managing) and Mr R. Wilkinson of Waltham, who took over the operation of the former Hancock's Palace of Pleasure opposite Hawkey's New Capitol Cafe; now to be known as The Arcadia.

Another welcome return to normality came in 1949 when the Promenade Illuminations were switched on again for the first time after the war.

97. Come Along Soon… Leicester Chronicle 27th March 1948

Crowded Cleethorpes

By 1950 visitor numbers had returned to pre-war levels and the resort was thriving once again. Cleethorpes again became prominent as the favourite seaside holiday destination for Sheffield folk and the surrounding areas. The Sheffield Daily Telegraph for Friday 28th April 1950 announced: "The Sheffield Telegraph and the Sheffield Star Ltd. have opened a fund and have chartered a special train for each of the four Thursdays in July to take parties of old people from Sheffield for a day by the sea at Cleethorpes. Each of the trains will carry 350 people, making a total of 1400 in all. The Old Age Pensioners' Association have been asked to pick out deserving cases to make the numbers, but any really needy people who are not members of the association will also be considered. The parties will have both men and women St John Ambulance nurses in attendance on the train and two hot meals will be provided in Cleethorpes".

Soon after, in the Sheffield Daily Telegraph for Monday 19th June 1950 came the heart warming story of the newspaper's support for the community: "FIVE HUNDRED SHEFFIELD CHILDREN who visited Cleethorpes on Saturday had their own ideas about the benefits of a trip to the seaside. They were guests of the Sheffield Children's

98. The Crowded North Promenade in about 1950

Grimsby Telegraph.

The Post-War North Promenade

Seaside Holiday Fund, organised by the "Sheffield Telegraph" and "The Star," and they were so certain that the effects of the seaside air would be felt immediately, that they made a beeline to practically every weighing machine in the town. So eager were the children to sample the joys of Wonderland with the free tickets provided that many wanted to forgo the dinner awaiting them on arrival. For Dennis Webster, of Hastilar Road, the beach was so fascinating that he nearly missed his tea".

Then on Friday 7th July 1950, the Sheffield Daily Telegraph reported: "PENSIONERS AT SEASIDE. An 80 year old Sheffield man, his cloth cap pulled well forward, got into his Dodgem car in the Wonderland amusement arcade at Cleethorpes, yesterday, I'll give these youngsters what for, he said as the car began its crazy careering. He did too. Happily humming "Down at the old Bull and Bush", he rammed as many cars as he could. His was a more vigorous way of enjoying himself than some of the 350 Sheffield old age pensioners cared to undertake, but they enjoyed themselves. As Mrs Edith Wood, aged 68, of 8 Worthing Road, Darnall, put it 'We've come to enjoy ourselves; I know I'm going to'. The trip to Cleethorpes was made possible by the newly established Old Folks Fund, organised by the Sheffield Telegraph and The Star. The Sheffield Branch of the National Federation of Old Age Pensioners' Association chose most of those who went on the journey, though they were not necessarily association members".

The town was outraged when Mr W. O. Hoskins, a lecturer from University College, Leicester, wrote disparagingly about Cleethorpes in a 'Festival of Britain' visitors guide book, published in 1951. He said: "Cleethorpes is best avoided by the casual visitor. It is a paradise for small children but something correspondingly less so for most of the remainder of the human race". Cleethorpes was incensed!! However, as is often the case when such outrageous statements are made, they generate unexpected extra publicity, and Cleethorpes found many allies. A good example appeared in the Yorkshire Post on Saturday 7th July 1951: "CLEETHORPES IS POPULAR – AND PROUD OF IT! The trouble with him, said the Cockle and Whelk stall proprietor thoughtfully, is that he's one of these Intellectuals; and we don't cater for Intellectuals. We never have done and if we've got any sense, we never shall. Cleethorpes is a working man's place – and proud of It. He had given the complete answer to Mr Hoskins, the Leicester University College lecturer, who had incensed the whole town. It's the answer almost everyone gives Cleethorpes, from the Publicity Manager downwards. There is certainly not much to offer the intellectual, unless he can work up any scientific enthusiasm for Gloria, 'The Girl in the Fish Bowl', or wishes to test his Freudian libido by discovering from a machine for a penny, whether he is cuddlesome, kissable, loveable, naughty, flirtatious, cautious or hot stuff. Even Intellectuals must be one or other".

The reporter went on: "I think it's demonstrated by the fact that each Sunday from now until the end of August, over 50.000 trippers will be arriving in 30 special trains and 500 coaches from Sheffield, the West Riding of Yorkshire, the Midlands and other parts of the country. They will whet their appetites on cockles, whelks, oysters, prawns and shrimps, and will then pass on through candy floss, giant lollies and chocolate snowballs to seven different varieties of Ice-cream, ranging from Mammoth Bricks at 1/10d, down to Pola Maids (with cones) at 3d. Then presumably, it will be time for lunch. The afternoon will be spent by most of them either in one of the Corporation's 10,000 deckchairs on the sands, or in the bracing air of Wonderland which, with its capacity for 20.000, is the biggest covered amusement park in the country. They will relax on the big dipper or the dodgem cars, and put themselves in the holiday mood by watching an actual working model of the pendulum knife the razor-sharp instrument of torture which swings slowly over its LIVE victim's head. Peculiar people, the Intellectuals may say with a sneer. He should look more closely at some these sideshows and ponder over the philosophy of the patrons which they reveal. The Mental Marvels, for instance. You pay 6d to visit the Mental Marvels and they are first-class entertainment. All academics do, is tell you what your troubles are!"

Of course, the attractions on the North Promenade changed year by year to keep up with the times. A walk along the North Promenade to observe what was on offer in say, 1951, would give a good impression of Cleethorpes in the post-war period. At the end of the North Promenade was the new Cafe with its magnificent views of the Humber estuary. This is where most Wonderland staff took their tea breaks. The new Cafe, later enlarged, had replaced the old Cafe & Bazaar (the former Kursaal), which dated back to 1906 and had latterly been used as a Boxing Booth where visitors could challenge a professional to three rounds!

Next to Wonderland is the open ground of a recently demolished arcade creating a 150ft open site, now occupied by Roy Cripsey's WALL OF DEATH which had returned for the 1951 season. Motor cycle stunt riders rode up the side of the near vertical twenty foot high circular wall at speeds of up to 45mph. One act included a rider on the wall of death with a female sitting on the handle bars!

Close by the Wall of Death is the still very new GAYWAY Amusement Arcade. The original Gayway had been enlarged by the addition of two annexes soon after the war, extending its modern promenade frontage to an impressive 160ft. The two annexes consisted of the Ritz Cartoon Cinema on the station side and an impressive addition of two gift shops and a smaller arcade on the Wonderland side. They were constructed in the same Art-Deco style as the Gayway and in keeping with the pre-war spirit of the 'Efforts for a Better and Brighter Cleethorpes', alluded to in the Grimsby Daily Telegraph on the 14th July 1939. These were also owned and operated by the East Coast Amusement Company. The Gayway was managed by Charlie Carrington, a ginger haired man, assisted by his daughter, Stella. The Ritz cartoon cinema was first mentioned in Wonderland adverting on 25th March 1953.

The Post-War North Promenade

99. The Gayway and Happidrome Amusement Arcade in about 1952.
Grimsby Telegraph.

In complete contrast to the Gayway, next is the historic Auckland Colonnade constructed in 1885 from which about fifty feet had been removed from its northern extremity to make way for the new Ritz Cartoon Cinema referred to above. This included the former brick built kitchens at the restaurant end of the Colonnade. Within the remaining Auckland Colonnade was Samuel Smith's (Taddy's) public house, followed by more gift shops and Hawkey's New Capitol Cafe, adjacent to the narrow railway passage off the Promenade. Hawkey's New Capitol Cafe was built in 1938 and complimented the Gayway in being part of the pre-war Better Cleethorpes scheme. The passage off the Promenade provided access to the railway facilities, locomotive turntable, etc, as well as to the rear of Hawkey's Cafe and Taddy's pub in the Auckland Colonnade. Opposite Hawkey's Cafe is the Arcadia, the former Hancock's Palace of Pleasure, built out from the promenade as a small pier on the sands.

Being weighed was a traditional British seaside resort attraction. The coloured postcard North Promenade from N. Cleethorpes, illustrated in Chapter 2 (Fig 17), shows a set of weighing scales on the Promenade with its lady attendant opposite the Kursaal Cafe & Bazaar in about 1911. Attending Weighing Scales in the 1950's was Wally Holley, another of the characters of the North Promenade. His scales were situated on the North Promenade close to the Big Wheel near the station. Walter E.

Miles of Smiles

100. Close up of the Auckland Colonnade in the autumn of 1955. The structure is in course of demolition. There are gaps in the roof of the colonnade. Little remains of Taddy's pub behind the front wall.

Author's Collection.

101. The North Promenade looking towards the station in 1958. In the centre is Hawkey's New Capitol Cafe. To its right is a small gift shop, then the last remaining section (approx 80ft), of the Auckland Colonnade which once extended to some 330ft along the promenade. The new Taddy's pub, opened in 1956, is on the right.

Doug Best.

The Post-War North Promenade

102. The popular postcard view of Cleethorpes showing the Slipway and North Promenade in about 1950. The Arcadia (centre right) was destroyed in the 1953 floods.
Author's Collection.

Holley lived on Suggitts Lane. He was a slim, jovial man who always had a big smile and was never short of a joke. He had the ability to gather a crowd around to make an entertainment of being weighed. On the serious side though, his were traditional weighing scales with balance weights, which could not lie!

After the railway passage, there are more amusement arcades, shops and bazaars in a variety of elderly wooden structures, including the Empire Colonnade. There was the Humber Pastimes automatic amusement arcade, established by Walter West in 1935, Browns Rock Shop, Hawkey's original Premier Cafe and a string of elderly ramshackle shops and amusement stalls, most with long standing promenade traders, before reaching the railway station. The only relatively new structure was Blakeman's ice cream shop with its attractive frontage of two windows and a single entrance, dating from 1948, situated very close to the station.

Beyond the station steps, the magnificent Victorian cast iron Victor Colonnade with its various arcades, bazaars and shops, still completely intact, extends along the North Promenade to its junction with Sea Road, completing our walk along the length of the North Promenade.

Miles of Smiles

The East Coast Floods of 1953

Being a coastal town, events of flooding, both minor and major occurred from time to time. Dr Alan Dowling in his scholarly work Cleethorpes the Development of a Seaside Resort alludes to a major flood in the area in 1571. The railway was the resort's commercial lifeline. The timeline of Lincolnshire Railway History in The Railways of North East Lincolnshire, Part Two by Paul King, records the branch line to Cleethorpes was breached for the first time on 18th October 1869.

A combination of a high spring tide, low atmospheric pressure and strong northerly gales resulted in the storms that battered the East Coast of England from Kent to the Tees on the night of 31st January 1953, causing major flooding and loss of life, particularly in East Anglia and the Mablethorpe area of Lincolnshire. Cleethorpes fared rather better, with no loss of life but extensive damage. The railway was washed away between Fuller Street and Suggitts Lane and flooding extended down Fuller Street and Suggitts Lane, crossing Grimsby Road. The sea wall was breached between Suggitts Lane and Wonderland and sections of the carriage sidings washed away.

On the North Promenade itself, the major casualty was the Arcadia (the former Hancock's Palace of Pleasure). This was built on a short wooden pier, a substantial part

103. Extensive flood damage to the sea wall and carriage sidings, seen from the high viewpoint of the Big Dipper looking towards Suggitts Lane.
Note the wartime tank traps on the sands.

Doug Best.

The Post-War North Promenade

104. Extensive flood damage and debris on the North Promenade in 1953.
Grimsby Evening Telegraph.

of which was washed away with the tide scattering amusements and slot machines as far away as North Sea Lane. All the amusement arcades and stalls along the North Promenade suffered water damage and debris was strewn everywhere.

Mrs Sadie Beal told the Grimsby Telegraph what became of the police box which was on North Promenade, opposite Hawkey's (probably Arcadia) Palace. "The storm uprooted the box and its contents and the wind carried it and deposited it in the bathing pool which had been drained for the winter", she said. Also recalling the incident as a teenager was P D Addison who said "The Bathing Pool was flattened and full of sand; the railings all along the promenade were bent, buckled or torn out completely". Lynn Wright said: "My abiding memory of the floods is that, as a small child, I went out on the Sunday morning of February 1 and saw the horses from the circular ride at Wonderland (actually the Arcadia) in the Bathing Pool".

The Grimsby Telegraph went on: "The worst destruction came in the area between Wonderland and the Pier, with special constables being called out as the night wore on to cordon off damaged properties and hold back hundreds of sightseers. The sands and promenade were strewn with debris, much of it from the Arcadia, which was reduced to a smashed-up shell of wood and masonry".

Geoff Maggs was 13 at the time and recalled he and his friends found time to hunt for pennies on the beach from the destroyed Arcadia slot machines. Also delighting in the sudden treasure was Frank Priest, who was just a boy when the floods struck. "I remember it well. I was only seven years old. At about 7pm, my mother called me to the front door and said: Come and look at the sea coming down the road". The sea was coming down the street very fast, whipped up by the wind, but stopped rising at our doorstep. He went on: "The next morning, a friend and I went onto the beach. We were astounded by the sight which met us. Debris was strewn the length of the North Promenade and the remains of the Arcadia (Hancock's Pleasure Palace) stuck out starkly against the heavily overcast sky. Making our way on to the beach, we saw the whole extent of the damage. It was only then I realised the full power of the sea. The promenade was severely damaged, with snapped and buckled railings and the beach was full of debris and broken slot machines. There were hundreds of people on the beach. We suddenly realised what they were doing. They were picking up money – loads of it! It was everywhere. We could not believe it; we were rich! I was wearing my school blazer and filled the pockets with my ill-gotten gains. I went back home, emptied my pockets, and ran back to the beach again three times to collect more money. I remember seeing a man taking a one-armed bandit off the beach using a two-wheeled wooden handcart".

Following the severe storm damage, the wrecked venue could not be salvaged; however the Council had served notice to the owners of the Arcadia to remove the structure a couple of years previously and it was in fact operating on a stay of execution at the time, so the storm had enacted the Council's wishes for them!

105 & 106. Salvage operations from the wrecked Arcadia following the 1953 storm and flooding.

Doug Best

The Post-War North Promenade

107. Damage to the slipway opposite Wonderland following the 1953 storm and floods.

108. Slipway Repairs under way.

Both: Doug Best.

Everything in full swing again at Cleethorpes

After the Floods

The cafe at the end of the promenade sustained severe storm damage but was rebuilt and enlarged afterwards. There was also considerable damage to many of the wooden arcade and shop buildings along the North Promenade as a result of flooding, prompting a re-awakening of some aspects of the pre-war 'Scheme For A Better Cleethorpes'. Whilst the aspirations of an Art-Deco frontage for Wonderland never materialised, considerable modernisation and rebuilding did take place along the North Promenade during the ensuing few years.

There was an amusing follow up to the floods reported in the Yorkshire Evening Post on Friday 15th May 1953. "DECK CHAIRS IN SEA FOR THREE MONTHS. About 130 deck chairs which were washed away from Bridlington in the storm at the end of January have been swept up at Cleethorpes after being in the sea for over three months. A total of over 700 deck chairs were washed away from Bridlington. The chairs were identified by initials on the canvas".

The sea however, had not finished with Cleethorpes, for the Liverpool Echo reported on Saturday 6th March 1954: "Railway repair men worked all night on the embankment near Cleethorpes. Lincs, where a 15ft section of the bank was partly washed away by the sea last night. Single-line working over the section was expected to be restored this morning. Before dawn, police in cars stood by to warn residents in the Suggitts Lane area if the sea swept over again, but the high tide passed without incident. The tide at 7pm is expected to be higher than last night's high water but its effect on the embankment depends on the force and direction of the wind. Air Ministry Meteorological Office report that only fresh to moderate winds are expected and they will be from the south-west. The weather generally today will be cloudy with rain at times".

Cleethorpes For Happy Holidays

The post-war golden age of the North Promenade was between 1946 and 1966 with thousands of visitors arriving by train every weekend during the summer season.

The Post-War North Promenade

109. Nottingham Journal 20th May 1953
110. 'Travel by Rail to Cleethorpes'. Nottingham Journal. 20th May 1953.

A typical summer Sunday in peak season would bring thirty or forty excursions or 'trip' trains, each with four or five hundred holidaymakers eager to have a good time! It was during this frenetic period of prosperity that various major improvement and modernisation projects were completed along the North Promenade.

Promenade Improvements

On the North Promenade next to Wonderland, was the new Happidrome amusement arcade. Erected on the open land of former amusements, latterly the Wall of Death, Happidrome opened in 1956 and is at the time of writing the Cleethorpes Indoor market.

Next to Happidrome were the two Gayway shops selling ice cream and gifts, the main cavernous Gayway amusement arcade, and the Ritz Cartoon Cinema. There was a model railway exhibition in the cartoon cinema for a time in the mid fifties, run by Jack and Arthur Newbutt. A miniature 'Royal Scot' locomotive ran on rollers outside on the Promenade to draw folk in.

Between the Gayway and Hawkey's New Capitol Cafe, the historic Auckland Colonnade with public house and shops was swept away during the 1955/56 close season. Newly built next to the Ritz Cartoon Cinema were much needed modern public conveniences and a brand new public house. The new Taddy's, opened in 1956, was owned and operated by Samuel Smith's Old Brewery (Tadcaster Ales). At that time there were still two vacant sites. The one between the conveniences and the new pub became the Savoy amusement arcade, opening in 1960. The other site became a block of three fancy goods and gift shops built in 1960 occupied by

Miles of Smiles

111. The 'O' Gauge Model Railway exhibited for a short time in the Ritz cartoon cinema by Arthur & Jack Newbutt in the mid fifties.

Doug Best.

Mr R. Samuels, Mrs M. Mendell and Mr S. Weiss, situated between Taddy's pub and Hawkey's New Capitol Cafe. Hawkey's Cafe was modernised and refurbished in 1960, catering for up to 600 diners (250 on the ground floor and 350 upstairs). In 1965, the menu included roast dinners or fish chips & peas for 6 shillings (30p). Chicken & chips was three shillings and sixpence (18p). Also on offer were hot dogs and takeaways.

Adjacent to Hawkey's Cafe the railway passage off the Promenade provided access to the expanded railway facilities catering for the new diesel trains introduced on East Lincolnshire lines. This included a fuelling point and carriage washing plant, as well as services to the rear of Hawkey's cafe and Taddy's pub. It also provided an excellent viewing spot of the end of the station of departing excursion trains at tea time and during the early evening; a grandstand for loco-spotters (including the author!) who were sometimes ejected by officious railway staff as trespassers. They would point to a cast iron railway sign: Trespassers Will Be Prosecuted. Can you read? Those signs are now collector's items!

The Post-War North Promenade

Modernisation along the North Promenade continued between the railway passage and the station, sweeping away a variety of small shops and attractions, most dating back to before the war, including the Empire Colonnade. First was a new Humber Pastimes amusement arcade, opened in 1955 still operated by Walter West with its modern facade of a barrel vaulted roof forming five canopies, which still exists. Next was a new shop opened in 1956 for that long established Cleethorpes seaside rock manufacturer Brown's (E.A. Brown & Sons). Even more radical was the impressive new Hawkey's Premier restaurant with rooftop dining area. It provided seating for 200 diners and replaced the earlier Premier restaurant and Cafe in the Empire Colonnade, which dated back to the thirties on the same site. Next to Hawkey's towards the station was Blakeman's ice cream kiosk from 1948. Being so close to the station, the railway tracks were immediately behind these buildings.

Continuing towards the station, there was a vacant 60ft long parcel of open land, and finally a block of three shops, built in 1951, before reaching the railway station itself. The three shops were operated by Catering Enterprises Ltd and consisted of the Marine Snack Bar and two more selling fruit, candy floss, whipped ices, rock and novelties.

With changing tidal patterns, amusements on the sands were confined to the area opposite the station which is still in use today. At various times, there has been a Big Wheel, a Peter Pan type railway, children's roundabouts, miniature aeroplane flight, helter skelter, swings and a host of smaller attractions, together with ice cream kiosks, refreshment stalls, deck chair hire and the like, all in full view of holidaymakers arriving at the station by train!

Also present on the beach in the fifties, in addition to the donkeys, were 'Duks', or more accurately DUKW's. These were General Motors ex-WWII US Army & Marine Core amphibious vehicles, which took holidaymakers on trips along the sands and out into the shallow areas of the sea. They were operated by well known local businessman and racehorse owner, Louis Furman, who ran a footwear store on Freeman Street in Grimsby and a garage on Grimsby Road, Cleethorpes selling cars. The DUKW's were a post-war version of the original 'Sea Cars'

112. Loco-spotters at Cleethorpes in 1952. Return excursion trains ready to depart.
H.D.R McNeill.

113. Crowded North Promenade on a wet day in 1954.
Grimsby Evening Telegraph.

operation of the 1920's & 30's (see Chapter 5). Ex WWII DUKW's were also found to be useful in providing 'sea trips' at other resorts where the tide could be some distance from the promenade and are known to have operated at Mablethorpe, Eastbourne and even for river trips on the Thames in London!

Beyond the station, the historic Victorian Victor Colonnade remained completely intact up to 1960, but re-development had commenced at the Sea Road end with a new brick corner kiosk built in 1961 adjoining the end of the Victor Colonnade. There were 20 units within the Victor Colonnade. The first five from Sea Road were amusement arcades operated by Norman Kaye & Co Ltd. These were in reality, new 1961 buildings with the Victorian colonnade frontage replaced by single storey concrete pillars with roof extending to canopy. The rest of the Victorian Colonnade remained original, but perhaps looking well past its best. Next to the amusement arcades moving towards the station was the long established Duke's Bazaar taking up three units with Colonnade frontage and cast iron supports. The next three consisted of Browns Cafe, Osborne's Fish Bar and a Snack Bar run by E.W. Parkinson & Son, again with original Colonnade frontage. The following two units were Duke's Bazaars Ltd shops, then Brown's Snack Bar and finally, five units consisting of a another Duke's Bazaar and four units of

The Post-War North Promenade

amusement arcades operated by Casino Amusements Ltd, adjacent to the Station Approach. This latter arcade, now completely transformed, dominates both the former Victor Colonnade and the skyline; all traces of the original Victorian Colonnade having been swept away.

Miles of Smiles

Impressions of Post-War Cleethorpes

Daily Mirror Monday 26th July 1954

"I haven't had any holiday yet. In fact, I was wondering if I should cancel the whole thing this year. After all, I said to my wife it's almost certain to rain. And how can people possibly enjoy themselves in this ruddy weather? I know the answer to that one now. To find out, I slipped a muffler in my Mac' and went north to Cleethorpes on the Lincolnshire coast where 100.000 people crowd the gaudy front on a fine day. It was early morning when I walked out of the station. It was gently raining and grey clouds trailed low across a sea that looked as inviting as corrugated iron.

The first wave of arriving holidaymakers overtook me pushing prams piled with suitcases and dragging children blowing pink plastic trumpets. As they vanished toward the boarding houses a thin man in a bathing suit and white cap ran across the prom and plunged into the sullen sea. Near the pier Joe Holmes set up his telescopes beside a placard saying 'See the Fishing Fleet'. Aye, but you'll see nothing in this mist." he said disgustedly. In twenty five years, I've never known a summer like it. Jimmy Crampton's 'Flights Around the Bay' has had only seven flying days in four weeks. Boatman Reg Higgins has reduced his prices by half and still mighty few takers. At a tea-stall employing three waitresses, I was told that receipts were often under five shillings (25p) a day.

A bucket and spade merchant said his total take for one day was one shilling and nine pence. And the deck chairs, boating and bathing pools and putting greens run by the Borough Corporation are doing only a quarter of last year's trade. The reason? By his weighing machine, Sid (Dead On) Mountain whipped out a calendar to prove that the town has had only eight fine days since Easter. It's driving people to the arcades he mourned. Up at Wonderland their eyeballs were dropping out from counting the takings! And standing in a puddle by the dodgems, Sid Smith, owner of Wonderland, known as the biggest covered funfair in Britain chuckled fatly as he shook the rain from his sodden hat.

Every cloud that sends them scurrying off the beaches brings me a silver lining he beamed. Yes sir, if there's one thing I like to see, it's a nice drop of rain. Cleethorpes is essentially for the family. The cheapest room on the front is 4/- (shillings) a night, 2/6d if you provide your own food, cooked without extra charge. How do these families manage when they are rained off the beach? They are not supposed to spend the day in the boarding houses.

IN THE STATION. A harassed porter has one quick answer 'They bring sandwiches and tea and pile into the station. You'd think the Queen was arriving to see the crowds. It's ideal for the kiddies, stare at the engines for hours, they do'.

The Post-War North Promenade

Len Wilson, on holiday from Nottingham with his wife and two children had another suggestion. The first few days we went to Wonderland, until we were spent up! Then we took the kids to the mock auction when it was wet. It was as good as the pictures and the children could sit on the floor with their comics.

OWN CONCERT. One torrential day thousands of people with sandwiches and spirit stoves streamed into the pier ballroom. They imagined their own concert party and sat around brewing tea and shrieking with laughter. As I strolled around the dripping front, I began to see that while the beach men prayed for sunshine and the arcade men hoped for squalls, the holiday-makers didn't give a dam either way. Under the shelter of the pier, four women, one with a child asleep in her arms played cards across a suitcase, a man in a Mac lay snoring nearby and a small boy with a shrimping net scooped a biscuit from the clutch of an outraged baby! The pubs opened at 11am and five minutes later one bar was so crowded that we were breathing by numbers. Someone started a sing song. Everybody joined in.

DEFIANT. Meanwhile in the arcades, small boys rammed pennies into the pinball machines. Pretty girls in jeans madly danced while a juke box blared 'With a Dime and a Dollar'. All around me, Cleethorpes was defying the salty rain from its chin and rocking with good humour. The rain that will kill the British holiday has yet to be invented!"

Chapter Ten

POST-WAR WONDERLAND

> **HOLIDAYS AT**
> **"WONDERLAND"**
> **CLEETHORPES**
> CAN BE ENJOYED **WET or FINE**
> OPEN DAILY from JUNE 8th INCLUDING SUNDAYS
> ENTERTAINMENT FOR THOUSANDS UNDER COVER

114. Holidays at Wonderland. Lincolnshire Standard 1st June 1946

Miles of Smiles!

The East Coast Amusement Company re-opened Wonderland for Whitsuntide on 8th June 1946 and then daily for the remainder of the summer season, but following the passing of George Wilkie in 1944, now under the sole direction of 'Ma' Wilkie, with Sid Smith as her General Manager.

The Big Dipper (New Dips) was quickly re-commissioned, as was the Boating Lake and the Skating Rink. In the Great Hall, the Dodgems track was re-laid and the Ghost Train revived. Other pre-war rides were brought back to life out of storage. Looping the Loop was re-constructed and the Brooklands Speedway, previously outdoors, was installed in the Great Hall near the Big Dipper boarding steps.

The outdoor area beyond the Great Hall was re-modelled with the opening of the new Wonderland Cafe at the very end of the promenade. New post-war attractions included the ELECTRIC WATER DODGEMS and the LAKESIDE MINIATURE RAILWAY giving visitors a ride behind a steam locomotive around the boating lake

Post-War Wonderland

115. Classic Wondersnaps shot of thrills on the Big Dipper. A seat was provided beside the lift hill of the Big Dipper for the cameraman.

Doug Best.

116. Running repairs to one of the (Brooklands) Electric Speedway cars in 1952. Arthur Taylor is replacing damaged electrical pick-ups under the car.

Doug Best.

(formerly Lakeland). The miniature railway boarding station was initially between the new Cafe and the Electric Water Dodgems, under a newly constructed canopy. The Electric Water Dodgems was a new ride, not to be confused with the pre-war Water Dodgems (motor boats) on the boating lake. Next to the Electric Water Dodgems was the GOLDEN GALLOPING HORSE ROUNDABOUT (Gallopers) and the ROLLER SKATING RINK, adjacent to the Wonderland Great Hall.

The canopy that had previously extended along the whole length of the promenade side of the Wonderland building was removed during the war, completely transforming its promenade appearance. Now fully exposed was the side wall of the Great Hall with its three entrances; the Station entrance, through which most visitors entered and exited Wonderland, the Centre entrance (always considered to be the Main entrance) and the Dock entrance, close to the skating rink.

A Golden Galloping Horse Roundabout was the centrepiece of any fairground or amusement park, so it is inconceivable it would not be mentioned in advertising or publicity, yet despite assertions to the contrary, and even some writings, there is no evidence to suggest a set of Gallopers ever operated at Wonderland before the war and there is no mention of them in pre-war advertising or news reporting. We can conclude therefore with some certainty that the Gallopers came to Cleethorpes out

Post-War Wonderland

117. Wondersnaps shot of the Water Dodgems in about 1953. Gallopers in the right background.

Doug Best.

of storage soon after the war. The Gallopers were first mentioned as an attraction in Wonderland advertising in 1949.

Older readers may remember the Gallopers being outside, next to the Miniature Railway and Speedway cars (which had replaced the Electric Water Dodgems in 1955), but the Gallopers were actually installed in the Great Hall as the centre ride at first. This may have been a temporary move, prior to the delivery of the new Cycledrome. Doug Best remembers there were complaints about the loudness of the organ playing in the Great Hall. Of course, a Gavioli fairground organ was never designed to operate indoors and the Gallopers were moved outside for the 1949 season. It was an ideal spot as the sound of the organ playing could still be heard within the Great Hall, drawing folk outside to see what else was on offer! The magnificent and historic Savage's Golden Galloping Horse Roundabout, located in the open air at the end of the Promenade, came to be regarded by many as the jewel in the crown of Wonderland. Complete with Gavioli organ that played all day, every day during the summer season, the Gallopers were the star attraction of Wonderland for more than 20 years and remained in its familiar spot until the late sixties. The horses were named after Wonderland staff. Also outdoors under a canopy on its pre-war spot, was the Skating Rink and close by, a set of Flying Chairs (Chair-O-Plane).

118. Wonderland in about 1950. The pleasure arch was fabricated in the Blacksmith Shop. The pre-war extended canopy has been removed, radically changing the promenade facade of the Wonderland building.

Doug Best.

119. The Jewel in the Crown of Wonderland! The newly positioned Gallopers (moved from inside the Great Hall), in action with visitors on a wet day in 1950. The Big Dipper is in the background. Under construction on the right, is the canopy over the Water Dodgems.

Grimsby Evening Telegraph.

Post-War Wonderland

120. The Roller Skating Rink looking down from the lift hill of the Big Dipper in 1950. This later became the site of the Peter Pan Railway.

Doug Best.

The basic pre-war layout of the Great Hall gradually returned with supporting Side-stalls, Dearden's Children's rides, Swings and Roundabouts. The brand new Robert Lakin 'Silver Rodeo' CYCLEDROME was installed as the centre ride during 1949. It cost an astonishing £12.000 (equivalent to £440,000 at the time of writing!) and was one of the largest and final pair of fairground scenic's produced by that long established South London fairground ride manufacturer. With motor cycles on the platforms, its capacity was about 80 riders. The Cycledrome was hugely popular and was usually operated by Jim Griffiths, the Park Foreman. Ride duration was about five minutes, less at peak times! Elsewhere in the Great Hall, the former Mirrored Maze was re-modelled to become the Crazy House. A new attraction close by was the Miniature Zoo.

The Lakeside Miniature Railway, opened in 1949 was developed in association with Jack Woolley of Model Exhibitions Ltd, Harrow. It was an instant success, but it soon became clear that both the locomotive and rolling stock were not robust enough for the intensive daily demands of summer visitors. Drastic action was taken during that first year of operation when the East Coast Amusement Company purchased five locomotives and carriages from the recently closed Kenton Miniature Railway, a private line that had run in the grounds of Kenton Grange, near Harrow, Middlesex. With the Kenton Grange railway assets, came its engineering manager, Jack Newbutt, a former London & North Eastern Railway (LNER) steam locomotive fitter, who moved

121. With shelter for 20,000 people! A busy scene inside the Great Hall of Wonderland in the fifties. In the foreground is Jack Wright's Convoy Ride roundabout and Little Wheel.

Doug Best.

122. The Wonderland Miniature Railway in 1950. The locomotive is 'Flying Scotsman' with Jack Newbutt at the controls. Under the canopy in the background are the Water Dodgems. The first carriage dates from about 1935 and is now owned by the author.

Michael Newbutt Collection.

to Cleethorpes with his family and took on the role of engineer for the whole of the Wonderland site. Also in 1949 came Doug Best who started work as a photographer for the Wondersnaps operation (described in Chapter 14). Doug had recently returned from active service overseas as a tank driver so had basic engineering experience which was put to good use assisting Jack Newbutt during the close season. He later took on the role of engineering manager himself and together they set about the task of making the Wonderland rides more robust, safe and reliable.

Hermann Goering's Armoured Car

Field Marshall Hermann Goering's armoured car was displayed at Wonderland for a week during the summer of 1949. It was displayed close to the Big Dipper, next to the fitters shop on the miniature railway and driven daily along the North Promenade from overnight storage in the town. Its visit to Cleethorpes was part of an extensive tour of the UK commissioned by the War Office to raise funds for the Soldiers, Sailors & Airmen's Families Association (SSAFA). There was a souvenir booklet on sale at the time with the history of the car which was overprinted with individual venues. It is not known if any 'Wonderland, Cleethorpes', stamped copies still survive.

The armoured car was a 1938 Mercedes 770K seven seat Pullman Convertible. It was one of seven built by Mercedes Benz for Nazi Supreme Commanders and was painted in Goering's favourite colour, Aviation Blue. Others were used by Adolf Hitler and those in High Command. The armoured cars weighed 4 tons 7 cwt (4420Kg), had under floor steel armour for protection from land mines, steel inserts in the doors and 1.75 inch, five ply bullet proof glass. They featured a retractable bullet proof shutter behind the rear seat for protection and even a trap door in the floor in front of the rear seat for rapid exit! Powered by a supercharged 7.6 Litre 8 cylinder engine the car was capable of speeds in excess of 100mph. Keeper and guardian throughout the tour was Captain J.F. Thirlby, who demonstrated its special features to enthusiastic visitors who paid 6d to inspect it! It was garaged locally overnight. Registered in the UK as JLY 819, Hermann Goering's armoured car was displayed at Wonderland complete with bullet splattered screen, though it later transpired that the bullet splattered screen was not as a result of enemy action, but by over enthusiastic 'Tommies' checking it was actually, bullet proof!

Wonderland made national news in the Daily Mirror on Tuesday 15th November 1949 when it played its part for the local community. "A GOOD SHAVE BY BARBER FRED OPENS A WONDERLAND FOR THE TOWN'S YOUTH: HUNDREDS of Cleethorpes (Lincs) youngsters feel that local hairdresser Fred Cripsey is just the tops when it comes to wielding a razor. For Fred, while shaving a local businessman managed to obtain a first-class sports stadium for the local youth centre. After using

123. Herman Goering's Bullet Proof Car was displayed at Wonderland in 1949. Cover of the Souvenir booklet.

Author's Collection.

a recreation ground for summer activities the youngsters badly needed an indoor stadium. Let Mr Cripsey, who helps coach at the centre tell the story of how they got it. 'I was shaving, Mr Sidney Smith, managing director of Wonderland, a big summer amusement arcade and told him of our trouble. The arcade is filled with dodgems, a cycledrome and a miniature zoo in summer. MR SMITH CAME BACK: Mr Smith must have been pleased with his shave because he came back the next day and agreed to let us have the arcade each Wednesday night without charge'. All the amusements are cleared away and 400 youngsters play table tennis, Badminton, heading tennis, volley ball and basket ball. When opened two weeks ago, Grimsby Town players gave a demonstration for us and we hope for similar sports shows. All it costs the boys and girls is one shilling subscription to the games centre for sixteen weeks' attendance".

The Lakeside Express goes to Sheffield!

For those not able to take a trip away, Sheffield City Council organised its own annual 'Holiday Week Gala' on the Farm Park Grounds in Granville Road, Sheffield, which included outdoor attractions and displays, such as the Police Motor Cycle Stunt Team in action. In 1950, in a complete role reversal, Sheffield City Council hired the 'Lakeside Express' from Wonderland, Cleethorpes, to operate at Farm Park during its Holiday Week Gala. At that time, the Lakeside Miniature Railway at Wonderland was only in its second season of operation and still finding its feet, but a steam locomotive and carriages made the trip to Sheffield to attend the event. The locomotive was probably the A1 Flying Scotsman, together with three of the sit astride carriages repainted and re-branded with Read the Sheffield Telegraph & Star logos. Unfortunately, the author has not been able to trace any photographs of the Wonderland Lakeside Express in action at Farm Park, but the Sheffield Evening Telegraph of Thursday 27th July 1950 announced: "MODEL TRAIN WILL BE GALA DRAW. The double tracked light railway from Cleethorpes Wonderland will be transferred to Sheffield for the 2nd Annual Holiday Week Gala at the Farm Grounds, Granville Road, which opens on Monday. The track will run along the side of the lake". A few days later on Monday 31st July, it followed this up with "Visit Holiday Week Gala and travel on the Popular Lakeside Railway especially brought from Wonderland, Cleethorpes. Proprietors: East Coast Amusement Co, Promenade, Cleethorpes. Tel: 61130". The Flying

124. Sheffield Daily Telegraph 31st July 1950

Miles of Smiles

125. The three sit astride carriages that went to Sheffield for the Holiday Week Gala repainted with 'Sheffield Telegraph & Star' logos, following their return to Cleethorpes. The portable ladder in the background was for emergency rescue on the Big Dipper. No-one can recall it ever having had to be used!

Michael Newbutt Collection.

Scotsman locomotive was later fitted with a streamlined casing, renamed Sheffield Belle and in this guise, carried a headboard Sheffield Flyer, but there is no evidence that it ever returned to Sheffield in subsequent years.

Wonderland and the Floods

The great hall of Wonderland escaped relatively unscathed as a result of the East Coast floods in 1953, but the outdoor area, the Skating Rink, Electric Water Dodgems and Cafe were all extensively damaged. Doug Best remembers only a few inches of water and mud on the floor of the great hall and no major damage. Fortunately, the gallopers were inside for the winter and the Gavioli organ was well above water level on its transport truck, however about a hundred books of music were lost when the shed by the miniature railway station in which they were stored was flooded. Not so lucky was the Cafe at the end of the promenade which was badly damaged, but was rebuilt and enlarged afterwards.

Post-War Wonderland

126. *The badly damaged end of promenade Cafe, seen from the high viewpoint of the Big Dipper. It was rebuilt and enlarged afterwards. Note the World War II concrete tank traps on the sands below.*

Doug Best.

127. *Flood repair men ready for action on the promenade in front of the Skating Rink in 1953. Big Dipper and Miniature Railway station in the background.*

Doug Best.

The Start of the Summer Season

The first day of a new summer season was Good Friday, but an exciting time was always the afternoon of the day before, Maundy Thursday, when all the rides in Wonderland were run-up on test in preparation for the first revenue earning day. A typical start to the season would follow an established pattern. On the Big Dipper, the cars would be tight after the close season lay-over, so as many people as could be mustered would ride them, all afternoon if they wished! The Big Dipper relied on speed and momentum to ride the dips as once the car left the tower at the top of the lift-hill, it was only gravity that allowed it to complete the run. To achieve a full weight car, sand bags might be placed in any empty seats to simulate passengers and maximise the load. Sometimes a car may not quite make it to the top of a dip and was held from rolling backwards by a safety device, so the test passengers would jump out and push it until gravity took over again! After a few circuits of the track, the bearings would free up and the Big Dipper was re-commissioned.

Most of the big rides in the Great Hall were dismantled and stored during the close season to allow other events to take place. The big rides, such as the Cycledrome, Loops and Jets were rebuilt and tested ready for the new season. This was routine as they were designed for rapid take-down and erection for use in travelling fairs. Park Foreman, Jim Griffiths and his 'heavy gang' undertook most of this work. Jim knew every nut and bolt on every ride.

128. A full train of happy holidaymakers on the Lakeside (Wonderland) Miniature Railway in about 1954. The locomotive is 'Henrietta', constructed by Jack Newbutt in 1947.

Michael Newbutt Collection.

Post-War Wonderland

Outside, the Brooklands Speedway Cars, which had replaced the Electric Water Dodgems in 1955 were tested with much flashing from the electric pick-up shoes underneath as the layers of contamination built up from the salt air during the winter were burned away. The Gallopers were re-assembled and the organ run-up on test. It may still have been very cold, but once the organ began to play, it seemed as if summer had already arrived! Nearby was the Lakeside Miniature Railway. This was always an exciting time for the author as one of the locomotives was steamed for the first time after its winter maintenance and annual boiler test. There was much shunting and re-arranging of carriages to be done as they were moved from the main line straight on the far side of the boating lake where they had been stored over the winter and brought back to the station. After a good hosing down to remove accumulated debris, the carriages were shunted into their respected positions ready for the first passengers. Minor derailments were dealt with at the same time.

129. 'Required Attractive Girl'. Grimsby Evening Telegraph 30th June 1956. Such an ad' would not be acceptable today!

Everywhere there was good natured banter from seasonal regulars meeting up for the first time since the end of the previous season. There were also plenty of opportunities for seasonal staff, particularly girls, to work the side stalls and rides. Frank Smith, Company Secretary, hired seasonal staff from his office next to the dock entrance.

Wonderland opened to the public at the start of a new season at 10.00am on Good Friday, and then Easter Saturday, Sunday, Monday and Tuesday. The start of the season could be disappointing in terms of visitor numbers as the weather was often cold, particularly if Easter

130. 'For Miles of Smiles'. Nottingham Journal. 25th March 1953

fell towards the end of March. After Easter, Wonderland opened at weekends until Whitsuntide and thereafter daily, including Sundays, through the high season until the weekend nearest the 20th September, which marked the end of the summer season. Peak season was late July and early August when literally thousands of visitors packed the North Promenade. It was a Wonderland tradition that all takings from rides were distributed to local charities on the final day of the season.

More Miles of Smiles!

Wonderland progress in the 1950's and 60's saw the introduction of some new rides and the re-location, rebuilding or disposal of others.

The Rotor, sometimes known as Ride-A-Wall was a ride demonstrating the power of centrifugal force. It was a post-war fairground innovation and a modernised version of the Edwardian Joy Wheel. Riders entered the circular drum and as it began to revolve, increasing in speed, they became pinned to the wall by centrifugal force. As the floor was lowered, they were riding the wall with no visible means of support. When the drum slowed, centrifugal force was lost and the riders slipped ungraciously down the wall before the floor had been completely raised to meet them, revealing

131. The Rotor at the end of the promenade, present during the 1951 season only.
Author's Collection.

perhaps rather more female leg than might be usual! It is thought a Rotor was in operation at New Brighton in 1948, almost certainly for the Wilkie's. The Cleethorpes Rotor was built by Orton & Spooner and located next to the Water Dodgems at the very end of the North Promenade. Its frontage read Max Myers Presents Hoffmeister's Rotor (German showman Hoffmeister was the patentee of the ride). Advertised as a Wonderland attraction, it operated for the 1953 season only, before moving on to Rhyl where it continued for many years afterwards.

The PETER PAN RAILWAY, a product of the Supercars Company of Warwick, replaced the Skating Rink

> **WONDERLAND**
> **AMUSEMENT PARK**
> The Finest Covered Amusement Park in the Country
> Main Hall accommodates 20,000 people
> **OPEN SEVEN DAYS A WEEK**
> with the Holiday Spirit every day!
> Attractions include: Big Dipper, Dodgem, Ghost Train, Flying Jets, Cartoon Cinema, Boating, Miniature Railway and scores of others
> **SPECIAL CONCESSION TICKETS FOR PARTIES**
> Write:—Wonderland, Promenade, Cleethorpes

132. Long Eaton Advertiser. 30th June 1956.

in 1953. It was located just outside the main hall on a site about 40 feet square fronted by the promenade and backing up to the start of the lift hill of the Big Dipper. It was a gentle ride for the little ones. The entrance platform was directly off the promenade and the whole of the ride could be viewed from virtually anywhere around its perimeter, such that children could wave to parents from any point on the ride. The track was either straight or in very sharp curved sections and weaved its way round, filling up the site. There was a chicane (later removed to obviate wear & tear on the cars) and a mock tunnel which had been fashioned from an old air raid shelter! The rest of the site was attractively laid out in the Peter Pan Neverland theme. There were five cars, each brightly painted in different colours named Peter Pan (blue), Captain Hook (black!), Tinkerbelle (yellow), Wendy and Michael. They were lined up in the station between rides.

The station was on an electrically dead section of track. After passengers boarded, an operator pushed the car forward a short distance, whence it made contact with the live track and set off under its own power. The ride was one circuit of the track, accompanied by much bell ringing and waves to parents by excited children! At the end of the ride, the car entered the electrically dead section in the platform. A member of staff would bring it to a halt safely and passengers alighted. The car would then be at the rear of the line up awaiting new passengers and moved forward as the cars in front took off. The layout was subtly altered from year to year.

Miles of Smiles

133. The Hurricane Jets was the last brand new ride at Wonderland. From the cover of the 1966 Cleethorpes Tourist Guide.

Author's Collection.

The HURRICANE JETS, manufactured by Lang Wheels in 1955 was the last new big ride supplied to the East Coast Amusement Company. It was located in the Great Hall at the foot of the steps leading up to the Big Dipper and replaced the Brooklands Speedway cars which had been moved outside again, in turn replacing the Electric Water Dodgems which had become unreliable due to leakage from the water tank. Each car held two adults. The rider was able to pull back a joystick that lifted the arm and controlled the height and angle of elevation of the car when the ride was in motion. The loud and abrupt blasts of air emitted simulated the launch of a space rocket, but could be quite frightening for the little ones.

The Cleethorpes Trade Fair

Wonderland occasionally hosted special events and exhibitions during the close season. One such event was the Grimsby Canine Society's Show in 1928, described in Chapter 5. It was used after the war as a youth sports centre for 16 weeks during each winter, also for Ideal Home Exhibitions, Christmas Fayres and the like.

Post-War Wonderland

134. Cover of the 1958 Cleethorpes Trade Fair programme. 57 local businesses had stands in the Great Hall of Wonderland.
Author's collection.

In 1958, the Cleethorpes Trade Fair was held in the Great Hall between Wednesday 1st and Saturday 4th October. It was promoted by the Cleethorpes Chamber of Trade and 57 local businesses had stands in the Great Hall of Wonderland. This must have been a frenetic time for Wonderland staff and contractors for the summer season had closed only ten days previous, on Sunday 21st September, with the annual Charity event.

The Trade Fair was opened by Mr T. B. Northcote, Managing Director of H. Mudd & Sons Ltd, Fish & Frozen Processors, Grimsby Docks, supported by The Worshipful, the Mayor of Cleethorpes, Councillor Woolf Solomon. A plan of the exhibition shows the Dodgems track was used as the Hall of Fashion and the Cycledrome, Loops and Jets had been cleared, along with virtually everything else in the centre of the hall, to make way for the exhibition stands, which were all brought in for the event. It appears from the exhibition plan that Stand No 6, the Milk Bar, was set up in the Jollysnaps Studio and Civil Defence on Stand No 9 was housed in the closed-off Main Entrance.

Three rows of exhibition stands were set up in the cleared centre of the hall and more rows set up in front of the Promenade Side Stalls, the Power House and Crazy House. On the Station side of the hall, the Tennis Ball Shooter became the Chamber of

Miles of Smiles

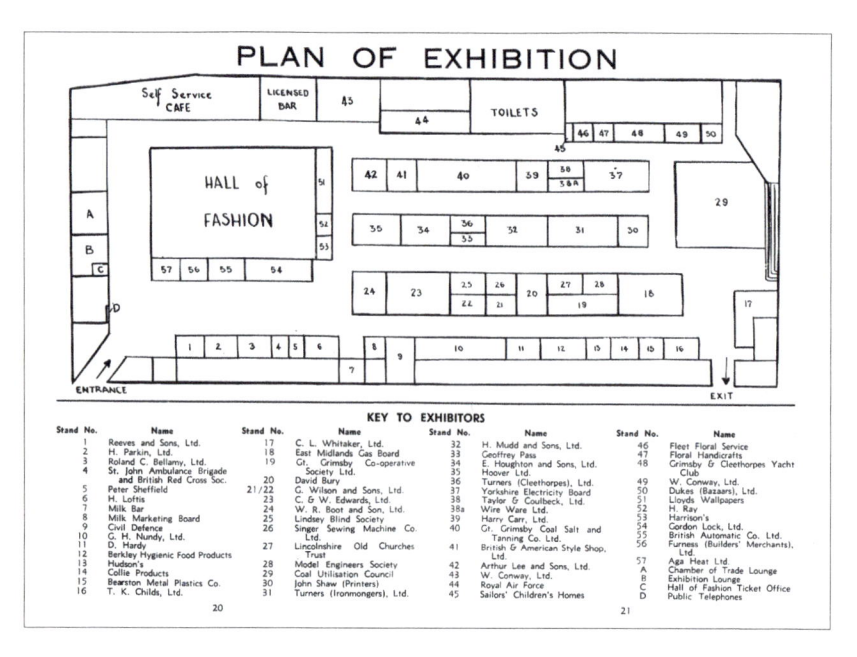

135. Plan of 1958 Trade Fair Exhibition

Author's collection.

136. The Redwings Ice Hockey Team on the frozen boating lake at Wonderland! Motor boats stored out of the water for the close season. Boating lake supplies shed in the background.

Doug Best.

Post-War Wonderland

Trade Lounge, the Bowling Alley became the Exhibition Lounge and Hall of Fashion ticket office, and in the frontage of the Bows & Arrows were Public Telephones. It is not clear whether the Cleethorpes Trade Fair was an annual event or a one-off, held in Wonderland that year.

Following the closure of the Ice Rink on Ladysmith Road in Grimsby, the Grimsby Redwings ice hockey team used the partially drained frozen boating lake at Wonderland as an impromptu ice rink. Doug Best, one of its leading members, obtained permission from Wonderland management and a number of informal local matches were played during the close season when weather conditions were favourable. John Lilee remembers these being quite successful but sand blown on to the ice tended to blunt the skates. Local teams who took part included the Red Hawks, Columbia and Lions.

Enter the Waltzer

In 1958, in a brave move to keep up with the times, the Cycledrome was converted to a WALTZER. This reduced its capacity by half to about 40 riders. Converting it was a massive job but was undertaken entirely in-house. There were 20 platforms, all of which needed additional strengthened hinges due the out of balance action of the Waltzer cars. The original gearbox to drive the ride proved inadequate and a bespoke replacement, manufactured by Crofts Engineers of Bradford, was supplied and fitted. The thinking

137. *The Waltzer (former Cycledrome) in the Great Hall of Wonderland in 1975. Dodgems in the background.*
Michael Smith / University of Sheffield.

may have been to keep up with the times, but revert to the motor cycles in peak season to maximise income, however the bikes were stored in the paint shop afterwards and never used again.

Another LOOP-O-PLANE was operated at Wonderland for one season only in about 1960. It was situated on the outdoor site beyond the Great Hall, next to the Peter Pan Railway. Similar to the pre-war one, it had two long arms, each with an enclosed car on one end and a counterweight at the other. Propelled by an electric motor, the arms swung in opposite directions to each other until they 'looped' taking the riders through a full 360 degrees. This Loop-O-Plane proved not to be universally popular and many were apprehensive about riding it. Doug Best operated it for a short time during a period of staff shortage. He remembered operators would hold the ride momentarily with the twin cars upside down, and then collect the change that had fallen out of the riders pockets, afterwards!

The Boating Lake was drained and converted to Go-kart operation in 1963. Looping the Loop (The Cages) remained as popular as ever but in 1965, after some vigorous action, one of the heavy counterweights came crashing down on the platform below after a pivot snapped, fortunately without injury. It was later discovered the arm had metal fatigue, so after 31 years the Loops were declared unsafe and dismantled.

Except for the historic Big Dipper, which was condemned in 1974 and replaced with a Mad Mouse roller coaster the following year, the basic content and layout of Wonderland remained, with only minor changes right up until its sale by the East Coast Amusement Company to Dudley Bowers (Leisure) Ltd in 1981, who went on to develop the Great Hall as a Sunday Market, together with outdoor rides.

Post-War Wonderland

Plan of Wonderland Great Hall image key:

1. Oyster Bar (Bill Anderson)
2. Coconut Shy (Dearden)
3. Bows & Arrows (Dearden)
4. Bowling Alley (Dearden)
5. Tennis Ball Shooter (Norman Murgatroyd)
6. Winchester Shooting Gallery (Norman Murgatroyd)
7. Madam Ruby (Palm Reader)
8. Wonderland Cafeteria
9. Slot Machine Arcade (Tony Felcey)
10. Ghost Train
11. Gents Toilets
12. Ladies Toilets
13. Electric Power House
14. Electrician Store
15. Blacksmith Shop
16. Photographic Dark Room (WonderSnaps)
17. Secure Store
18. Store (Under Dips Platform)
19. Competition Darts Gallery (Peggy Bailey)
20. Crazy House / House of Laughter (George Blyth)
21. Pet's Corner (Ken Hood)
22. Side Stall (Not used)
23. Big Dipper Boarding & Alighting Platform
24. Offices / Dips Car Shed
25. Motor Boats Fuel Store
26. Lakeside Miniature Railway Station
27. American Whipped Ice Cream Stall
28. Peter Pan Railway
29. Spider & Fly (Mr & Mrs Scruton)
30. Admin & Wages Office
31. Nails (Reuben Felcey)
32. Roll-A-Ball (Reuben Felcey)
33. Hammers / High Strikers (Bill Shotton)
34. Seasonal Side Stall
35. Cork Shooter (George Blyth)
36. Cans (Mops)
37. Jollysnaps Studio
38. Wondersnaps Counter
39. Madam Eileen (Palm Reader)
40. Laughing Clowns (Dora Lockley)
41. Roll-A-Ball (Peter Jones)
42. Ice Cream Parlour (Bessie Wilkie)
43. Derby Racer (Dearden)
44. Kiddie Roundabout (Dearden)
45. Hoop-La (Dearden)
46. Hook-A-Duck (Colin Blyth)
47. Dive Bomber (Peggy Cripsey)
48. Gift Stall
49. First Aid Centre
50. Kiddie Swing-boats (Jack Wright)
51. The Little Wheel (Jack Wright)
52. Convoy Ride Roundabout (Jack Wright)

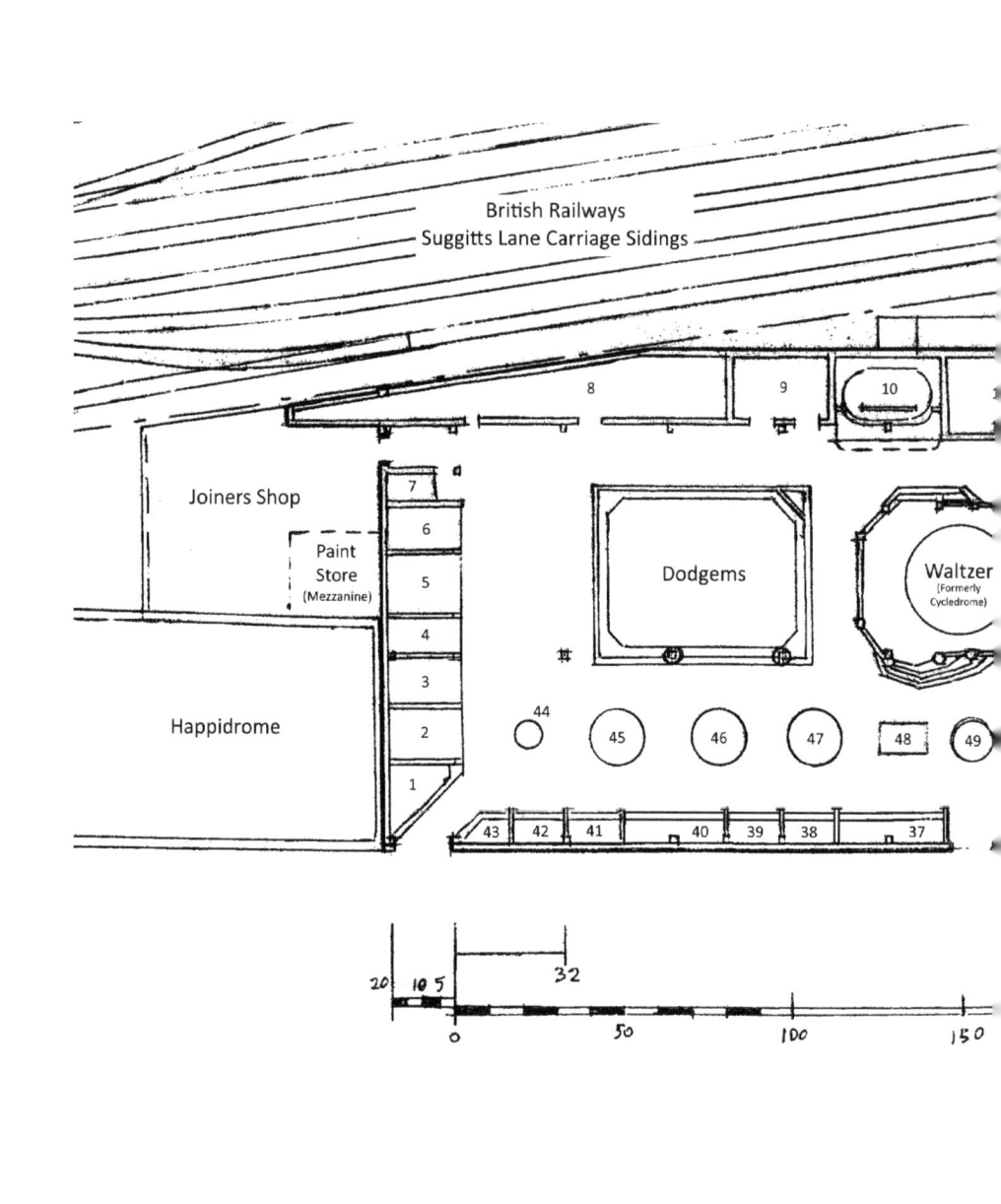

British Railways
Suggitts Lane Carriage Sidings

8   9   10

Joiners Shop

7
6
Paint Store (Mezzanine)
5
4
3
2
1

Dodgems

Waltzer
(Formerly Cycledrome)

Happidrome

44 45 46 47 48 49

43 42 41 40 39 38 37

20 10 5   32
0   50   100   150

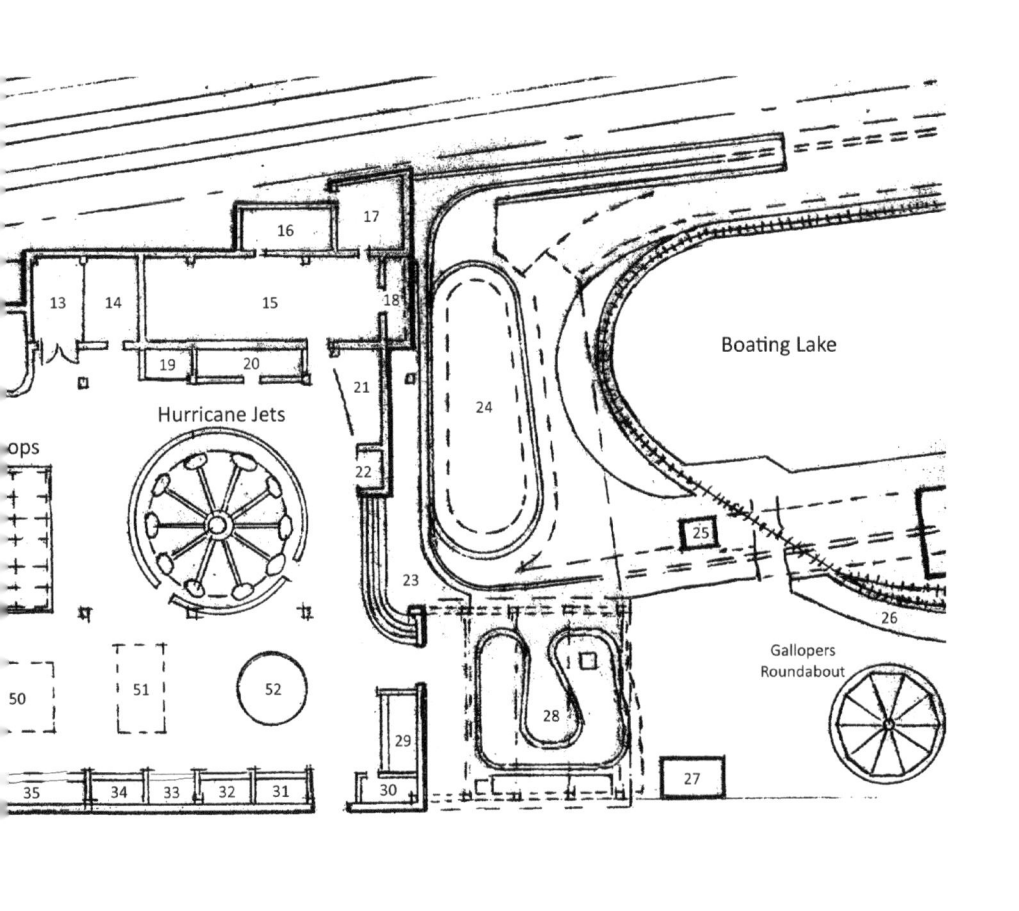

16
17
13 14 15 18
19 20
21
Hurricane Jets
22
24
Boating Lake
ops
23
25
26
Gallopers Roundabout
50 51 52
28
29
35 34 33 32 31 30
27

FEET 1:500
0 250

138. Plan of Wonderland c1960
Plan by Chris Dibben.

Chapter Eleven

WONDERLAND RIDES – A CLOSER LOOK

The East Coast Amusement Company tended to be loyal to known and established suppliers of fairground rides and equipment. Prominent amongst these were Robert Lakin, Supercars and Lang Wheels. Wonderland has a proud history and some of its long established big rides deserve examination in more detail. These are described in roughly chronological date order from its opening in 1926.

The Big Dipper, or New Dips, was the re-constructed former Dip-the-Dips roller coaster moved from the Promenade during the 1925/6 re-modelling of the site. Doug Best remembers being told a friend of the family, a Mr Hutchinson of Robson Road was involved in the re-construction.

The Big Dipper was a Miller design side friction roller-coaster. John A. Miller (1872-1941) was a key figure in the technical development of roller coasters. In side friction roller coasters, flanged wheels carry the weight of the car on the track, while the 'side friction' guide wheels run against vertical boards keeping the car central on the track. This allowed steeper inclines and tighter, faster curves. The vertical side boards were visually pleasing, conveying a sense of assurance to the observer that the car was secure on the track. The Big Dipper was an impressive structure of Canadian pitch pine located adjacent to the main line railway carriage sidings, and occupying part of the site of the former Figure-8 Railway. It was one of the main opening attractions of the new Wonderland complex in 1926. The tower at the highest point of the structure proclaimed it to be New Dips. Each year, a quantity of Canadian pitch pine was delivered for repairs during the close season.

The post-war manager of the Big Dipper was Barney Samuels. Its operation was largely self- sufficient from the rest of the Wonderland site. The twin cars each seated six passengers, making a maximum payload of twelve. Cars were released from the boarding station by operating a floor mounted lever which released a friction brake under the car, allowing it to roll forward by gravity into a shallow dip, at the bottom

Wonderland Rides – A Closer Look

139. Looking down upon Wonderland and the North Promenade from the summit of the Big Dipper prior to 1953. A car is racing down one of the dips on its final circuit. Under the canopy on the left is the Skating Rink. On the right is the Big Dipper car shed and just visible below it, the Boating Lake.

Doug Best.

of which it engaged an endless rope to haul it to the summit of the lift hill. A loud click-click-click sound could be heard from the ratchet system, a safety feature that prevented a car from rolling back in case of failure.

At the summit (under the tower), the car was released and travelled by gravity alone. A bell at the boarding station sounded when it was safe to release another car. Speeds of up to 40mph were possible with a full car. As on any railway the surface of the track became polished with regular use as the cars passed over it, however Ray Crome recalls that a very short section of track on the descent of the double dip never did attain the shine of the rest of the circuit, indicating the cars were travelling so fast, they momentarily left the rails at that spot! There was of course no danger as the side rollers kept the car secure in the centre of the dip.

Slowing the car to a safe stop at the end of the ride was again by a friction brake applied to the underside. The final run in was through a long covered tunnel, necessary because if it was wet, the car would not stop! Before the war, there was an additional

Miles of Smiles

140. *The impressive structure of the Big Dipper which surrounded the Boating Lake with a car on the top level. The building in the lower part of the image is the Dips car maintenance shed.*

Rob Foxon.

short tunnel with an emergency brake on the middle level, overlooking Suggitts Lane. This was a safety feature allowing more cars to be released at peak times. The emergency brake was applied by a large ship type capstan wheel located at the boarding station, though no one recollects it ever having been used. Tensioning the haulage rope was a daily operation to allow for expansion and contraction due to outdoor climatic conditions. A tight rope could lift the car off the track! This was a laborious job as the hand wheel was located very close to the ground and required both hands to turn it. Doug Best later made a device coupled with a turning handle at waist height which made the job much easier. He made many friends as a result of this! The haulage rope was replaced every two years and the old one laid aside in-situ as an emergency spare.

There were five twin cars which were maintained in the car shed behind the boarding station. Access was via a circular loop line running through the car shed. There was also a pink coloured car which was used for parts as its floor had been damaged in an incident many years before. The wheel bearings on the cars were ground in annually with valve grinding paste. Engineering Manager, Jack Newbutt introduced an improved technique latterly.

Wonderland Rides – A Closer Look

There was a serious fire in 1952 which started near Bill Shotton's Hammers side stall, located between the Dips boarding steps and the Zoo. It severely damaged the Dips platform, offices and the Zoo, fortunately without loss of human or animal life. It was thought the cause was an electric fire being left switched on. It put the Big Dipper out of action for several months whilst repairs were carried out.

The Big Dipper ceased operating in 1974 following a safety inspection which revealed several of the massive main supports required replacing and that it was no longer possible to source Canadian pitch pine of sufficient size. It was demolished during the winter of 1974/5 and replaced on the same site by a 'Mad Mouse' roller coaster aquired second hand from the Ocean Beach Amusement Park in Rhyl. For the historic Wonderland Big Dipper however, it was a sad end to a ride that had thrilled Cleethorpes visitors for almost fifty years.

The WONDERLAND DODGEMS may well have been the very first in the UK. They were advertised as an attraction from the opening of Wonderland in 1926. The cars were small half barrel shape and clearly of US origin. The track was approximately 60ft x 50ft with probably, twenty bumper cars.

The origin of the fairground Dodgem car is not easy to understand. It is generally accepted that the concept of bumper cars (dodgems or auto skooters), originated with

141. Cars pass very close to the fitters shop on the final level of the Big Dipper. One of the structural supports protruded into the engineering workshop shop itself!
Rob Foxon.

Miles of Smiles

142. The sad sight of the landmark Wonderland Big Dipper in course of demolition in 1974. The Big Dipper replaced the Figure 8 Railway in 1926 and thrilled Cleethorpes holidaymakers for almost 50 years.

Grimsby Evening Telegraph.

the Stoehrer Brothers in America, who filed a patent in December 1920. They went on to create the Dodgem Company. Dodgems were an instant success at Coney Island and soon became big business. They found their way into the UK, some of the first examples being at Butlin's, Skegness in 1928, however Dodgems were advertised at Wonderland from its opening in 1926, so may have actually been the very first examples in the UK.

The National Fairground Archive describes the history of Dodgems: "The Dodgems as we know them today were introduced in Britain in 1928 by Messrs Lusse Brothers (a competitor of the Dodgem Co). Earlier models of this type of ride had been in existence before this time, but they did not gain popularity in the UK until they were presented in the fairgrounds by a number of British firms including Robert Lakin and Orton & Spooner".

It seems unlikely the original 1920's dodgem cars would have survived for very long in Wonderland for dodgem car development was very rapid throughout the thirties. Substantial streamlined dodgem cars manufactured by Supercars were in use in Wonderland in the fifties. These were probably new post-war models which in turn, were replaced by more modern streamlined dodgems, also by Supercars, in about 1960. The Wonderland Dodgems were still operating in their original place in the Great Hall (with the 1960 cars) up until the sale to Dudley Bowers in 1981.

Wonderland Rides – A Closer Look

THE BOATING LAKE, originally known as LAKELAND, was another of the original attractions. The Boating Lake measured 300ft x 80ft and was located within the Big Dipper. It originally had children's paddle boats, but for the 1929/30 seasons, the lake was drained and converted into a huge open air roller skating rink, which it claimed to be the largest of its kind in the country. "A special composition floor had been laid, at great cost and was said to be equal to ice" was reported the Hull Daily Mail on Wednesday 19th June 1929. For the 1931 season, the lake was restored and roller skating relocated closer to the promenade.

SPEEDBOATS were advertised as the new lake attraction for 1931, but there is no visual evidence of anything resembling a speedboat! For 1933, WATER DODGEMS were advertised as 'new', however for 'Water Dodgems' read either 'Speedboats' (from 1931), or perhaps more accurately, Motor Boats! These were the two seat motor boats referred to in all subsequent thirties advertising as WATER DODGEMS. The little two seat motor boats powered by two stroke petrol engines shown in the 1934 display ad' (plate 87), were to become a feature of the Boating Lake for the next thirty years. Between the wars, there were rowing boats and even a passenger carrying boat seating

143. Wondersnaps Ref: 1196/28. Mum and daughter on the Dodgems, circa 1955. They would have been presented with a card after the ride advising their photograph would be ready for collection in two hours. Three 3.5" x 2.5" size prints cost 2/6d (13p)!

Doug Best.

up to 24 persons. An island in the centre of the lake, accessed by a bridge, boasted a WATER CHUTE (in 1938/9 advertising) and even a miniature golf course, at various times.

After the war, the attraction was marketed as Motor Speed Boats! They were actually the same pre-war motor boats, seating two persons and still proving to be very popular. Powered by a 98cc Villiers two stroke engine (pop-pop) with centrifugal clutch drive to the prop shaft, the engine was started by pull chord. Boating lake operators had well developed right arms as starting could sometimes be difficult! With heavy passengers, the boat might be low in the water, sometimes covering the exhaust and stalling the engine! Duration of ride depended on demand on the day, but probably about ten minutes. Come in number 5, your time is up!

The motor boats were constructed and maintained in the joiners shop. A boat that had been completely rebuilt with new wood would be set back into the water and left to sink for a few days to allow the wood to swell, after which it would become watertight. After being lifted out of the water and pumped dry, the engine would be installed and it would be good for another period of service. The Boating Lake was drained each winter and was sometimes used for ice skating by the staff. It was finally drained in 1962 and the boats replaced by Go-Karts for the 1963 season.

The GHOST TRAIN was announced as a new ride in 1931. The cars were basically a travelling bench seat for up to three adults. The track was a single rail. A front bogie

144. The Boating Lake in the late fifties. The sturdy little two seat motor boats were powered by 98cc Villiers two stroke petrol engines and were already about 30 years old!
Doug Best.

Wonderland Rides – A Closer Look

145. The Boating Lake converted to a Go-Kart track in 1963. It was ideal for the purpose but the area is already beginning to look run down.

Rob Foxon.

clamped to either side of the rail with electrical pick-ups guided the car which was powered from the motor driven fixed rear axle, similar to a tricycle.

The ride was operated by Harold Scherzlinger for many years. He was a veteran of Wonderland. The cars lined up at the station on an electrically dead section of track. Those out of use were stored off track behind the station. Riders boarded the front car. A push from the operator set the car in motion through a set of double doors dead ahead, then turning sharp right through a second set of double doors into the 'Lost World' dark spooky cavern. There were many sharp turns, illuminated skeletons and ghostly sirens, before emerging through the exit double doors, turning 90 degrees right again and back into daylight where an operator brought the car to a safe stand behind the other waiting cars. The haunted cavern was actually quite small. A red light above the entrance doors illuminated briefly when it was safe to release another car. There could be as many three cars in action at once at peak times. With a new frontage, the Ghost Train was still in operation in 1977 and is thought to have continued after the sale of Wonderland to Dudley Bowers in 1981.

The LOOPS or Cages were actually devised, manufactured and constructed in-house at Wonderland in 1934 and patented by George Wilkie. A circular wire cage which could hold two adults was attached to six swinging arms with counterweights. The ride was of timber construction and there were six cages in the set. The action was that of a playground swing, swinging back and forth, but with super-human

Miles of Smiles

146. The colourful frontage of the Ghost train obscures any view of the cars. The Ghost Train was new in 1931 and still working fifty years later!
Dick Price / University of Sheffiled.

147. The Speedway outdoors again, next to the Gallopers beside the Miniature Railway, having replaced the Water Dodgems in 1955. As the Brooklands Racing Track, they occupied this same spot when new in 1936.
Grimsby Evening Telegraph.

effort, the cage could be made to swing through a full 360 degrees (Over the Top in a Swing), hence it looped. Ride duration was at the discretion of the operating staff but a brake was fitted which could be applied if it was deemed a rider had had his allotted time!

The BROOKLANDS SPEEDWAY was manufactured by the Supercar Company Ltd, then of Leamington Spa, and supplied new for the 1936 season. It was originally on the open ground beside the Big Dipper at the end of the Promenade. Advertising in 1938 declared "Come and Learn How to Drive a Car", showing it in place next to the Big Eli Wheel and Flying Chairs. After the war, it was in the Great Hall near the Big Dipper boarding steps. In 1955 it was moved outside again back to its original pre-war site, but now under the canopy of the former Electric Water Dodgems, which it replaced. Its place in the Great Hall was taken by the brand new Hurricane Jets ride. The Speedway track was oval with an island in the centre on which was situated the control cabin. The electric cars picked up power at 110 volts from adjacent parallel plates on the interleaved metal track. Staff needed rubber soled shoes for this ride as they could get an electric shock if walking on the track with the power on. Anyone wearing hobnail boots might find themselves welded to the track!

The Speedway cars seated two adults, had conventional pneumatic tyres and were of very robust construction. The rear wheels were chain driven from an electric motor set behind the seat. The driver had only two controls, the steering wheel and a foot switch to start the car. There were no brakes! The ride could be very jerky when the electrical pick-up shoes made intermittent contact with the track accompanied by much sparking and flashes from under the car. Cars stopped for maintenance or repair were lifted on to the central island and tipped on their side to access the underneath. Broken electrical pick-ups due to protruding screw heads on the track were the most common problem. Modern day Health & Safety would have had a field day with this ride but it was inherently safe, for when the power was off (between sessions), no car could move.

Prospective riders jumped into any empty car on the track between sessions. Staff moved quickly from car to car to collect the fares and issue tickets. Change was not given and had to be claimed from the cashier after the ride! With the track clear of people, the power was switched on and the ride commenced. Problems during the ride usually related to crashes or a car slewed across the track following a shunt. A slewed car could not usually be recovered and needed manual assistance in the form of a burly member of staff to 'bounce' it back into play. Ride duration was about 5mins (less at busy times!). Arthur Taylor managed the Speedway. It was still operating well into the seventies, having moved again back into the Great Hall following the rationalisation of the outdoor rides. There it was squeezed in between the Waltzer and the Jets, and re-branded the Indianapolis 500!

Miles of Smiles

148. The Indianapolis 500 Speedway in the Great Hall of Wonderland c1975. This nomadic ride was supplied new as the Brooklands Race Track, situated outdoors in 1936. It was moved inside the Great Hall after the war, then outdoors again as the Electric Speedway in 1955, before finally returning inside the Great Hall again re-branded as the Indianapolis 500, in about 1970. The Jets are in the background but the Big Dipper has already gone. In the right background can be seen Jack Wright's Convoy Ride roundabout and Little Wheel kiddie rides, but the side stalls all appear to have closed.

Grimsby Evening Telegraph.

The LOOP-O-PLANE was introduced into the UK in 1937. It was announced as a new attraction at Wonderland in a feature about Cleethorpes Carnival Week in the Hull Daily Mail on Wednesday 27th July 1938. Manufactured by the Eyerly Aircraft Company of Salem, Oregon, it was a fairground adaption of their flying simulator used by the US Air Force for training pilots. The Loop-O-Plane had two long arms, each with an enclosed car seating two riders at one end and a counterweight at the other. Riders were seated back to back. Propelled by an electric motor, the arms swung pendulum style in opposite directions to each other until they 'looped' taking the riders upside down through a full 360 degrees. It was advertised as a Wonderland attraction from 1937 to 1939.

The CHAIR-O-PLANE or Flying Chairs, was located on the outdoor area of Wonderland on the Promenade next to the Brooklands Speedway and shown in Wonderland adverts for the 1938 season, however a Chair-O-Plane is also mentioned in earlier advertising for the launch of Wonderland in 1926 & 1927. This is almost

Wonderland Rides – A Closer Look

149. This magnificent Chair-O-Plane (Flying Chairs) on the Wonderland outdoor site beyond the Great Hall in 1952. Chair-O-Planes are known to have operated at Wonderland from its opening in 1926 to 1938. This splendid example was at Wonderland in 1953.

Doug Best.

certainly the one shown in Plate 26 in action on the sands back in 1912. Little is known about the actual machine itself, which was probably of US manufacture, as it rotated anti-clockwise, unlike British and European convention for circular rides.

After the war, a Chair-O-Plane featured in Wonderland advertising from 1951 to 1953. It was located next to the Skating Rink. There are no further references to it after 1953 so it is not known for exactly how long it remained, but photographic evidence shows it to be an excellent example, probably of German origin.

Post-War Wonderland Rides:

The post-war Wonderland star attraction was its magnificent set of Gallopers. The Golden Galloping Horse roundabout, complete with Gavioli fairground organ was the oldest ride on the site, though little is known of its history. Sid Smith, General Manager suggested the organ was 54 years old in an article published in the Grimsby Telegraph in 1954. He was probably about right and the Gallopers of similar age, but it is not known when they came into Wilkie ownership. It seems likely the Gallopers were aquired by

Miles of Smiles

George Wilkie complete with organ well before the war, but prior to that the merry-go-round and organ would have had quite separate lives. To be technically correct, they were steam powered, three horse, crank axle Gallopers, manufactured by Savage & Co of Kings Lynn around the turn of the 20th century.

Best loved of all merry-go-rounds, the Gallopers owe much of their origin and development to that renowned manufacturer of fairground rides, Frederick Savage & Co. Their Platform Gallopers imparted a vigorous rocking motion to the platform mounted horses when the roundabout was in motion, hence the horses Galloped. His patent Platform Slide also allowed the horses to swing out slightly by centrifugal force as the roundabout gathered speed, adding to the Illusion of Galloping Horses. The horses themselves were manufactured in the Savage's factory by skilled craftsmen. Each horse took about ten days to make. The body consisted of about 30 pieces of yellow pine whilst the legs were made of beech. Savages proudly proclaimed that only the glass eyes and the horsehair tail were out-sourced.

Having been initially installed in the Great Hall (possibly a temporary move) the Gallopers were moved outside beside the Big Dipper, probably during the 1949 season and remained there until the late sixties. During the close season, they were dismantled and taken inside. In 1950, the barge boards were replaced and in 1952, the

150. The magnificent set of Gallopers, with organ, in about 1952. The Flying Chairs (see previous image) are on the extreme left. The Big Dipper and Lakeside Miniature Railway station are in the background. The Gallopers remained on this spot until the mid sixties.
(R.A.Taylor/ University of Sheffield).

Wonderland Rides – A Closer Look

151. A close season view of the Gallopers, situated under the canopy of the former Peter Pan Railway in 1969.

Ron Kinder / University of Sheffield.

organ was enlarged to 89 keys by Ben Barretti (of Chiappa Ltd, London) using parts from the dismantled former Custer Cars organ stored in the paint shop. This gave it the very distinctive sound which later attracted fairground organ lovers from all over the country. The bargeboards were painted with Wild West themes (said to be based on images in comics!) by artist Cyril Creswell and were superb!

Despite some assertions to the contrary, it has been confirmed the Gallopers were never steam operated in Cleethorpes. Indeed, although the original Savage's steam engine was still in place, it was incomplete and could never have been steamed indoors in the Great Hall in any case. A large electric motor mounted on the steam engine powered the ride at Wonderland. The crown wheel was the most vulnerable part and Doug Best recalls travelling to Kings Lynn on several occasions to procure an emergency replacement and then working late into the night with Jack Newbutt to fit it, ready for opening the following day. It was in about 1960 that it was discovered the wooden cradle containing the steam engine was severely weakened. The engine was removed and the existing electric motor, coupled to a second hand ex-fairground gearbox mounted on the ride. The Savages steam engine was stored in the joiners shop for a while afterwards then sold, it is thought to Jonathan Potts, local scrap metal dealer (valuable copper boiler).

Miles of Smiles

152. The Gallopers, now known as the Wells Fargo Carousel, in the Great Hall without organ and with a stagecoach on the platform, replacing missing or broken horses.
Dick Price / University of Sheffield.

Following the rationalisation of the Wonderland outdoor site in the late sixties, the Gallopers were moved under the cover of what was formerly the Peter Pan Railway, where it is believed to have worked for several seasons, however its condition and that of the organ, was rapidly deteriorating. The organ was sold in 1975 and the merry go round moved into the Great Hall, re-branded as the Wells Fargo Carousel.

Shortly before the sale of Wonderland to Dudley Bowers, the Wonderland three abreast Gallopers were sold to Hatherop Castle Girl's School in the Cotswolds, reportedly for £15,000 and erected in the school grounds. The story attracted the attention of ATV Local Television News who aired a short item on 5th March 1981. It included an interview with headmistress, Dr Pandora Moorhead. How long the Gallopers remained at the school is not known but they were later reported as being aquired by Mr Jack Schofield of Retford, Notts, who was engaged in rebuilding the ride. Its present day whereabouts and status are unknown.

The Wonderland Gavioli organ is a happier story. In an article about the Cleethorpes Gavioli published in the Autumn 2007 issue of Key Frame, the quarterly journal of the Fair Organ Preservation Society, Phillip Upchurch described the organ as having been sold to Screeton Bros at Barton on Humber in 1975, where it was only part restored. The article goes on to describe the organ as being aquired subsequently by an American mechanical music enthusiast who had it completely refurbished in the UK, before shipping to the US in 2007. Now known as the Diamond Jubilee Gavioli (it was thought to have been new in 1897, the year of Queen Victoria's Diamond Jubilee),

Wonderland Rides – A Closer Look

153. Wondersnaps shot on the Cycledrome.

Doug Best.

154. The former Cycledrome, now Wonderland's Disco Waltzer, with crowds in 1981.

Stephen Smith / University of Sheffield.

Miles of Smiles

155. Wondersnaps shot of the Water Dodgems in the early fifties. Promenade and sea in the background.

Doug Best.

it is mounted on a trailer and tours fairground functions and exhibitions throughout North America, playing to delighted crowds.

The new post-war centrepiece in the Great Hall was the CYCLEDROME supplied in 1949 which replaced the Gallopers. It was a massive 'Silver Rodeo' four hill Scenic Ark manufactured by Robert J. Lakin of 67 Besley Street, Streatham, South London and one of the largest and last that firm produced. With motor cycles on the platforms, its capacity was about 80 riders. It remained original, as supplied, until being converted to a Waltzer in 1958.

Operating under a variety of names such as New Waltzer and Disco Waltzer, it remained on its original site in the Great Hall of Wonderland until being loaned out by Dudley Bowers to other operators from about 1987. It returned to Wonderland in 1992, this time located on the cleared and re-modelled outdoor site of the former Big Dipper.

There is reference to the Wonderland 'Silver Rodeo' Cycledrome in the National Fairground Archive (Ref: Ark A170) which suggests the Lakin Cycledrome was actually supplied new to Charles Manning at Felixstowe in 1946, before moving to Cleethorpes soon afterwards, however Wonderland staff have always maintained it was supplied new to them in 1949.

Wonderland Rides – A Closer Look

The National Fairground Archive also refers to a smaller Orton & Spooner Easy Rider Cycledrome Speedway Ark (Ref: A148) being at Wonderland between 1979 and 1984 owned by Michael Miller & Son (Son-in-law of Dudley Bowers). This was in the Wonderland Great Hall for a short time next to the Waltzer, before being moved outside around 1982. It later moved on to Funland at Mablethorpe.

The ELECTRIC WATER DODGEMS was a post-war creation. In 1949 a large open sided covered area was created alongside the end of the North Promenade, close to the Cafe. This was the site of the Brooklands Speedway cars when new in 1936. Under the canopy was installed a giant surplus ARP water reserve tank. The water dodgems were essentially a water-borne version of the electric dodgem cars in the great hall, energised by power from an overhead mesh via a mast attached to the rear. They operated at 110 volts, the return current path being through the water. A chemical added to the water to aid conduction gave it a yellow tint. The Water Dodgems would have been a Health & safety nightmare today!

156. *The Wonderland Miniature Railway in 1950. The locomotive is the American Pacific built in 1933. During that first season, trains ran anti-clockwise around the lakeside circuit. This locomotive operates today on the Grimsby & Cleethorpes Model Engineers track at Waltham Windmill.*

Michael Newbutt Collection.

157. Locomotive 'Henrietta' with Arthur Johnson at the controls, at Lakeside station in 1957. Gallopers in the background. 'Henrietta', now owned by the author, operates today on the Grimsby & Cleethorpes Model Engineering Society track at Waltham Windmill.

Michael Newbutt Collection.

The Electric Water Dodgems were a gentle ride and a popular target for Wondersnaps cameramen for there was more light outdoors and the action much slower than on the big rides. Leaks from the water tank caused its eventual demise. In 1955 they were disposed of and replaced by the Electric Speedway cars (formerly Brooklands), returning to their original pre-war place from the Great Hall. It is possible, but unconfirmed, that some of the water dodgems may have had engines installed afterwards for further use on the Boating Lake as the designs were very similar.

The WONDERLAND MINIATURE RAILWAY or Lakeside Miniature Railway was the third miniature railway to operate at Wonderland and this time, a permanent feature of the outdoor area beyond the Great Hall.

The steam operated seven and a quarter inch gauge Lakeside Miniature Railway was created for the 1949 season by a Mr John (Jack) Woolley of Model Exhibitions Limited, Harrow, who is believed to have been a dealer in miniature railway equipment. The railway ran around the perimeter of the boating lake and under the Big Dipper, forming a circle of over 200 yards. The original station was at the end of a short spur between the Water Dodgems and the Cafe at the end of the promenade. There were no platforms, passengers simply climbing aboard. The original steam locomotive was a Bassett Lowke scale 'Royal Scot' class which hauled its train of sit astride carriages

Wonderland Rides – A Closer Look

away from the station spur and on to the main line around the boating lake in an anti-clockwise direction. The ride proved very popular but soon revealed its Achilles heel, in that it was simply not robust enough to be operated on a commercial basis.

Drastic action was taken late in 1949 when the East Coast Amusement Company purchased the locomotives and rolling stock from the former Kenton Miniature Railway which had closed earlier that year. This was a long established line created originally by businessman Joseph Jeffress in 1931 and set in the grounds of his home, The Grange, Kenton, North London. The Kenton Miniature Railway had its own resident engineer by the name of Jack Newbutt, an ex LNER main line steam locomotive fitter who moved to Cleethorpes with his family in late 1949 to take charge of the fledgling Wonderland Miniature Railway and indeed, the engineering requirements of the whole Wonderland site.

With but one exception, even the Kenton locomotives proved inadequate for the heavy demands of running with full trains seven days a week and one by one, were disposed of. The exception was a North American outline Hudson type locomotive named Henrietta (after Jack's wife), which had been constructed in 1947 at Kenton by Jack himself from a kit of parts supplied before the war. The Wonderland engineering fitters shop was located on the railway and a track laid into it. Gradually Jack, assisted now during the close season by Doug Best, brought the railway up to commercial standard, rebuilding carriages, relaying track, etc. A passing loop was laid and a turntable installed enabling two trains to operate at peak times. A new station was constructed with platforms (and eventually an overall roof!) on the main running line adjacent to the Water Dodgems and Gallopers. Thereafter, trains ran in a clockwise direction around the main line.

A key moment in the life of the line was the construction of an entirely new steam locomotive named Grimsby Town in 1955. This was to be a sister engine for Henrietta and finally solve the problem of inadequate motive power. It was designed by Jack Newbutt himself and constructed in the Wonderland workshop. The design incorporated all the features of modern main line steam locomotive practice (superheater, roller bearings, etc) and proved to be easily capable of hauling trains of 30 plus passengers all day, every day. Thanks to Jack Newbutt and Doug Best, the Wonderland Miniature Railway, though not widely known, was probably the most intensively used and successful seven and a quarter inch gauge railway operating anywhere in the country. The steam locomotives were particularly admired by the British Railways footplate crews that had brought the 'trips' to Cleethorpes and were mingling with the holidaymakers during their mid-day breaks. They often struck up deep conversations with the Wonderland drivers and were particularly impressed to learn the miniature locomotive was superheated and operated at a boiler pressure of 125psi, similar to their own main line steeds!

Miles of Smiles

158. Doug Best (left) and Jack Newbutt putting the finishing touches to the new steam locomotive 'Grimsby Town', which was designed and constructed in the Wonderland engineering fitters shop.

Michael Newbutt Collection.

159. The classic shot of Lakeside station on the Wonderland Miniature Railway on a busy Bank Holiday Sunday in 1958 with two trains in operation. Left is locomotive 'Grimsby Town' with Ray Crome at the controls; right is 'Henrietta' with Mike Newbutt.

Michael Newbutt Collection.

Wonderland Rides – A Closer Look

160. The Peter Pan Railway in the sixties. This was the site of the former skating rink. Note the Big Dipper lift hill top left, Lakeside Miniature Railway station in centre background and Gallopers, top right.

Grimsby Evening Telegraph.

Two circles of the boating lake for 6d making a ride distance of about a quarter of a mile was the order of the day and very busy it was at peak times with sometimes two trains running. It is believed the last trains ran in 1969 prior to the rationalisation of the outdoor amusements area at the end of the North Promenade.

The PETER PAN RAILWAY: Peter Pan Railways were once a common sight at seaside resorts, holiday camps and amusement parks around the UK. The Disney feature film version of the classic John Barrie story released in 1953, popular in cinemas at the time, was the inspiration for this new ride.

The Peter Pan Railway was a kiddie ride manufactured by the Warwickshire Supercars Company utilising conventional railway technology. It used 2ft gauge track, 12lb rails and normal flanged wheels. The centre rail was energised at 110 volts. The cars were in the form of a steam outline locomotive but electrically powered from a centre rail pick-up. A four wheel front bogie guided the car around the sharp curves. There was a powered fixed axle at the rear, making it a 4-2-0 in railway parlance! Each car had two bench seats, the front one for children with easy access to a bell and the rear which could seat two adults. They had steel bodywork and could be supplied in various styles. The body was supplied fully fabricated and painted. The chassis was in kit form for assembly locally.

Miles of Smiles

161. New in 1955, the Hurricane Jets was the last new big ride at Wonderland. It operated in the Great Hall by the boarding station of the Big Dipper, however the Big Dipper had gone by the time of this 1977 picture. The Jets were sold on to a Scottish fairground operator the following year.
Dick Price / University of Sheffield.

The Peter Pan Railway at Wonderland was located just outside the main hall on a site about 40 feet square which was formerly the skating rink, fronted by the promenade and backing up to the start of the big dipper lift hill. It was constructed and laid out by Jack Newbutt and Doug Best from parts supplied. The Peter Pan Railway was out of use by 1967 (probably worn out!) and was replaced by the Gallopers, now under cover for the first time in many years.

The HURRICANE JETS produced by Lang Wheels of Hillingdon, Middlesex in 1955 was the last new big ride supplied to Wonderland. It was located in the Great Hall at the foot of the steps leading up to the Big Dipper, taking the place of the (Brooklands) Electric Speedway, which had moved outside again.

The first Jet rides were constructed by George Maxwell & Sons of Mussleburgh, Edinburgh in 1952 and unusually, operated in an anti-clockwise direction. Lang Wheels began to manufacture them in 1954 operating in the conventional clockwise direction and they soon became the major fairground demand ride of the 1950's, producing an estimated 18 standard sets in addition to many more variations. The ride was approximately 55ft diameter with 12 rider controlled jet cars, which were tubular in shape with a round front headlight, contemporary with Dan Dare and the space exploration themes of the day. Each car held two adults. The rider was able to pull back a joystick which released a pressure valve that lifted the arm and controlled the height and angle of 'flight' (elevation) of the car when the ride was in motion. The loud and abrupt blasts of air emitted simulated the launch of a space rocket.

The Hurricane Jets were sold on to Scottish fairground owners in 1978 and subsequently travelled extensively in Scotland, before becoming part of the Horton's Steam Fair operation. They are now available for hire; a small reminder of Wonderland still operational today!

Perhaps the lowest point in Wonderland history was in the 1974 season when the only rides and attractions on offer were those situated in the Great Hall. The demise of the historic Big Dipper had left a large void in visitor attractions and a replacement big ride was urgently required. The solution came with acquisition of a MAD MOUSE roller coaster, purchased from the Ocean Beach Amusement Park in Rhyl, to whom it had been supplied new in 1961. The Mad Mouse was one of a newer generation of roller coasters of steel construction, designed and manufactured by George Maxwell & Sons of Musselburgh, Edinburgh. A feature of the Mad Mouse was its very small cars riding on top of a track with very sharp unbanked curves, throwing the rider from side to side. The cars were actually wider than the track giving the rider the illusion of no visible means of support and when approaching a curve at speed, the impression it may fly off the end.

The Mad Mouse was constructed on the footprint of the former Big Dipper during the 1974/5 close season and operated at Wonderland from 1975 until 1979, when it was taken out of use following an accident and scrapped. The nature of the accident remains unclear but the impending sale of Wonderland the following year may well have influenced the decision to dispose of it. This then created a new outdoor open space for development by the new owners.

Chapter Twelve

WONDERLAND SIDE STALLS AND ATTRACTIONS

No Fairground or Amusement Park would be complete without its supporting side stalls and attractions with games and prizes to win. Wonderland had an excellent selection of side stalls located along the Promenade and Station sides of the Great Hall, together with a number of free standing round stalls.

As Wonderland was an amusement park, these tended to be more permanent and many remained little changed over the years. Prizes were displayed on shelves in layers behind the operator according to the number of wins required to secure them. There was the two wins shelf, up to as many as six wins. A single win would be rewarded with a minimal prize, such as a plastic comb, whistle or the like. Better prizes would be on offer on the second shelf for two wins, etc. The big prizes on the top shelf would be tempting, but virtually impossible to win! Here in summary, are some of the side stalls in Wonderland as they were in about 1960, many of which, older readers may remember.

The SPIDER & FLY was located at the Docks end of the great hall, close to the Big Dipper boarding steps. Before the war, this was Turner's Modern Darts Saloon. The Spider & Fly was a game for up to twelve players operated by Mr & Mrs Scruton, who were both still there when well into their eighties. In the centre of a giant spiders web behind the operator was the fly and radiating from it around the perimeter, dart board style, were the spiders, each connected by a wire to the player's operating handle on the counter. Player's turned the handle to move the spider towards the centre of the web; the first to reach the fly being the winner. Players needed to turn the handle as quickly and as smoothly as possible to achieve the desired result and win the game. This required a certain amount of skill, as there was a slipping clutch in the mechanism and vigorous action resulted in no progress! The winner received a prize, or collected a card to save for a bigger prize after more wins. Because of the nature of the game and

Wonderland Side Stalls and Attractions

162. The long established Spider & Fly side stall in Wonderland in the sixties with Mr & Mrs Scruton. Inset: An earlier Spider & Fly on the North Promenade in the thirties. It is not clear if it was this that moved into Wonderland after the war.
Grimsby Evening Telegraph.

the mass of connecting wires involved, this was a permanent stand and may have been unique to Wonderland. There is however photographic evidence of a Spider & Fly on the promenade in the thirties, next to Hawkey's Premier Restaurant. It is possible this moved into Wonderland after the war.

The LAUGHING CLOWNS (or Clowns) were operated by Mrs Dora Lockley. She was well known for drumming up custom by walking around with a big prize Noddy (Enid Blyton) in her arms. It was one of many variations of a Roll-A-Ball with six balls to play. A clown's head with open mouth moved back & forth through a 120 degree arc. Players dropped a ball into the mouth of the clown which directed it into one of six numbered chutes. All six balls in either chute 1 or 6 were required to win a big prize. Needless to say these would be slightly narrower to add difficulty! Doug Best remembers her rushing to the fitters shop in a very distressed state crying, "I've lost my Noddy!" The worn out mechanism had become disconnected facing chute 6, so she had to surrender her much loved big prize Noddy. A regular prize would have been a plastic whistle or comb!

The DERBY RACER: Sometimes known as the Kentucky Derby, was operated by the Dearden family and located on the promenade side of the Station entrance; the first attraction visitors entering Wonderland would see. It was a mechanical horse racing

Miles of Smiles

163. The Laughing Clowns was operated by Mrs Dora Lockley. Winners received a prize, or collected a card to save for a bigger prize after more wins. The bigger prizes were displayed on the shelves behind. She was well known for walking around with a big prize Noddy (Enid Blyton) in her arms, but lost it due to mechanical failure! The Laughing Clowns was one of many variations of Roll-A-Ball with six balls to play.
Grimsby Evening Telegraph.

track for up to seven players and cost one penny (1d) to play. Pull the lever back to 'kick' one of the seven horses into action, sending it rushing forward along the race track. The one that stopped closest to the winning post was the winner. Prizes were considered 'good' on this stall. A regular prize was a big stick of rock (which cost 6d), so a profit of at least a penny was made with every race (early 1950's prices!).

DEARDEN'S had a presence in the Wonderland Great Hall from its opening in 1926. Their juvenile attractions included Hoop-la, Kiddies Roundabouts and various other attractions, all situated close to the Station entrance.

Next to the Oyster Bar just inside the Station entrance, was the COCONUT SHY operated by the Dearden family. A traditional coconut shy with coconuts embedded in either sawdust or sand. Three attempts with wooden balls to win; not easy! It was said amongst Wonderland staff that only a fit shot-putter might succeed!

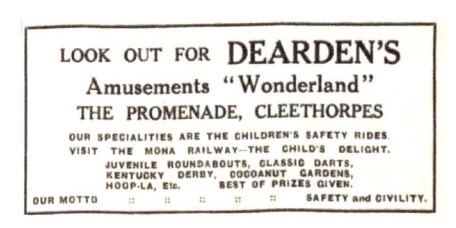

164. Look Out For Dearden's. Hull Daily Mail 27th July 1938.

Wonderland Side Stalls and Attractions

Next was BOWS & ARROWS, again operated by the Dearden family with targets for three players; the aim of course being to achieve a Bull's Eye.

The BOWLING ALLEY, operated by Dearden's was sometimes known as Skee Ball. The player bowled the ball as rapidly as possible down the alley but instead of knocking down skittles, the ball was launched up a (skee) ramp into the air, landing in one of a number of circular targets. The balls were wood and about three inches in diameter. Points were awarded based on how close to the centre of the target a player achieved. The Bowling Alley was between the Bows & Arrows and the Tennis Ball Shooter.

The TENNIS BALL SHOOTER was located on the station side of the hall, opposite the Dodgems. It was operated by Norman Murgatroyd. The aim was to land a tennis ball into one of the buckets pinned to the target wall. A direct shot into the bucket would usually result in it bouncing out again!

The WINCHESTER SHOOTING GALLERY on the station side of the hall was next to the Tennis Ball Shooter, also operated by Norman Murgatroyd. This was the real thing with live bullets! Genuine Winchester rifles firing 2.2 bullets (actually 'fairground shots', supplied locally by Lightwood's Gun & Fishing Tackle shop) were aimed at various static and moving targets. It was very popular with ex-servicemen (and boys aspiring to be servicemen). A few more shots, Sir?

The CORK SHOOTER was on the Promenade side of the Great Hall. Cork shooting pistols aimed at targets on a shelf opposite. The aim was to knock targets off the shelf to win prizes. It was operated by George Blyth.

The HOOK-A-DUCK round stall for the little one's near the Station entrance was operated by Colin Blyth (Son of George). Hook-A-Duck with the rod and line and lift it out of the water to win a prize. As a prize every time stall, it was always a favourite with the little one's (and their parents)!

Near the Dodgems was the DIVE BOMBER, a round stall operated by Peggy Cripsey, daughter of showman Roy Cripsey (Wall of Death). There was also a Round Stall close to the Waltzer selling gifts. A new attraction close to the Waltzer was a PUNCH-BALL machine that could measure the power and strength of the players punch; very useful for impressing the girlfriend!

The HAMMERS: Otherwise known as High Strikers, were between Pet's Corner and the Big Dipper boarding steps at the Docks end of the hall. They were operated by Bill Shotton. Strike the hammer and ring the bell at the top. This was traditional fairground fare. Original fairground hammers could be as high as 25 feet, but those in Wonderland were much less! The 1952 fire was thought to have started here, after which the Hammers moved to a side stall on the Promenade side of the Great Hall.

The NAILS: Drive a nail into a substantial block of hard wood with three strikes of the hammer without bending it. This was run by Tony Felcey and was the first side stall on the Promenade side of the Great Hall. It was almost impossible to win!

165. The Cans were located next to the Wonderland main (Centre) entrance off the Promenade. Ten cans were arranged on a shelf in a pyramid with four at the bottom, rising to a single can at top. Knocking them all off the shelf with four mops won a prize.
Grimsby Evening Telegraph.

ROLL-A-BALL: Other variations of Roll-A-Ball on the Promenade side of the Great Hall were Reuben Felcey's stall near the Docks entrance and that of Peter Jones, next to The Clowns.

The CANS (or Mops); also known as Can-Can, were located next to the Main (centre) entrance off the Promenade. Ten cans were arranged on a shelf in a pyramid with four at bottom rising to a single can at top. Knocking them all off with four mops won a prize; not as easy as it appeared! Again, a regular prize was a plastic comb, etc. This was operated by seasonal staff.

KIDDIES RIDES: There were various gentle rides for the little ones operated by Jack Wright located in the centre of the hall near the Docks end. There was the Little Wheel (a miniature big wheel) with very attractive enclosed gondola type cabins, a set of swings and the Convoy Ride roundabout with tanks, jeeps and army motor cycles painted in camouflage colours. Before setting a ride in motion, Jack would be heard to cry 'Stand Cleee-arr!'

COMPETITION DARTS: Another traditional fairground side stall was the Competition Darts Gallery operated by Peggy Bailey with prizes for those who scored 65 or more with three darts. It was located near the Power House, next to the Crazy House on the Railway side of the Great Hall.

The CRAZY HOUSE. With a superb crooked house frontage, the Crazy House (also known as the House of Laughter) was a simple entrance and exit attraction. Visitors entered and climbed the wobbly stairs (be careful!) into a hall of mirrors with uneven floors. Exiting was down more stairs and via a short guided walkway back into the main hall. It was operated by George Blyth, a veteran of Wonderland who before the war ran the Mirrored Maze on the same spot.

PET'S CORNER: Previously known as the Monkey House, Animal House or Miniature Zoo; Pet's Corner was operated by Ken Hood. It was a simple entrance and exit with display screened off from the main hall, located at the Docks end of the Great Hall between the Blacksmith Shop and the Hammers. Small animals (rabbits, etc) were on view in appropriate settings. Following Ken's passing, it became an exhibition venue with a different attraction each season. In 1961 it was home to a model railway exhibition (much to the delight of the author!).

Add to these Bill Anderson's Oyster Bar, Bessie Wilkie's Ice Cream Parlour, Madam's Eileen & Ruby (Palm Readers) and various Gift Stalls, all supporting the big rides in the largest covered amusement park on the East Coast. Pleasure the weather can't spoil!

Chapter Thirteen

SOME AMUSEMENT MACHINES ON THE NORTH PROMENADE

Amusement machines, or automatic machines, were all designed for the same purpose; that is parting visitors from their hard earned cash! The earliest amusement arcades were in Edwardian times and were sometimes known as Automatic Arcades or Mechanical Exhibitions. Another form of mechanical exhibition was Moving Pictures, or Bioscope shows. There was one shown next to the Slipping the Slip helter skelter in a tent like structure in an Edwardian coloured postcard in about 1906 on a site close to what later became Wonderland.

Amusement slot machines in Wonderland and other arcades along the North Promenade were largely mechanical in the fifties and as such, incurred no actual running costs. Prominent were flick ball slot machines, known as 'Allwins' (after the original US manufacturer). They came in numerous variations, were always brightly coloured and with different themes, from a number of British manufacturers. Insert a penny and the polished steel ball dropped into play. Flick the ball with the sprung lever and it would spin around until losing momentum and fall into one of the (usually losing) cups. If you were lucky enough to win, you recovered your prize (usually your coin returned and a free play) by rotating the knob in the bottom left corner of the machine clockwise. Some versions had sweets (small tube of Polo mints, etc), cigarettes or even cigars, as prizes. Local schoolboy John Lilee remembers an Allwin in the Gayway which had Kit-Kat chocolate bars as a prize. He and his friend got the knack of working this machine and when the manager saw how many bars of chocolate they had won, they were promptly thrown out and banned! Allwins were upright and came in polished wooden cabinets mounted on shelves. There was the traditional FiveWin which had seven cups, the outer ones being losers. Others included the Elevenses, Gap Win, Canon Ball, Carousel, Speedway, Photo Finish and many more. In Happidrome, there were several impressive four sided Allwin consoles, each a different model and theme to catch the eye.

Some Amusement Machines on the North Promenade

Another long established arcade favourite were the Cranes with their claw grabbers. Set in a floor mounted cabinet was a well engineered crane with a three claw grabber which reached out over an array of tempting gifts. The grabber opened, hopefully lifting an item, but usually dropping it before reaching the delivery chute. The player had some control of the placement of the crane, but the grabber was larger than the gifts, so the possibility of winning was diminished. Sometimes, the failed prize of a previous player would fall and land in a position on top of others making it easier to lift. Similar modern and much more sophisticated machines are to be found on the promenade at Cleethorpes today, proving the enduring popularity of the Cranes as an amusement attraction.

166. Playing an Allwin slot machine. Such machines were numerous in seaside amusement arcades throughout the country.
Doug Best Collection.

Another large machine was the Arms or Pushers. Set in the corners of a large floor mounted display cabinet were four traversing arms reaching over a slowly revolving turntable with prizes set upon it. Insert a coin and the arm moved in an arc from its rest point in the centre of the turntable towards the perimeter, hopefully pushing a prize over the edge of the turntable and into one of the winning chutes. This was very difficult as the foot of the arm was round, thus deflecting items on the turntable away. The player had control of the arm, but only its first two thirds of arc movement, after which it completed its travel to the perimeter uncontrolled. If a player did succeed in nudging a prize to the edge, but not winning it, a deflector by the prize chute safely brought it back into the centre again, so the next player had no advantage!

An attractive Prize Every Time machine was The Treasure Cave or Elephant Gift Vendor. In a cabinet was a pirate's cave and under it a circular turntable upon which was mounted an elephant. The elephant had a tray on its back. Insert a coin and the turntable was set in motion. The elephant disappeared out of sight under the set, re-appearing with a small white box on its back which it deposited into an open treasure chest (delivery chute), before coming to rest, ready for the next player. There were gifts for boys or girls, usually a plastic ring, a car, or the like selected by which coin slot was used. The Elephant Gift Vendor was produced by Whales of Redcar, who also manufactured a large range of Allwin flick ball machines (see above). Such machines were in the Gayway and several other amusement arcades along the North Promenade.

Miles of Smiles

A vintage machine, even in the fifties, was the Laughing Sailor or Laughing Policeman. Players could not help but laugh along with him! There was one in Norman Kaye's amusement arcade in the Victor Colonnade on the corner of Sea Road. Similarly was the Palm Reader. Insert a coin and place the palm of your hand firmly on the metal plate. Protruding metal fingers felt your hand and calculated whether you were strong, cuddly, loveable, or the like, and printed a card to confirm it! In an upright glass cabinet was the Love Tester. Squeeze the handle with increasing pressure to see if you are anything from clammy and harmless, to passionate and hot stuff!

In the fifties, there was a model railway in a large glass top display cabinet in the Gayway. It was a large gauge railway, probably Gauge 1, with a 2-4-2T tank locomotive of distinctly London & North Western Railway appearance on an oval of track with a small station and very simple scenery. Inserting a coin set the loco off around the track very gracefully. The aim was to stop it in the station by pressing a button. Of course, there was a delay before it began to slow down and it usually rolled through the station and came to a halt elsewhere! If you did succeed in stopping it in the station, you won your coin back. Being realistic, it took up a lot of floor space for probably very little return!

Mechanical Play Football cabinets were popular on the North Promenade. Operating one or the other team's lever triggered a footballer to 'kick' the ball (ball bearing). The 'ground' was uneven to ensure the ball landed by another footballer's foot to continue the game. Ball bearing shooters were also in many of the amusement arcades before the introduction of shooting galleries in the sixties. Players aimed the ball bearing gun at targets at the other end of the glass cabinet. There were a variety of themes, the most popular perhaps being the Territorial Shooting Range. The Army Territorial's had a big profile in post-war Britain.

Then there was the Driving Test (Super Steer-A-Ball). There was one in Norman Kaye's Victor Colonnade amusements. The rocking tray inside the cabinet was controlled by a large steering wheel on the front of the machine. On the tray was a series of curved channels with connecting crossovers in a townscape type setting. Insert a coin and a large polished steel ball dropped on to the tray, the object of the game being to carefully steer the ball through the route and into the finish channel. This was not easy as the ball was heavy and once on the move was difficult to control, gathering momentum, losing control and falling off the end of the tray! Manoeuvring into the various channels that got progressively narrower nearer to home required great skill, patience, and an element of luck!

More sophisticated was the Drive Yourself Road Test. This was a mechanical sit-on machine where the player had to steer the car on the ever changing rolling road, safely.

Modern machines being introduced at the time included Rifle Ranges, with an air gun shooting at both static and moving targets through a window. There were a

Some Amusement Machines on the North Promenade

number of variations and themes. Targets included ducks, rabbits, and even enemy aircraft! One Arm Bandits were becoming more sophisticated but several original American mechanical Bandits were still in use in the Wonderland slot machine arcade opposite the Dodgems. Pre-war Pinball machines were still to be found in amusement arcades along the North Promenade, but newer models had flippers to keep the ball in play longer and these were beginning to appear. Pinball machines have reached amazing sophistication today, again proof of their enduring popularity.

There were many others including The Punch Ball, that measured the strength of the player's punch, vintage What The Butler Saw peep show machines and more, but ever increasing numbers of modern one arm bandits were becoming the norm and Bingo was taking over large areas of amusement arcades by the 1960's, displacing many of the traditional machines. The now universal coin pusher or Penny Falls appeared in 1966 and today dominates most modern amusement arcades.

Chapter Fourteen

WONDERSNAPS

167. The Wondersnaps counter close to the main entrance. Just visible on the left is the Jollysnaps studio.

Doug Best.

Wondersnaps cameramen candidly photographed (snapped) visitors in Wonderland and roamed freely amongst the crowds. They took up strategic positions to get the best views and snapped visitors on the rides and amusements. The photographs were all processed in-house and were ready in two hours, so visitors could take them home with them and show friends what an enjoyable time they had at Wonderland.

The Wonderland 'Wondersnaps' operation was launched in 1949 by local photographer, Jim Henschel who operated a small photographic business from his upstairs front bedroom studio at 192 Grimsby Road, Cleethorpes. Doug Best, recently

Wondersnaps

168. A classic Wondersnaps shot of thrills on the Big Dipper.
Doug Best.

returned from active service, was his neighbour at 194 and Jim taught him the fundamentals of photography. This was to be Doug's introduction to the East Coast Amusement Co (Wonderland) as an assistant cameraman working for Jim. It soon became a big operation with as many as five roaming cameramen in action during high season. A Wondersnaps card presented to visitors identified their photograph by a unique number which was printed, following instructions from the Wondersnaps counter. The card advised the photograph(s) would be ready for collection from the Wondersnaps counter in the Great Hall in two hours.

Strategic positions were provided for the cameramen beside some of the rides. On the Big Dipper there was a seat beside the lift hill above the dips power house which had a prime view of the last but one dip before the end of the ride. From here the photographer would present a Wondersnaps card to the front seat passenger of a passing car as it slowly climbed the lift hill at the start of the ride, and then photograph it passing at speed, near the end of the ride.

They would snap the pale faced passengers on the Ghost Train as it emerged from the darkness of the Lost World haunted cavern at the end of the ride, then move in swiftly to present Wondersnaps cards as they alighted with instructions on how to redeem their photographs from the Wondersnaps counter afterwards. Having identified and snapped their targets, cameramen would often jump on and off moving rides (Cycledrome, Gallopers, Dodgems, etc), then hang on for dear life to present cards to the riders before the ride stopped. This could be quite frenetic as during busy periods, ride times were often shortened in order to maximise revenue! Cameramen covered the outside rides such as the Motor Boats, Peter Pan Railway, Gallopers, etc, but were not always favourably received by the ride operator. Arthur Taylor, who ran the Speedway cars, disapproved of photography. Bringing the cars into the centre to give out Wondersnaps cards disrupted the operational flow of the ride.

Doug Best was a Wondersnaps cameraman during the summer season and assisted Jack Newbutt in the Engineering Fitters shop during the close season. Following the

Miles of Smiles

169. Candid photography sometimes produced unexpected results. This unfortunate 1950's shot on the Cycledrome caused some amusement amongst Wondersnaps staff, but Doug recalled the father went on to order an enlargement!

Doug Best.

departure of Jim Henschel, Doug managed the Wondersnaps operation assisted by Colin Govis, another of the roaming cameramen until 1959, when he became the full time engineering manager for the whole site. Cameramen were equipped with 35mm cameras and a huge electronic flashgun for use in the Great Hall. The flash unit was about the size of a car headlight and was mounted on a pole about a foot long. The base unit contained two batteries and the whole thing was quite cumbersome. They used a variety of cameras, both reflex (SLR) and viewfinder models of the types in general use at the time, shooting on high speed film, typically Ilford HP3 (400ASA) for the low light conditions of the great hall.

The films were processed and printed in the dark room situated at the rear of the hall behind the Blacksmith Shop. Access was strictly limited for obvious reasons; the password being 'HP3' (the Ilford film in use!). The darkroom was manned by Frank (Nimrod) Carver during University vacations. David Wilkinson also worked in the darkroom. Doug recalls them working well into many nights during high season, loading cassettes of 35mm film from 200ft bulk rolls ready for the following day's shooting. Normal camera 35mm film cassettes were used but loaded only to 30 exposures (rather than the usual 36) to increase reliability and prevent jamming. The

Wondersnaps

170. A rare view of the railway side of Wonderland in 1960 showing the Big Dipper and its run-in tunnel. The square building in the centre is the secure store, a wartime addition. The Dark Room is the low roofed building to the right of the secure store.
Doug Best.

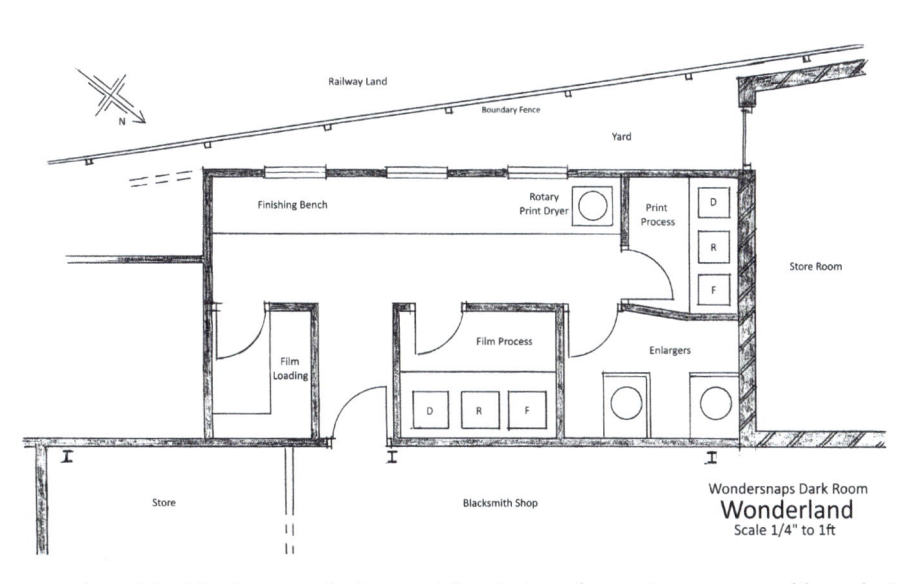

171. Plan of the Wondersnaps darkroom. After drying, photo prints were speedily packed and dispatched to the Wondersnaps counter in the Great Hall.
Chris Dibben from a sketch by Doug Best.

Miles of Smiles

172. Wondersnaps prints were stamped on the back with a unique reference number enabling visitors to order repeat prints or enlargements afterwards. In this case it was exposure 25 from film number 360.
Doug Best.

cassettes would normally be good for a whole season, but it is worth remembering that an entire film (30 exposures) could be used up in just three rides of the Cycledrome or Dodgems!

Each film was given a unique number. This was followed by the exposure number to identify the actual image required afterwards. It was all done in-house and a black & white photographic print would normally be ready for collection in two hours. The dark room was a busy place! Doug recalls the most film cassettes used by any cameraman in one day was 33, an astonishing 990 Wondersnaps pictures shot by Doug himself, though what percentage of these materialised into actual orders is not recorded!

The Wondersnaps counter close to the main entrance was the public face of the operation. It was staffed by Christine Wilkinson, Alice Horner and Sylvia Govis, amongst others at various times. Next to the Wondersnaps counter was the 'Jollysnaps' studio where visitors could have their portraits taken, or be photographed looking through one of those much loved saucy seaside postcard type panels, or as a barman, or even as a prisoner in jail! The studio camera was a Zeiss Ikon Ikoflex twin lens reflex camera which used 120 roll film. Brian Best (Cousin of Doug) supervised the Studio. Later, Photomation was added. The Photomation booth was an early version of the fully automatic photo machine, similar to the passport digital photo machines in use today.

There must be many thousands of Wondersnaps photographs recalling happy holidays, still in sideboard drawers even today!

Wondersnaps

173. Everything in this Jollysnaps Studio picture is fake, except the holidaymaker!
Doug Best.

174. The Water Dodgems.

175. The Cycledrome. Happy family holding tight!

176. Children on the Peter Pan Railway.

177. On the Speedway Cars.

All – Doug Best.

CHAPTER FIFTEEN
WONDERLAND PEOPLE

Senior Management:

George Wilkie, founder of Wonderland was a pioneer of the British fairground. He was also founder of the Cleethorpes Advancement Association, a long standing member of the Freemasons, a Cleethorpes Councillor for a while, and was largely responsible, either directly or indirectly, for the development of the North Promenade. Doug Best remembers he drove a big American car, so his presence was always known. George was a very benevolent man and on the last weekend of each summer season, he donated the takings from Wonderland rides to local charities. The first Charity Day in 1926 raised £500 for the Red Cross and other good causes. This continued long after his passing, in fact right up until the sale of Wonderland to Dudley Bowers. George Wilkie died in 1944 in Wallasey.

In partnership with Cleethorpes businessman Matthew Dowse, the East Coast Amusement Company was aquired by George Wilkie in 1921, from Anthony Hill and J.H. Thomas MP. George Wilkie, a Geordie from Tynemouth, had already established an amusement arcade business in New Brighton back in 1912 which is still operated by Wilkie descendants today. He remodelled the site at the end of the North Promenade in Cleethorpes in 1926 into what became Wonderland and ran it with his sister in law Elizabeth (Ma) Wilkie.

178. George & his Sister in Law, Elizabeth 'Ma' Wilkie.
Grimsby Evening Telegraph.

Wonderland People

'Ma' Wilkie with daughters Hilda and Bessie, continued to run Wonderland after the war. Hilda Wilkie married Sid Smith, who joined the board in 1946 as Managing Director. Elizabeth Smith, daughter of Sid & Hilda Smith worked on the Dips. Their (young) son, Michael set up a Trix Twin railway layout in the ghost train out of season! Sid Smith moved on to manage Funland at Mablethorpe. Ma Wilkie died in 1965 aged 87yrs, but daughters, Hilda and Bessie continued to run Wonderland until selling to Dudley Bowers in 1981.

So Wonderland was a family run business. Bessie Wilkie ran the ice cream parlour located just inside the station entrance. She married Reuben Felcey who operated the first two side stalls next to the Docks entrance. He carried around a Rugby ball as a big prize. Tony Felcey, son of Reuben and Bessie, ran the slot machine arcade next to the Cafeteria, opposite the dodgems.

Frank Smith (no relation) was Company Secretary. He worked in the office next to the Spider & Fly, and hired the seasonal staff.

Supporting Staff:

The post-war years were a time when many had nicknames and some of the more colourful characters of Wonderland would only respond to them. For example there was 'Snowy' Trash, a very fit and athletic young man with blonde hair who worked on the Speedway. Similarly, there was a retired Yorkshire man known only as 'Fat Pump' who worked on the Lakeside Miniature Railway in the early fifties. Now in Yorkshire, grease was known as 'fat' and as one of his daily duties was to grease the locomotives, he was known as 'Fat Pump'. His real name was only recalled with some difficulty as Bill, but no one ever knew his surname!

An organisation such as Wonderland required many and varied skills to keep it running smoothly. Almost all work was done in-house. There was the joiners shop, blacksmith shop, engineering fitters shop, paint shop and photographic darkroom, all within the complex. The combined skills and versatility of the Wonderland team was quite remarkable. It had to be, for everything was done on minimal budget including, it was said, the wages! Nonetheless, Wonderland was a happy place and many stayed a long time. Here are some of the people who worked at Wonderland in the post-war period. There are probably many more!

Jim Butcher was the Park manager and a Cleethorpes Councillor. Arthur Taylor became Park Manager later. Jim Griffiths was the Park Foreman. Before the war, he was a travelling fair showman and had many a tale to tell particularly involving the fairground steam engines!

Miles of Smiles

The Heavy Gang:

The heavy gang was a regular full time team headed by Park Foreman Jim Griffiths, who set up and dismantled the big rides between seasons when the Great Hall was being used for exhibitions, fairs and the like. The heavy gang consisted of 'Snowy' Trash, Eddie Robotham, Arthur Taylor, Harold Scherzinger and Roy Drinkall, all of whom worked various rides during the summer season (see below).

Painters:

Eric Hardman was the painter/artist after the war. He later moved on to Funland at Mablethorpe and was replaced by Ralph Smith as Foreman Painter. Ralph was assisted by painter/artist Cyril Creswell, a master of fairground art who created most of the colourful signs used throughout Wonderland. Particularly fine was his work on the Wild West barge boards of the Gallopers.

179. The Old Showman. Jim Griffiths, Park Foreman.

Doug Best.

Electricians:

Frank (Frankie) May was the Electrician from 1946. He was versatile and highly thought of. He maintained everything electrical on-site from the power house in the Great Hall to repairing the big electronic flash guns used by the Wondersnaps cameramen! Noel Gray became Electrician after Frank May. He was followed by his son, John Gray. Later still it was Cliff Colebrook, with his son doing his apprenticeship at Wonderland.

Joiners:

John Stone and Chris Beer were the Carpenter Joiners. They worked on the Big Dipper during the summer season.

Blacksmith:

The blacksmith for many years was Horace. When answering the telephone, he would always reply, 'Horace here'. His surname was thought to be Rose, but no one is sure

Wonderland People

because he never used it! He fabricated the Wonderland Arch of Pleasure which spanned the North Promenade by the Station entrance of the Great Hall.

Contractors:

Charlie Jackson was the contract plumber for Wonderland who attended as required.

Ben Barretti called at Wonderland annually to service and re-tune the Gallopers organ. He worked for Chiappa Ltd of London. The Principal was Victor Chiappa who was interviewed in a local TV News item that can be viewed on the East Anglian Film Archive website (film No 135985). Chiappa was, even in the sixties, one of the very few remaining specialists in mechanical music. Ben Barretti enlarged the Gallopers organ to 89 keys in 1952 using parts from the former Custer Cars organ. He set up a facility in the Wonderland paint shop to repair the card music for the organ and to cut and punch the music stencils. Over the years, Ben Barretti came to love Cleethorpes so much he moved from London to one of the Cul-de-sac's off Brereton Avenue.

Engineering:

Jack Newbutt was the Engineering manager for ten years, from 1949. He was an Ex London & North Eastern Railway (LNER) steam locomotive fitter who had worked at both Annesley (Nottingham) and Neasden (North London) locomotive sheds on all the big main line steam locomotives of the day. He was later engineer to the Kenton Miniature Railway in North London. When this closed just after the war, most of the Kenton miniature locomotives and rolling stock were aquired by the East Coast Amusement Co and moved to Wonderland, bringing Jack and his family to Cleethorpes. He returned to North London in 1959.

Doug Best started at Wonderland in 1949, soon after returning from active service overseas. He began as a photographer with the Wondersnaps operation, but having wartime engineering experience as a tank driver, assisted Jack Newbutt in the fitters shop during the close season. After Jack Newbutt had moved on, Doug became engineering manager for the whole site.

180. Engineering Manager, Jack Newbutt on his way to a job in the Great Hall.
Michael Newbutt Collection.

Miles of Smiles

After 17 years at Wonderland, Doug moved on to Torbinia (local engineers) in the spring of 1966, having given two week's notice. He was replaced at Wonderland by Roger Bush who came from Torbinia. It is only due to Doug's clear and remarkable memory, that this book has been possible!

The Big Dipper:

Barney Samuels was the Big Dipper manager. Barney had worked on the pre-war Custer Cars and is thought to have been at Wonderland since its opening in 1926. He was still working the Big Dipper in the 1960's when he died suddenly following a heart attack on the Big Dipper boarding steps.

Barney's Tale: Barney Samuels would tell new staff a tale about a couple of redundant steam engines that were dumped out of use under the Big Dipper, close to the railway in the early thirties. He said they attempted to take them out to sea for disposal but they would not sink so were buried on site by the railway. There was a thread of truth in the tale, in that the two steam engines really did exist close to the Big Dipper and were there for some time. Doug Best remembers playing on them as a schoolboy and lighting a fire in one of them. It is thought they had worked rides on the sands and may have been damaged by an extraordinary high tide. Their ultimate disposal remains a mystery, but Barney always maintained that dig close to the railway and you will uncover the chimney of one of them – an unlikely story!

Elizabeth Smith, daughter of Sid & Hilda Smith also worked on the Dips, as did joiners John Stone and Chris Beer during the summer season.

181. Barney Samuels, Big Dipper Manager with a young Michael Newbutt, son of Engineering Manager Jack, outside the fitters shop on the miniature railway. Michael Newbutt Collection.

The Gallopers:

Eddie Robotham was the manager of the Gallopers. He not only lovingly maintained the Gallopers, but also its Gavioli organ and its precious music books. He was assisted by Joe Daniels, Dave Philpotts and Sid Horner. Mrs Horner (Mum of Sid) was cashier

Wonderland People

182. Jack Newbutt, Arthur Johnson & Mrs Brown with locomotive 'Henrietta' at Lakeside station. The Gavioli music books for the Gallopers organ were stored in the shed behind. Alas, many were lost following the flooding of the site in 1953.
Michael Newbutt Collection.

in the pay box. Daughter Alice worked on the Wondersnaps counter in the Great Hall. Sam Brumby and Frank Priest are also known to have worked on the Gallopers in the late sixties.

The Boats:

Bill Dempsey managed the motor boats in the boating lake (formerly Lakeland) within the Big Dipper. He had very distinct curly hair. In 1963, the boating lake was drained and converted to Go-Kart operation. Dave Rogers became manager of the Go-Kart track. His father was a trawler skipper (one of Grimsby's top Skippers).

Wonderland (Lakeside) Miniature Railway:

Jack & Michael Newbutt, Ray Crome, Doug & Armas Best, Arthur Johnson, Bill Hart, Jack Bradshaw, 'Fat Pump' (see above), Rob Foxon (author) and Mrs Brown, cashier in the pay box. Rides were 6d (5p) for two circuits round the lake, about a quarter mile.

Undoubtedly Wonderland's highest ever achiever was Rod Temperton, who went on to become famous as a song writer, record producer and musician. Rod was a junior on the Wonderland Miniature Railway in the 1960's. Later a Grammy award winner, he wrote hit songs for many well known artists of the Seventies and Eighties. He was in the hit 70's band Heatwave and wrote the title track for the biggest selling title album of all time, 'Thriller' for Michael Jackson.

Miles of Smiles

Arthur Johnson was a regular driver on the Wonderland Miniature Railway in the fifties. He passed away in 1958. Bill Hart, known as Blower Bill when his loco was short of steam, was a regular WMR driver throughout the 1950's. He was still there in 1963, by then well into his eighties. Bill was a well known local model engineer who constructed a working model fairground with rides. He moved to the East Coast from Leicester and exhibited regularly at the annual Grimsby & Cleethorpes Model Engineering Society exhibition in St Aiden's Church hall in Cleethorpes.

Michael Newbutt, son of engineering manager Jack, was a schoolboy helper and casual driver on the WMR until he left the area with his family in 1959. Ray Crome, friend of Michael was also a schoolboy helper and casual driver. After a working career on British Railways as a steam locomotive fitter at Immingham depot, Ray left the railway industry at the end of the steam era and worked as an engineer in the food industry. He was engineer to the Cleethorpes Coast Light Railway for many years and is an active member of the Grimsby & District Society of Model Engineers, based at Waltham Windmill.

Mike Newbutt and Ray Crome, both juniors on the Wonderland Miniature Railway at the time, remember having the 'task' of consuming the left over American whipped ice cream from the kiosk next to the Peter Pan Railway on the promenade, at

183. The author age 13 years on locomotive 'Grimsby Town' in 1960. Electric Speedway Cars in the background.

Doug Best.

the end of the day. An unexpected bonus of this new form of confectionary was that it could not be stored overnight, so any left over's were eagerly awaited and they came away with metal tea cans filled to the brim with ice cream!

Jack Bradshaw was another regular WMR driver. He had moved to Cleethorpes in 1947 from Chadderton, Oldham, Lancs, after having lost the end of a finger in an accident on the belts in the cotton mills. He lived on Whites Road and moved from the Bathing Pool to work at Wonderland. He was still there in 1963. Jack was never seen without his cap!

Armas Best, son of Doug, was also a schoolboy helper on the WMR. Rob Foxon (Author) worked as a schoolboy helper from 1957 (aged 9 years!) until the end of the 1962 season. He spent six gloriously happy seasons on the Wonderland Miniature Railway, fell in love with steam locomotive Henrietta (built by Jack Newbutt in 1947) and went on to purchase her 50 years later, in 2012! Restored by Ray Crome, Henrietta has returned to the East Coast and operates on the Model Engineers track at Waltham Windmill.

The Speedway:

The (Brooklands) Electric Speedway was managed by Arthur Taylor, ex-RAF, later Park Manager. He was assisted by Snowy Trash and Roy Drinkall. They went on to operate the Jets.

The Loops/Cages:

George (Big Tool) Russell managed the Cages (or Loops). This was one of the oldest rides on site, having been constructed in-house in Wonderland back in 1934. There were six cages in the set. It required a burly operator to handle some of the intimidating hopefuls!

Ghost Train:

The Ghost Train, dating back to 1931, was another vintage ride. It was managed by Harold Scherzinger, assisted by seasonal extras.

Promenade Cafe:

Hilda Scherzinger, wife of Harold, managed the Cafe at end of promenade where staff took their breaks. There was a separate counter for Wonderland staff in this very busy establishment. A regular visitor to the nearby engineering fitter's shop, it was recalled Hilda seemed to need quite a lot of attention to her water softening and tea making plant!

Miles of Smiles

184. The Wondersnaps team in about 1958.
L to R Back row: Brian Best, Dave Wilkinson, Eileen, Local Casual, Local Casual;
Centre row: Frank Carver, Doug Best, German Casual, Christine Wilkinson, German Casual;
Front: Ron Ewell.

Doug Best.

Wondersnaps/Jollysnaps:

Jim Henschell was the original photographer who started the Wondersnaps operation just after the war. Photographers included Doug Best, Colin Govis and many other seasonal casuals. In the darkroom was film processor Frank (Nim) Carver. The name 'Nimrod' was bestowed upon him by Jim Henschel and he was always known as 'Nim' thereafter. He later graduated with a BSc and PhD in chemistry from Leeds University. He went on to work in Australia and later, in rocket research. Seasonal jobs often launched prominent careers! David Wilkinson worked in the darkroom. Christine Wilkinson was a Wondersnaps cashier, together with Eileen (surname unknown), Alice Horner and Sylvia Govis. Brian Best (Cousin of Doug) worked the Jollysnaps Studio and Photomation Booth.

Side Stalls and Amusements:

Ken Hood ran the Animal House, later known as Pet's Corner. Mr & Mrs Scruton operated the Spider & Fly; joined later by nephew Geoff Hallam, ex Coldstream Guards. Mrs Dora Lockley ran the Laughing Clowns. She carried around a Noddy (Edith Blyton character) as a big prize but lost it due to mechanical failure when it was won by a lucky visitor! Peter Jones ran the Roll-A-Ball, next to the Clowns. The Derby Racer, by the

Wonderland People

Station entrance to Wonderland was run by the Dearden family. Bill Anderson ran the Oyster Bar on the other side of the entrance. The Dearden family also ran the Coconut Shy and some Kiddie rides. Jack Wright worked the Juvenile Swings, the Little Wheel and the Convoy Ride roundabout, located near Big Dipper steps.

Norman Murgatroyd, assisted by Jack Peals, operated the Winchester Shooting Gallery. Norman was a regular visitor to the fitters shop when any of his rifles were in trouble. He also ran the Tennis Ball Shooter next to the Winchester Rifles. An annual winter time task in the fitters shop was the checking and servicing of the Winchester rifles. During this time, the fitters shop was known as the barrel bending department (not literally, of course!). The rifles were tested afterwards by firing at a target attached to one of the giant Canadian pitch pine timber legs of the Big Dipper which protruded through the fitters shop itself. It is said that that leg was full of lead!

Peggy Bailey ran the Competition Darts Gallery next to the Crazy House; score 65 or more with three darts to win! Bill Shotton ran the Hammers, otherwise known as High Strikers. George Blyth, another veteran of Wonderland, managed the Crazy House (pre-war it was a Maze) and the Cork Shooter. Colin Blyth, son of George, ran the Hook-A-Duck round stall.

Madam Eileen was one of the Palm Readers. Her booth was situated next to the Wondersnaps counter in the Great Hall. No one knew who she actually was, such was the mystique of the profession, but she was there for many years! There was also Madam Ruby. Her small booth was next to the Winchester Rifle Gallery, opposite the Dodgems. The First Aid Post, located by the Wonderland Main (centre) Entrance, was attended by Mrs Daniels (mum of Joe Daniels above).

There were many seasonal extra's operating the rides and as well as the regulars, this provided an opportunity for school leavers from the age 14 years to actually get paid to enjoy themselves! One such person was John Prior, who spent a couple of seasons as a casual in about 1960/1. He recalled first spending a short time on the Miniature Railway, then on the Gallopers from where he developed a lifelong love of fairground organs and music. He went on to do a spell on the Cages where he recalled the most outrageous thing he ever did was to assist two girls not strong enough to move the cage, by swinging it into motion hanging on to the outside, eventually going 'over the top in a swing'! His favourite ride though was the Waltzer. The Waltzer was a very powerful machine that was run up to three quarter speed on test at the start of each day but was never operated at more than half power with riders. His 'party piece' was to step on to the moving platform backwards with two mugs of coffee without spilling a drop!

These are just some of the folk known to have worked at Wonderland during its post-war heyday. There will have been many more, together with seasonal extras, whose names have been lost in the passage of time, but who all made up the family that was Wonderland. This book remembers them as well.

Chapter Sixteen

SEASIDE EXCURSIONS OR 'TRIP' TRAINS

Cleethorpes as a resort was developed by the railway which still owned the land of the North Promenade, leasing it to amusement proprietors. The railway was the resort's lifeblood until well into the 1960's and amusement operators, including Wonderland, planned their day by the number of 'Trip' trains expected. These excursion trains, also known as 'Specials' or 'Extras', arrived in Cleethorpes on summer Saturdays and Sundays in a steady stream from about 10.30 in the morning, often until well after 2.00pm.

The busiest time at the height of the summer season was the last week of July and the first week of August when the steel industry in Sheffield and surrounding area

186. Nearly there! A seaside excursion approaching New Clee in August 1963. Passengers would have their first glimpse of the sea after Fuller Street bridge, about a mile further on. The locomotive is British Railways Standard Class 5 No 73138.

Rob Foxon.

Seaside Excursions or 'Trip' Trains

HOLIDAY EXCURSIONS

DANCING IN PIER PAVILION, CLEETHORPES
Daily:—11.30 a.m. to 12.30 p.m. — 7.30 p.m. to 10.0 p.m.

DEAN and DAWSON'S EXCURSIONS TO

EDWINSTOWE, OLLERTON, LINCOLN, GRIMSBY DOCKS

AND

CLEETHORPES

Mondays, 9th July to 27th August inclusive
(6th August excepted). For 1, 4, 6 and 8 days.

FROM	Times of Departure.	\multicolumn{2}{c}{Edwinstowe.}	\multicolumn{2}{c}{Ollerton.}	\multicolumn{2}{c}{Lincoln.}	\multicolumn{2}{c}{Grimsby Dks.}	\multicolumn{2}{c}{Cleethorpes.}
		Day.	Period.	Day.	Period.	Day.	Period.	Day.	Period.	Day.	Period.
	a.m.										
LEICESTER (CEN.)	7 25	5 10	8 0	6 0	8 3	6 6	9 9	9 0	17 9	9 0	18 3
Rothley	7 30	5 4	7 3	5 6	7 6	6 6	9 0	9 0	17 0	9 0	17 0
Quorn and Woodhouse	7 40	4 11	6 9	5 1	7 0	6 0	8 6	8 6	16 0	9 0	16 6
Loughborough (Central)	7 45	4 8	6 3	4 10	6 6	6 0	8 0	8 6	16 0	9 0	16 0
Ruddington	8 0	3 6	5 0	3 8	5 0	4 9	6 6	8 0	14 0	8 6	14 6
Arkwright Street	8 5	3 0	5 0	3 2	5 0	4 2	5 9	8 0	13 3	8 0	13 9
NOTTINGHAM (VIC.)	8 15	3 0	5 0	3 2	5 0	4 2	5 9	8 0	13 3	8 0	13 9
Edwinstowe .. arr.	9 5										
Ollerton .. ,,	9 10										
Lincoln (L.N.E.R.) ,,	9 40										
Grimsby Docks ,,	11 4										
Cleethorpes .. ,,	11 12										

Passengers holding **DAY EXCURSION** tickets return **SAME DAY ONLY** as under:—

From—	At p.m.
Cleethorpes	7 39
Grimsby Docks	7 45
Lincoln (L.N.E.R.)	9 5
Ollerton	9 40
Edwinstowe	9 45

Those holding **PERIOD** tickets return on the following Thursday (4 days), Saturday (6 days) and Monday (8 days) as under:—

From—	Thursday and Monday. At p.m.	Saturday. At p.m.
Cleethorpes	12 39	1 40
Grimsby Docks	12 53	1 45
Lincoln (L.N.E.R.)	12 30	3 5
Ollerton	3 5	3 35
Edwinstowe	3 9	3 40

For Excursions on 6th August, see Special Announcements.

No. 993.

LNER

185. LNER Holiday Excursions bill of 1928.

Author's Collection.

Miles of Smiles

187. An aerial view of the extensive railway facilities at Cleethorpes. Bottom left are the carriage sidings, next to Wonderland. In the centre behind the Gayway is the locomotive turntable and ash pits. Top right is the station.

British Railways Board.

closed for the annual summer holidays. It was during these two Sheffield Weeks, that special trains arrived in Cleethorpes every day and it seemed as though the whole of Sheffield had visited the resort, for at least a day.

The most frenetic day ever was August Bank Holiday Sunday, 1956 when Cleethorpes was host to no less than 52 'trip' trains, each loaded to ten or eleven carriages bringing in around 400 happy holidaymakers. Trip trains were unusual in railway terms because they were made up with a parcels carriage marshalled in the centre of the train. The reason for this became obvious when the train arrived and the doors were flung open to reveal the carriage packed full from floor to roof with prams and push chairs! Standing at the buffer stops at Cleethorpes station might be two or more other 'trips' with crowds heading to the beach. Sometimes the steam locomotives carried headboards. There was one with a circular headboard covering the entire locomotive front proclaiming it to be the Sheffield Children's Homes Sunshine Holiday Express, or words to that effect.

Seaside Excursions or 'Trip' Trains

With passengers gone, the empty carriages were propelled into Suggitts Lane carriage sidings adjacent to Wonderland. The locomotive was turned on the turntable behind the Gayway and the train moved forward over Suggitts Lane crossing and on to New Clee sidings, where it would lay over for the day. In late afternoon, the locomotive would propel its train of carriages back into Suggitts Lane sidings and await its turn for a platform, ready to take its happy but weary charges home. Return trips began departing from just after five until well after nine o' clock. There was also the occasional evening 'Illuminations Special', late season.

Suggitts Lane crossing was a very busy place and the author often spent time there watching the trains arriving during the morning, before signing on at the Wonderland Miniature Railway at one o'clock and staying often until well after nine at night. As the 'trips' reversed slowly over the crossing, loco spotters read the destinations pasted on the carriage windows. Familiar places were Doncaster, Sheffield, Leeds, Nottingham, etc, but some of the return destinations were more obscure, such as Wadsley Bridge, Kiveton Park, Neepsend and South Elmsall. These were as a result of local Working

188. Excursion train in Suggitts Lane sidings awaiting its call to the station for the return journey to the Midlands. Just discernible behind in the right distance is a second train. Number one siding was long enough to accommodate two complete excursion trains consisting of eleven carriages each, plus locomotives! The locomotive is an LMS 'Crab' type, based in the industrial Midlands for use mainly on goods traffic, which has been 'borrowed' for this seaside special.

Author's Collection.

Miles of Smiles

189. Loco-spotters in the railway access passage behind Hawkey's New Capitol Cafe in 1952 observing return excursions ready to depart.
H.D.R McNeill.

Men's Clubs, Village Clubs, Church Organisations and the like, reserving one or more carriages in the train.

By the mid sixties however, special trains had become a victim of both market forces and railway modernisation. Holiday patterns were changing with the increasing popularity of package holidays overseas and family motoring was becoming more the norm. Seaside excursion traffic was still substantial however, and using British Railways own figures for rail borne visitors to Cleethorpes, there were 220,343 in 1963 and 234,218 in 1964.

The Beeching cuts of the early sixties included a proposal to close the line to Cleethorpes, but local management had established a diesel railcar servicing and fuelling point on the North Promenade (the current Network Rail facility) and this helped to make the case to retain it. The effects of the Beeching cuts did however, have a severe impact on Cleethorpes when after 1965, the running of seaside specials virtually ceased, leaving only the regular timetabled services. This rapid reduction of special trains however, was not due to any targeted decision making on the part of British Railways, but more a result of less rolling stock being available due to the effects of railway modernisation.

In the sixties, British Railways had a large float of carriage stock, some used only at weekends, and much more in longer term storage. This could be confirmed by the long lines of carriages by Sterling Street and Harrington Street, fronting New Clee sidings; some not moving for months. The Beeching report identified 5,500 carriages in daily main line use, plus a float of 8,900 vehicles for extra summer and high peak services. Of these, 2,000 were in use less than ten times a year. Interesting, was a green set of carriages from the Southern Region

190. Smoke and steam from the locomotive obscure the Big Dipper as passengers take a last glimpse of the sea before the train passes under Fuller Street Bridge. August 1963.
Rob Foxon.

Seaside Excursions or 'Trip' Trains

191. An unusual visitor was this Southern Railway brake third carriage No S3790 from Bournemouth, part of the rake of green livered carriages spending the week laying over in New Clee sidings, before returning south the following Saturday. The 7.14am Cleethorpes to Birmingham service train was extended to Bournemouth on summer Saturday's.
Rob Foxon.

which arrived in Cleethorpes from Bournemouth every other summer Saturday, then laid over in New Clee sidings until the following weekend. This was the corresponding return working of the daily 7.14am service train from Cleethorpes to Birmingham which was extended to Bournemouth on summer Saturdays, where the Cleethorpes based carriages would lay over until the following weekend.

By the mid sixties, large numbers of older pre-grouping carriages were being condemned and despatched to the scrap yards. A number of immaculate ex-works Gresley LNER teak bodied carriages could be seen stored fronting New Clee sidings and then being condemned with a white cross, probably never having turned a wheel since being overhauled and repainted. These would have been a heritage railway dream purchase today!

'Trip' trains were arranged through the British Railways Special Traffic & Trains Unit in the area of origin. Such units existed in all the British Railways operating centres. Many of the 'Trips' to Cleethorpes would have been organised through the Sheffield Special Traffic & Trains Unit, however not only was it becoming more difficult to arrange 'extras' due to less rolling stock being available, a similar situation was also arising with motive power and crews, as diesel traction took over.

Steam locomotives were being replaced with lesser numbers of main line diesel electric locomotives which were being more intensively worked due to their greater operating availability, thus making motive power for 'extras' also more difficult to identify. Add to this less footplate crews, the single manning agreement with its restrictions on working hours, overtime payments and the result was that it had become almost impossible to plan seasonal 'extras' within the framework of modern railway practice.

The Beeching Report summed it up in a couple of paragraphs: "Extra trains are very expensive to run, and may easily cause a loss which more than offsets any gain from increased traffic on the regular trains, especially if the extras are themselves only part filled and if there is no balancing return working for engines, vehicles and men. Such trains give rise to a high proportion of overtime working and they depend upon the availability of reserve coaching stock which is expensive to supply, maintain and assemble, and which is idle for most of the year". It goes on: "Since the beginning of 1959 the number of passenger carrying gangway coaches has been reduced by 5,584 and by the end of 1965 stock will not be available for use at high peak periods".

192. LNER open third class carriage of the type commonly used in excursion trains. No E13287 was built in 1936 and is one of a long line of carriages in New Clee sidings condemned and awaiting scrapping in the summer of 1963.
Rob Foxon.

The inevitable result was that Cleethorpes lost its life blood of rail-borne day trippers. Also in 1965, came a further blow when British Railways announced the sale of its seafront commercial property on the North Promenade (see next chapter) so within the year, the railway that had created Cleethorpes as a resort had almost completely retreated from it.

Unlike some other resorts where the railway has been cut back into the town, Cleethorpes station remains on the promenade and happy holidaymakers can still arrive beside the sea, just like those from the golden age of the British seaside, more than 50 years ago!

193. In complete contrast, LNER brake third carriage No E16761, dating from 1940, is newly overhauled and repainted, but probably never turned a wheel again in revenue earning traffic. This would have been a heritage railway dream acquisition today!
Rob Foxon.

Chapter Seventeen

SALE OF COMMERCIAL SEA FRONT PROPERTY ON THE NORTH PROMENADE

Seafront Under the Hammer

It was the Manchester, Sheffield & Lincolnshire Railway (later, Great Central Railway) that transformed Cleethorpes into a thriving resort. It owned the entire land of the North and Central Promenade's, had an interest in the Pier which opened in 1873 and had invested well over £100,000 in developing and beautifying the seafront. It created the Pier Gardens (now Alexandra Gardens) for those desirous of a peaceful visit. For those seeking more excitement, the start of the North Promenade between Sea Road and the station was complete with the Victor Colonnade of amusements, bazaars and stalls, opened by Prince Albert Victor, son of King Edward VII, on July 2, 1885.

The lessening of the railway's stranglehold on Cleethorpes began with the sale by the then London & North Eastern Railway Co, of railway owned land on the Central Promenade between Sea Road and High Cliff, including the Pier and Alexandra Gardens, to the Urban District Council for £27,500 in February 1936.

By the 1960's holiday patterns had changed. Package holidays in the sun and the universal ownership of motor cars had had a dramatic effect on traditional British seaside resorts, such as Cleethorpes. Add to this the reduction in British Railways excursion traffic or 'trip' trains, and Cleethorpes had lost a substantial part of its life blood. Whilst this had no direct bearing on events to follow, the British Railways Board was keen to reign in as much capital as possible from its remaining land assets, so British Rail Area Managers found themselves under pressure from the British Rail Property Board to release non-operational land.

Miles of Smiles

By order of the British Railways Board, a sale of the railway owned commercial sea front property on the North Promenade was held at the Yarborough Hotel in Grimsby at 2.30pm on Friday 17th September 1965. This was the remaining railway owned land that had been aquired by the former Manchester, Sheffield & Lincolnshire Railway in the nineteenth century, during the development of Cleethorpes as a seaside resort.

The forthcoming sale was widely reported, but this insight from the September 1965 issue of Railnews, the British Railways staff newspaper, sets the scene:

Headline: "BR's PROM IS UP FOR SALE the BR axe becomes an auctioneer's hammer this month when the famous Golden half mile at Cleethorpes is offered for sale. Going, going, gone! And at the fall of the auctioneer's gavel, British Railway's golden half mile of seafront will be sold, marking one of the biggest property sales in North Lincolnshire for years".

194. Cover of the sale brochure. Author's Collection.

"The sale includes the best known part of the North Promenade – the Wonderland area fitted with amusements and incorporating the old boating lake, big dipper and cartoon cinema. Other lots include a public house, two large cafes, shops and novelty bazaars, and platform 6 at Cleethorpes railway station".

"But for many of the tenants, the auction sale came as a bombshell. Walking through the brilliantly lit row of souvenir shops and cafes in the Victor Colonnade, I (Railnews reporter) came to number 11, a spotlessly clean snack bar which has been run by the Parkinson family for over 40 years. I first heard about the sale from the auctioneers late in July and it shook be rigid said Mr Parkinson. All my neighbours view the position with grave concern. We have been very happy with BR as landowners and until we know who the new landowners will be – and their intentions – our future seems uncertain. What is more, the auctioneers have lumped my property with numbers 10 and 9 and made them one lot – which makes it difficult for me to buy my own property".

"Not all tenants are as pessimistic about the forthcoming sale as Mr Parkinson and his neighbours. Several leaseholders told me they have experienced difficulty in the past in selling due to the land not going with the property. "This new move may help us to sell in the future, said one".

Sale of Commercial Sea Front Property on the North Promenade

No Difference

Others said they had their feet well and firmly on the ground. At Wonderland which has attracted millions of holidaymakers since it was built in 1926, Mr Frank Smith, secretary to the management commented "It doesn't really matter who will be our new landlords. We have a 21 year lease with an option for a further 21 years when it expires. We'll be carrying on as usual'" and the Hawkey family, who run two large cafes, are not in the least concerned about the future of their businesses. "My property is fairly new and covered by a good lease" said 65 year old Frank Hawkey. "I shall attend the auction and if the price is right, I shall buy".

A spokesman for Henry Spencer & Sons of Scunthorpe and Retford, the firm of auctioneers and estate agents handling the sale, said it's unlikely that any of the tenants livelihood's will be jeopardised by the sale. "I doubt if any old features of the promenade or old established firms will disappear from the front," he said".

It went on: "The Pier Gardens and promenade were railway owned until 1936, when they were sold to Cleethorpes Corporation. On September 17, British Railways will be selling what is left because, I was told, the land is not required and the capital which will be realised from the sale will be used to finance new railway projects".

The sale consisted of 21 lots, being the whole of the sea front property stretching from Sea Road to Wonderland, with the exception of the station itself and some public toilets, but including a seafood shop on the station approach, some property and undeveloped land on Grant Street. The total sum realised from the sale amounted to £328,990; approximately £6.5 million today. Lot 19 was for both the Wonderland and Gayway Amusement complexes, which together realised £97,000.

It is interesting to note from the sales catalogue that many of the lessee's along the North Promenade had erected buildings (arcades, shops, etc) at their own expense and that on the expiry of their lease, those buildings were either to be removed by the lessee, or transferred to the new landowner.

The normal lease agreement of railway land included a Railway Works Determination Clause, allowing the railway to change the conditions of, or terminate any lease if it required the land for further railway development or use, however in the case of the sale of railway property on the North Promenade, the reverse was the case. In a minor railway rationalisation scheme, the decision had been made to sell Platform 6 and an associated siding to release additional land for commercial development. This applied to several Lots which backed up to parts of the station (Platform 6) and associated tracks, hence the Special Conditions attached to Lots 7 to 12 in the sales catalogue:

"Notwithstanding the provisions of Special Condition 3 (that completion must be by 22nd October 1965) the Vendor shall retain after completion without any payment to the Purchaser that part of the lot as at present forms part of Platform 6 to Cleethorpes

Miles of Smiles

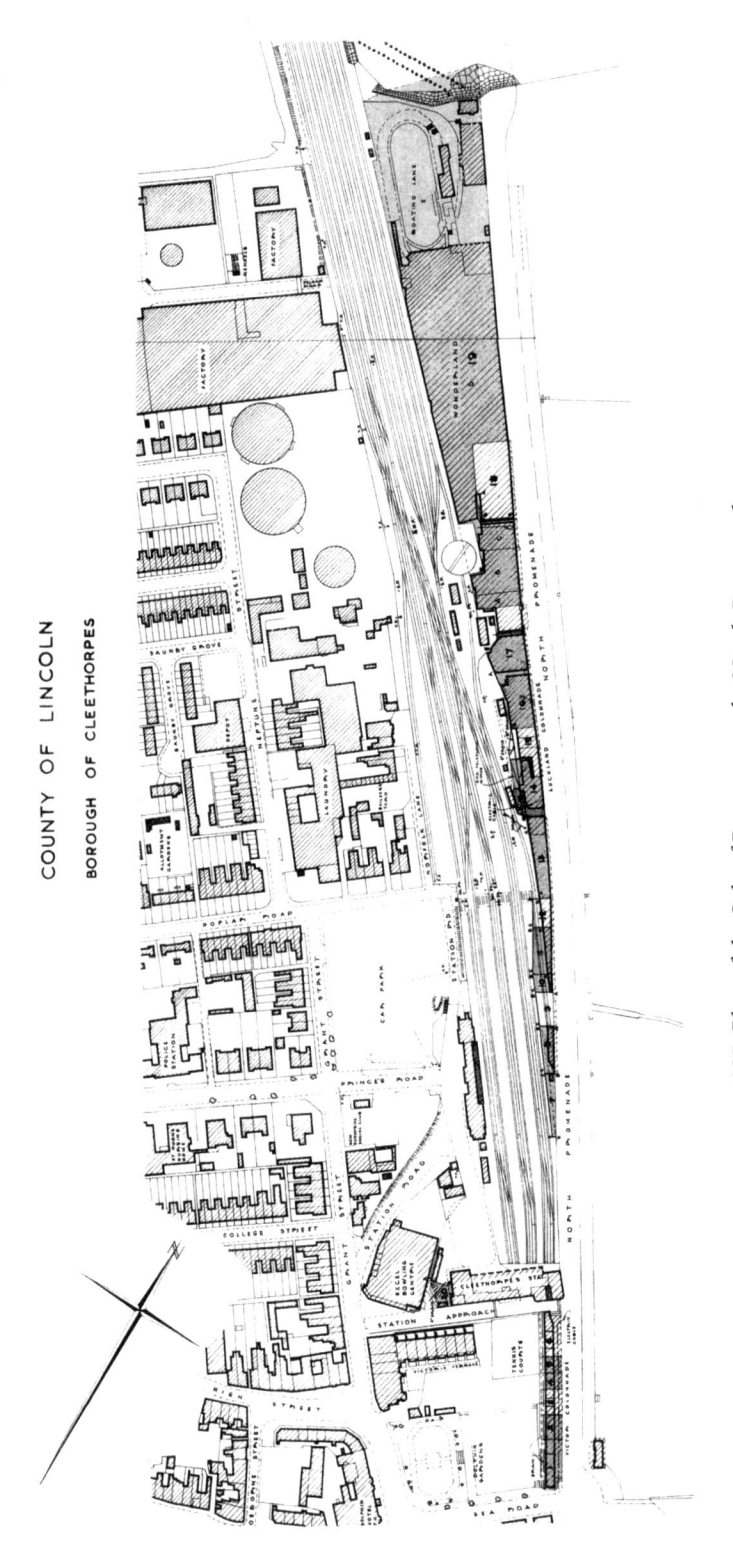

195. *Plan of the Sale of Property on the North Promenade. British Railways Board.*

Sale of Commercial Sea Front Property on the North Promenade

Key to image 195:
Lot 1.   1A & 1 to 5 Victor Colonnade
Lot 2.   6 to 8 Victor Colonnade
Lot 3.   9 to 11 Victor Colonnade
Lot 4.   12 & 13 Victor Colonnade
Lot 5.   14 & 15 Victor Colonnade
Lot 6.   16 to 20 Victor Colonnade
Lot 7.   Vacant Site, The Promenade
Lot 8.   Snack Bar & Shops, The Promenade
Lot 9.   Vacant Site, The Promenade
Lot 10. Ice Cream Kiosk, The Promenade
Lot 11. Premier Cafe (Hawkeys), The Promenade
Lot 12. Shop & Arcade, The Promenade
Lot 13. Amusement Arcade & Bazaar. The Promenade
Lot 14. New Capitol Cafe (Hawkeys), The Promenade
Lot 15. Three Shops, The Promenade
Lot 16. Licensed Premises, Auckland Colonnade
Lot 17. Savoy Amusement Arcade, Auckland Colonnade
Lot 18. Happidrome, Auckland Colonnade
Lot 19. Wonderland, The Promenade – Included Ritz Cinema, an Arcade, a Bazaar, an Amusement Hall and an Amusement Park
Lot 20. Shop, Station Approach
Lot 21. Freehold Site – Includes Undeveloped Land, House @ 20 Grant Street, a Betting Shop, The Sunny Side Club, 2 Sites for Store Sheds and a Site for a Store

196. *Aerial View of the North Promenade. All this land was railway owned and sold by auction in the September 17th 1965 sale of commercial sea front property.*
British Railways Board.

Miles of Smiles

station and the siding equipment railway tracks, etc, adjoining the same. The Vendor will remove such part of Platform 6 and the other items above referred to as are included in (Lots 7 to 12) as soon as is reasonably possible and in any event by not later than the 31st March 1966 when possession thereof shall be given to the purchaser".

So platform 6 alongside the promenade, one of the highlights for seaside excursionists arriving by train, was to be taken out of use, subsequently becoming a headshunt for the train servicing point.

The following details have been extracted from a surviving copy of the Auctioneers Sale Catalogue published by Henry Spencer & Sons for the sale by order of the British Railways Board on 17th September 1965. The details of the various tenants and lessees reveal many are long standing sea front traders and provide an excellent insight into the occupation of the North Promenade at the time. The prices realised for each Lot are those pencilled in by the unknown holder of the catalogue attending the sale, so may not be accurate or reflect the final situation. The report in the Birmingham Post on Saturday 18th September 1965 (see below) indicates significant differences in the figures.

The sale comprised of twenty one Lots as under:

197. Lot 1. Victor Colonnade, corner of Sea Road and the North Promenade.
British Railways Board.

Lot 1: Prominent Freehold Site of 1a, 1, 2, 3, 4, and 5 Victor Colonnade.

Buildings: 1a Corner Kiosk. Single storey 11 inch brick built in 1956.
Buildings: 1 to 5 Amusement Arcades. Single storey brick with concrete piers, single pitch bituminous and concrete roof extending to canopy, built in 1961.
Promenade Frontage: 92ft 4 inches.
Lessee: Norman Kaye & Co Ltd. By a lease dated 10th December 1963 for 21 years.
Annual Rent: £1500.00
Price realised at auction: £16000

Sale of Commercial Sea Front Property on the North Promenade

198. Lots 2 & 3. Victor Colonnade.

British Railways Board.

Lot 2: Freehold Bazaar 6-8 Victor Colonnade.

Buildings: Timber frame with corrugated asbestos roof, extending to form a canopy with cast upright supports.

Promenade Frontage: 47ft.

Tenant: J. Dukes by a tenancy dated 25th March 1953 terminable by 6 months notice.

Annual Rent: £483-15-0.

Price realised at auction: £6750

Lot 3: First-class Freehold Premises 9 to 11 Victor Colonnade.

Buildings: Timber frame with corrugated asbestos roof, extending to form a canopy with cast upright supports.

Promenade Frontage: 46ft 6 inches

Tenants: No 9, E.A. Brown & Sons (shops) Ltd by a tenancy commencing 6th April 1954 with 3 months notice. Annual Rent £300.00

No 10 A.&W. M. Osborne by a tenancy commencing 24th June 1956 with 6 months notice. Annual Rent £ 165.00.

No 11. E.W. Parkinson & Son by a tenancy commencing 25th March 1948 with 3 months notice. Annual Rent £250.00

Total Rent: £715.00

Price realised at auction: £6750

Miles of Smiles

199– Lots 4, 5 & 6. Victor Colonnade close to the station.
British Railways Board.

Lot 4: Important Freehold Bazaar 12 & 13 Victor Colonnade.

Buildings: Timber frame with corrugated asbestos roof, extending to form a canopy with cast upright supports.

Promenade Frontage: 31ft.

Tenant: Dukes Bazaars Ltd by a tenancy commencing 24th June 1956 with 6 months notice.

Annual Rent: £330.00.

Price realised at auction: £4540

Lot 5: Freehold Snack Bar 14 & 15 Victor Colonnade.

Buildings: Timber frame with corrugated asbestos roof, extending to form a canopy with cast upright supports.

Promenade Frontage: 31ft 1 inch.

Tenant: E.A. Brown & Sons (shops) Ltd by a tenancy commencing 24th April 1961 with 6 months notice.

Annual Rent: £500.00

Price realised at auction: £4500

Lot 6: 16-20 Victor Colonnade. Adjoining Station Approach with maximum footfall.

Buildings: Timber frame with corrugated asbestos roof, extending to form a canopy with cast upright supports.

Promenade Frontage: 77ft 6 inches.

Tenant: No16 J. Dukes by tenancy agreement dated 25th March 1953 with 6 months notice.

Sale of Commercial Sea Front Property on the North Promenade

Annual Rent £161 and five shillings.
Tenant: No's 17-20. Promenade Casino Amusements Ltd by tenancy agreements dated 29th September 1961 and 25th March 1963 with 6 months notice.
Annual Rent £1000.00
Price realised at auction: £11250

200. Lot 7. Platform 6 site for re-development.
British Railways Board.

Lot 7: The Promenade: Important Freehold Vacant Site.

Buildings: Site with vacant possession for development. Outline planning permission submitted for amusement, recreation and entertainment use.
Promenade Frontage: 120ft.
Price realised at auction: £12500

201. Lots 8, 9, 10 & 11. Marine snack bar, site for re-development, Blakeman's ice cream kiosk and Hawkey's Premier Cafe.
British Railways Board.

Miles of Smiles

Lot 8: The Promenade: Valuable Freehold Site of Snack Bar and Shops.

Buildings: Three inter-connected single story units in 9 inch brick with concrete bitumen covered roof. Five display windows and two entrances.
Promenade Frontage: 90ft.
Lessee: Catering Enterprises Ltd by lease dated 3rd April 1950 for 21 years.
Annual Rent: £360.00
Price realised at auction: £7000

Lot 9: The Promenade: Important Freehold Vacant Site.

Buildings: Site with vacant possession for development. Outline planning permission submitted for amusement, recreation and entertainment use.
Promenade Frontage: 60ft 6 inches.
Price realised at auction: £14000

Lot 10: The Promenade: Freehold Site of Ice Cream Kiosk.

Building: Single storey with 9 inch brick built in 1948 with concrete bitumen covered roof. Two display windows and single entrance.
Promenade Frontage: 37 ft 9 inches.
Lessee: C.H. Blakeman for 21 years from 29th September 1949, later assigned to E.A. Brown & Sons (Shops) Ltd on 18th November 1964.
Annual Rent: £100.00
Price realised at auction: £2700

Lot 11: The Promenade: Freehold Cafe Site, Premier Cafe.

Building: Two storey single unit of brick with concrete roof and verandah to first floor and roof area. Five display windows and three entrances. Seating for 350. Built in 1956.
Promenade Frontage: 89ft 6 inches.
Lessee: John Hawkey Ltd for 30 years from 24th June 1955.
Annual Rent: £500.00
Price realised at auction: £7250

Sale of Commercial Sea Front Property on the North Promenade

202. Lots 12 & 13. Brown's rock shop and Humber Pastimes amusement arcade.
British Railways Board.

Lot 12: The Promenade: Freehold Site of Shop and Arcade.

Building: Single storey unit of brick and concrete with mineral and flat felted roof. Built in 1956.
Promenade Frontage: 54ft 11 inches.
Lessee: E.A. Brown & Sons (Shops) Ltd for 21 years from 24th June 1955.
Annual Rent: £325.00
Price realised at auction: £6000

Lot 13: The Promenade: Freehold Site,
Humber Pastimes Amusement Arcade and Bazaar.

Building: A modern single and double story brick and rendered building with concrete barrel vault roof extending to form five bay canopy with roll up doors. Built in 1955.
Promenade Frontage: 158ft 3 inches.
Lessee: Walter West for 30 years from 24th June 1955.
Annual Rent: £1,100.00
Price realised at auction: £14750

Note: That between Lots 13 & 14, there exists a Right of Way, reserved at all times by the Vendor (British Railways Board) and the owner of the adjoining properties to the South West, for use at all times.

Miles of Smiles

203. Lots 14 & 15. Hawkey's New Capitol Cafe and Shops.
British Railways Board.

Lot 14: The Promenade: New Capitol Cafe and Restaurant.

Building: Two storey 9 inch brick with slated roof built in 1938, modernised and improved in 1960.
Promenade Frontage: 59ft 6 inches.
Lessee: John Hawkey Ltd for 14 years from 29th September 1949.
Annual Rent: £1.150.00
Price realised at auction: £17500

Lot 15: The Promenade: Excellent Freehold Site of Three Shops.

Building: 9 inch brick with flat concrete bitumastic roof built in 1960. Three separate windows and entrances.
Promenade Frontage: 95ft.
Lessees: R. Samuels for 21 years from 25th March 1960, later assigned to R.G. Samuels on 14th May 1965.
Annual Rent: £400.00
Lessees: Mrs M. Mendall for 21 years from 25th March 1960.
Annual Rent: £400.00
Lessees: S. Weiss for 21 years from 25th March 1960.
Annual Rent: £700.00
Total Rent: £1500.00 per annum.
Price realised at auction: £16750

Sale of Commercial Sea Front Property on the North Promenade

*204. Lots 16 & 17. Taddy's Pub and Savoy amusement arcade.
The toilet block on the right next to the Savoy was not included in the sale.*
British Railways Board.

Lot 16: Auckland Colonnade: Freehold Site of Licensed Premises (Taddy's).

Building: Modern Public House and Flat, in 9 inch brick with concrete and asphalt roof. Built in 1956.
Promenade Frontage: 185ft.
Lessee: Samuel Smith Old Brewery (Tadcaster) Ltd for 30 years from 25th March 1957.
Annual Rent: £1,100.00
Price realised at auction: £14750

Lot 17: Auckland Colonnade: Freehold Site of Savoy Amusement Arcade.

Building: Modern single storey with 11 inch cavity brick walls and mineral and boarded roof on timber trusses, forming a large arcade and roll up doors. Built in 1960.
Promenade Frontage: 70ft 3 inches.
Lessee: Sydney Kravis Ltd for 30 years from 25th March 1957.
Annual Rent: £1,250.00
Price realised at auction: £15000

Miles of Smiles

205. Lot 18. Happidrome Amusement Arcade.
British Railways Board.

Lot 18: Auckland Colonnade: Freehold Site of Amusement Arcade 'Happidrome'.

Building: A part two storey building with modern design, 9 inch brick with flat part concrete and bituminous roof and part asbestos. Six bays with roll up doors. Built in 1956.

Promenade Frontage: 150ft 10 inches.

Lessee: Mrs Mavis Glass for 21 years from 25th December 1947.

Annual Rent: £750.00

Price realised at auction: £31500

206. Lot 19. The Gayway complex, including Ritz cinema and adjoining shops. Wonderland on the extreme right was included in Lot 19.
British Railways Board.

Sale of Commercial Sea Front Property on the North Promenade

Lot 19: The Promenade: Freehold Amusement Arcade & Park 'Wonderland'

This was split into five units to be sold as one lot. Units A, B & C comprised the Gayway Amusement complex constructed in 1939:

Building Unit 'A': Ritz Cinema: Single story building in 9 inch rendered brickwork, with arcade and a corrugated asbestos ridge roof.

Promenade Frontage: 26ft 10 inches.

Building Unit 'B': Gayway Arcade: A mainly single storey building with facade constructed of brick with a corrugated asbestos roof and tiling at the front, rollup doors and twin sales kiosk.

Promenade Frontage: 80ft.

Building Unit 'C': Bazaar: Single storey building with facade, constructed of rendered brick, with asbestos corrugated roof.

Promenade Frontage: 53ft 9 inches.

Building Unit 'D': Wonderland Amusement Hall: Extensive building with brick facade constructed of steel stanchions and trusses, brick, timber roof trusses and uprights and corrugated roofing. Constructed in 1926. The building includes 15 kiosks with office and workshop accommodation.

Promenade Frontage: 402ft.

Building Unit 'E': Wonderland Amusement Park: Area of land with boating lake, timber snack bar and cafe. Note that all the buildings on this lot are included except for the Big Dipper and the Lessee's trade fixtures.

Promenade Frontage: 275ft.

Total Frontage: 837ft 7 inches.

Lessee: East Coast Amusement Company for 42 years from 1st January 1964.

Total Rent: £13,775.00 per annum.

Price realised at auction: £97000

Lot 20: Station Approach: Freehold Site of Shop

Building: Timber construction owned by the Tenant.

Station Approach Frontage: 24ft.

Tenant in Part: J. Dukes commencing 25th March 1953 with 3 months notice.

Annual Rent: £100.00

Price realised at auction: £2500

Lot 21: Important Freehold Site for Development.
The site incorporates Station Road and frontage to Grant Street

Buildings include The Sunny Side Club, a Betting Shop, a Dwelling House being 20 Grant Street, sites for store sheds and a large area of undeveloped land including public

Miles of Smiles

conveniences owned by the Cleethorpes Borough Council who have undertaken to remove them before completion.
Annual Rents: Dwelling House £60.00; Betting Shop £100.00; Sunny Side Social Club & Tea Room £350.00; 3 x Store Sheds totalling £66.00 together with Allotments at £1 One shilling and Sixpence.
Total Rent: £577 Six Shilling and Sixpence.
Price realised at auction: £20000

The sale was widely reported:

Coventry Evening Telegraph Tuesday 7th September 1965.

> "SEA FRONT COMING UNDER THE HAMMER. A HALF MILE stretch of sea front comes under the hammer on Friday, September 17, when British Railways will auction 41 acres of a holiday resort in Cleethorpes, Lincolnshire. Most of the property for auction is on the North Promenade and comprises the "Wonderland" amusement arcade and park, shops, a public house, cafes and bazaars. Annual rents for the 21 lots offered bring in £27,000. Also included is an acre near the main shopping centre. The land owned by the British Railways Board was acquired a hundred Years ago by the old Manchester, Sheffield and Lincolnshire Railway when it extended its line to Cleethorpes, then a quaint seaside village. The railway went Into the resort business and the public opening was performed by Prince Albert Victor, son of King Edward VII, on July 2, 1885"

Birmingham Post Wednesday 8th September 1965

> "RESORT SEAFRONT TO BE AUCTIONED. A half-mile stretch of seafront will be auctioned on September 17th when British Rail puts up for sale four and a quarter acres of holiday resort In Cleethorpes. Most of the property for auction is on North Promenade and comprises the "Wonderland" amusement arcade and park, shops, a public-house, cafes and bazaars."

Birmingham Post Saturday 18th September 1965

> "WONDERLAND IS EXPECTED TO FETCH £l00,000. A total of £220.000 was raised at an auction at Grimsby, Lincolnshire, yesterday of the 'Golden Half-mile' of Cleethorpes, North Promenade. But the biggest lot of 21 originally advertised on behalf of British Rail—the site of a big amusement centre "Wonderland" was withdrawn when bidding reached £75.000. Later the auctioneer, Mr. Michael Spencer said the Wonderland site would be sold by Monday for about £100.000. A public house was withdrawn at £14.500."

Sale of Commercial Sea Front Property on the North Promenade

Footnote: The Gayway complex was again advertised as being for sale in the showbiz newspaper The Stage edition of 18th April 1985. Its purchaser is not known, but was likely British Rail, who had released the land twenty years earlier in the 1965 sale. With the land for sale in private ownership, the Railway Works Determination Clause earlier mentioned would not have been applicable and the British Rail agent would have had to bid competitively with others at the sale. Sadly, the Art-Deco Gayway complex was subsequently demolished and the site is now occupied by the expanded Network Rail train servicing depot, used at the time of writing by Northern Trains.

Chapter Eighteen
WONDERLAND FINALE

207. The Mad Mouse roller coaster replaced the Big Dipper for the 1975 season.
Doug Best Collection.

The rationalisation of the outdoor area of Wonderland was well under way, even by 1970. The Miniature Railway, Go Karts and Speedway had all gone and the Gallopers moved under cover on the site of the former Peter Pan Railway, now accessible directly from the Great Hall, where they worked for a number of seasons. The Big Dipper lingered on until a safety inspection resulted in its closure in 1974. Following the demolition of the Big Dipper during the winter of 1974/5 by Robotham's of Waltham, the boating lake was filled in, the cafe and the canopy over the former Speedway removed, and the whole outdoor site levelled.

The Big Dipper was replaced for the 1975 season by a Mad Mouse roller coaster aquired from Rhyl, which operated until 1979 and was then dismantled. The Gallopers moved again, this time into the Great Hall next to the Waltzer. By this time it was known as the Wells Fargo Carousel, but only a shadow of its former glory without

Wonderland Finale

organ and with the odd stagecoach on the platform to replace missing or broken horses. The Jets were sold in 1978 and the Gallopers in 1980, just prior to the sale of Wonderland to Dudley Bowers (Leisure) Ltd.

1981 – 2013

The new operators lost no time in re-modelling the Wonderland Great Hall for its new use as an undercover Sunday Market venue. The Dodgems and Ghost Train remained in place a while longer but the side stalls were dismantled and all other rides moved to a new outdoor amusement area, created on the levelled site of the former Big Dipper and Mad Mouse. Both the Waltzer and the smaller Custom Rider Speedway Ark had moved outdoors by 1982, the latter being disposed of to Funland at Mablethorpe in 1984. Also moved outdoors were the various kiddie rides including a roundabout with cars, two ladybird roundabouts and an Octopus ride, clearing the Great Hall for the rapidly expanding Sunday Market operation which was attracting as many as 300 stalls each week.

An Astroglide was erected at the end of the North Promenade in about 1970. This allowed six riders to race down the slide at once. History was repeating itself, for the

208. Dudley Bowers Sunday Market

Dudley Bowers.

Miles of Smiles

209. The North Promenade with Astroglide on the right, in 1979.
Author's collection

Astroglide was a late 20th century development of the original Victorian (Slipping the Slip) helter skelter, proving yet again that some fairground ride concepts have endured the passage of time. Unfortunately the Astroglide was destroyed following a severe gale in 1985.

The Dodgems, Ghost Train and Waltzer continued in use with the new operators into the eighties. The Waltzer was outside from 1982 until being loaned to various other fairground operators for a period of five years from 1987. National Fairground Archive records suggest the Waltzer (ref: Ark A170, former Cycledrome) was loaned from 1987, moving first to Levitt's at Redcar, then to West Sands at Selsey and finally, to Lightwater Valley at Ripon. An image of the outdoor site in 1982 includes an advertising sandwich board stating: "WONDERLAND. The Following Rides are Inside: The Dodgems, The Twist, The Waltzer, The Ghost Train, Carousel Snack Bar and American Burger Bar", but the Waltzer was already outdoors and can be clearly seen in the background of the image.

Other rides known to have worked at Wonderland during the Dudley Bowers years include the Sky Glider (1979 – 1995), Chair-O-Plane (1987 – 1997), the Zinger (1982 – 1984), Snow Storm (Jolly Tubes ride, 1982 only) and the Custom Rider Speedway (1979 – 1983). This latter ride was the previously mentioned Orton & Spooner Easy Rider Cycledrome Speedway Ark (National Fairground Archive Ref: A148) at Wonderland between 1979 and 1984, owned by Michael Miller & Son (Son-in-law of Dudley Bowers). There was also of course the original Wonderland (Disco) Waltzer which returned to Cleethorpes ex-loan in 1992 but was alas, destroyed by fire in 1997.

Wonderland Finale

Views of Wonderland in about 1982.
210. Wonderland promenade exterior.
211. Wonderland outdoor amusement area. Sandwich board highlights indoor amusements including the Ghost Train and Dodgems, still operating in the Great Hall.
Grimsby Evening Telegraph.

212. Wonderland outdoor amusements with Ladybird rides. Waltzer in the background.
Grimsby Evening Telegraph.

Miles of Smiles

213. Wonderland Sunday Market. 2nd July 2004.

Dudley Bowers.

It is not clear how long the outdoor site remained an amusement park before becoming the Sunday Market car park, but Wonderland was sold on in 2005 to Town & Country Markets, and again in 2011. The Sunday Market continued until the spring of 2013 when the Grimsby Telegraph reported its closure at short notice. The news was not received well by stallholders (Appendix 8). Michael Miller, son-in-law of Dudley Bowers said "People won't come down this end of the promenade once the market has gone and it will spell the death knell for other businesses down here". The passing of time has proved him correct.

To their credit, the Local Authority have spent a great deal of money repaving and enhancing the North Promenade making it a very pleasant walk and a good environment for business, but the hoped for revival of the promenade has sadly not materialised. The Wonderland Great Hall became a Go-Kart

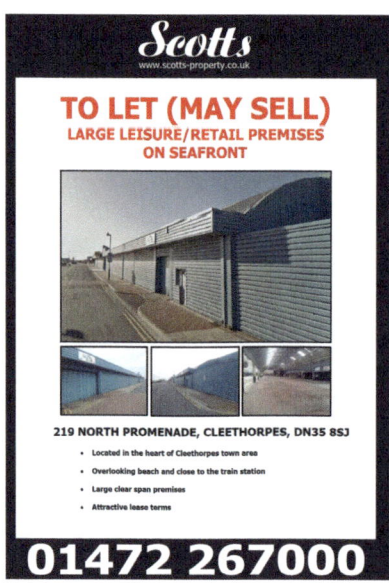

214. Wonderland for sale again in 2011. Author's Collection.

Wonderland Finale

track and Airsoft war gaming centre. As creditable as these might be, they have not lured visitors to the end of the North Promenade, with the result that attractions fizzle out soon after passing the railway station, leaving the once thriving Golden Half Mile a rather desolate place.

Chapter Nineteen

THE NORTH PROMENADE TODAY

Together with a Potted History of each site

This chapter describes the North Promenade at the time of writing (2021) and helps the reader to identify sites of historical significance, enabling them to be compared with the scene today.

The North Promenade has changed considerably since the post-war golden age of the British Seaside, however most buildings from the post-war period are still extant, albeit some heavily disguised. Nothing remains of the original Victor Colonnade between Sea Road and the Station, but the Amusement Centres and shops that have replaced it are today, the busiest part of the North Promenade. Between Sea Road and the Station today is Fantasy World (Casino Amusements), Taylor Made Fun amusement arcade, more Fantasy World, Brown's Cafe & Restaurant (Est. 1880) and finally, more Fantasy World amusements. This was previously the site of the Victor Colonnade, the first major leisure attraction on the North Promenade opened by Prince Albert Victor, son of King Edward VII, on July 2, 1885. It represented Lots 1 to 6 in the 1965 British Railways sale of commercial seafront property.

Over the road on the beach side of the North Promenade today is Darracotte's Coffee Shop & Ice Cream Parlour, MacDonald's Ice Cream, Cleethorpes Rock Co, MacDonald's Cafe and Daisy's mobile Seafood Bar.

The Mermaid Fish & Chip Restaurant is in the former Station Refreshment Rooms opened in 1884 and altered in the 1950's. The historic Refreshment Rooms and Clock tower are by Lockerbie and Wilkinson of Birmingham for the Manchester, Sheffield and Lincolnshire Railway, station enlargement scheme of 1880. The Refreshment Rooms have cast iron framework, with timber and glass walls and are Grade II listed.

Long standing attractions remain on the sands opposite the station including the Big Wheel, Junior Switchback Railway, Roundabout and Chair-O-Plane.

The North Promenade Today

215. The start of the North Promenade today at its corner with Sea Road. Inset: The scene in 1965.

Michael Foxon.

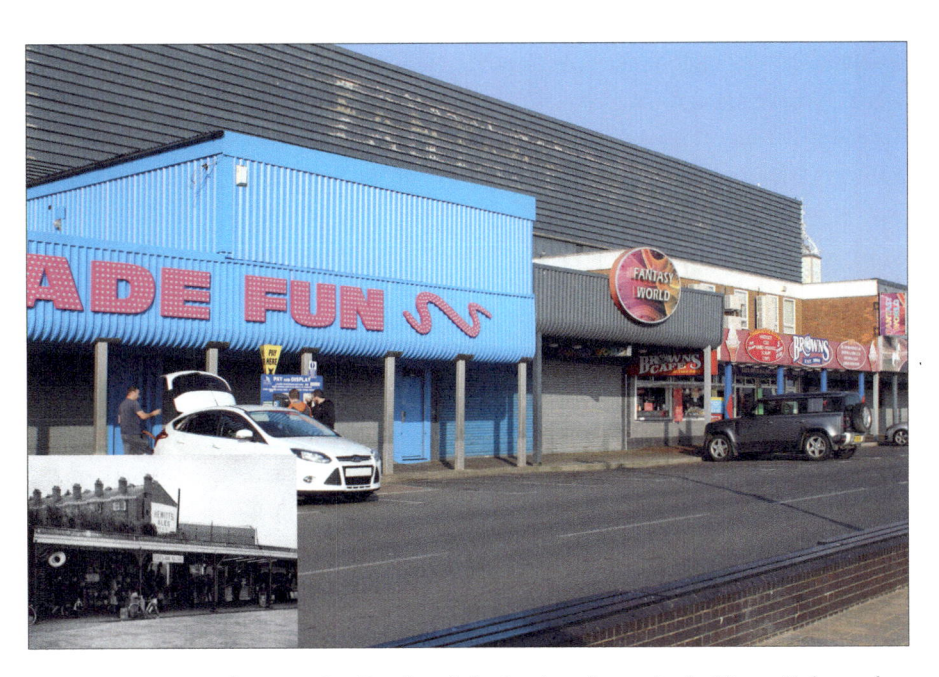

216. Amusements between Sea Road and the Station, formerly the Victor Colonnade. Inset: The same location in 1965.

Michael Foxon.

Miles of Smiles

217. Amusements closer to the Station, formerly the Victor Colonnade. Railway station on the right. Inset: The same location in 1965.

Michael Foxon.

Between the station and Wonderland, the first Block of Shops are now 177-179 North Promenade and comprise the Naughty But Nice Rock Shop and Fryer Tuck's Takeaway & Cafe. This was Lot 7, a 120ft frontage of undeveloped land in the British Railways sale of commercial seafront property in 1965, which was formerly platform 6 of the station.

No 185 North Promenade is today The Smile Factory (toys and gifts) and Buttercups & Daisy's (gift shop). This was formerly the three inter-connecting promenade shops operated by Catering Enterprises Ltd, built in 1951 and sold as Lot 8 in the sale of commercial seafront property.

Adjacent is Scoops Ice Cream. This was formerly the 60ft frontage of undeveloped land sold as Lot 9 in the British Railways sale of commercial seafront property. Next to it is The Chippy. This was Lot 10 in the British Railways sale and has been built on the site of the former attractive Blakeman's ice cream kiosk of 1948. Before the war, this was promenade amusements and gift shops; the beginning of a series of ramshackle kiosks, shops & kiosks which extended from the station along the Promenade to the railway access passage (see Edwardian postcard North Promenade, Cleethorpes c1905).

The next three buildings were part of the post-war Better Cleethorpes modernisation programme:

The North Promenade Today

218. The historic Grade II listed Mermaid fish & chip restaurant today, formerly the Station Refreshment Rooms opened in 1884, altered in the 1950's.
Michael Foxon.

219. 'Naughty but Nice' Rock Shop and 'Fryer Tuck's' Takeaway & Cafe, built on the site of Platform 6 of the station. Inset: Platform 6 before the sale in 1965.
Michael Foxon.

Miles of Smiles

220. The remains of platform 6 are on the right. November 2021.

Steven Foxon.

221. The Smile Factory (toys and gifts) and Buttercups & Daisy's (gift shop), formerly Promenade Shops operated by Catering Enterprises Ltd, dating back to the 1950's. Inset: Catering Enterprises in 1965.

Michael Foxon.

The North Promenade Today

222. Candiland and Fabulous Fudge in the former Hawkey's Premier restaurant which when new, had a rooftop dining area.

Steven Foxon.

Today, Candiland and Fabulous Fudge are in the former giant Hawkey's Premier Restaurant (with rooftop seating) of 1956. This was Lot 11 in the British Railways sale. Previously it was the site of an earlier Hawkey's Premier Cafe and adjacent Empire Colonnade of shops. Originally this was the site of Hawkey's tiny Photographic Shop and Cafe, dating back to Edwardian times.

The Rock Shop was formerly Brown's Seaside Rock, still in its post-war (1956) building. This was Lot 12 in the British Railways sale of commercial seafront property. E.A. Brown & Son were the long established seaside rock manufacturers mentioned in earlier chapters. Behind their impressive Promenade Shop before the war was Brown's Model Rock Factory (see it being made), which was adjacent to the railway tracks.

Next is the Humber Pastimes amusement arcade, again in its post-war (1955) building with concrete barrel vault roof. This was Lot 13 in the British Railways sale. Humber Pastimes is the oldest and only traditional amusement arcade remaining on the North Promenade today. It was established in 1935 as Walter West's Humber Automatic Exhibition on the same site in an attractive timber arcade building with gable frontage which dated back to Edwardian times.

Next to Humber Pastimes is the original railway access passage, now an outdoor catering area for the adjacent pub. The Punch Bowl & Lacey's public house and

Miles of Smiles

223. The Rock Shop and Humber Pastimes amusement arcade in little changed 1950's buildings with shutters transformed as part of the 'Longest Visual Art Gallery' creation. Inset: The scene in 1965.

Michael Foxon.

224. The Punch Bowl & Lacey's Public House & Restaurant today. This is a radical conversion of the former Hawkey's New Capitol Cafe building, incorporating its three adjacent shops.
Inset: Hawkey's New Capitol Cafe & Restaurant in 1965.

Michael Foxon.

The North Promenade Today

Restaurant is a radical conversion of the former Hawkey's New Capitol Cafe building, incorporating its three adjacent shops. These were Lots 14 &15 in the British Railways sale of commercial seafront property. Originally Hawkey's New Capitol Cafe of 1938, it was enlarged in 1960 and three new shops built adjacent. This was previously the site of the original Capitol Cafe & Restaurant in a distinctive white gabled timber building. Next to it were the promenade public toilets which dated back to Edwardian times, on the site of the three shops.

A couple of modern single storey units now stand next to the Punch Bowl. These are the Walkers Fitness Centre and Reemas Beauty Salon. This site was Lot 16 in the British Railways sale of commercial seafront property.

The former Moon on the Water music venue and the Ebb and Flo water sports shop are in the radically altered 1956 former Taddy's public house building and collectively form 201-203 North Promenade, sometimes known today as 'The Steps'. This was previously the site of Sam Smith's pub at the south end of the historic Auckland Colonnade (1885-1955). Sadly, the Moon on the Water cafe, bar & live music venue, which had been established on the North Promenade for a number of years, has announced it will not be re-opening, following the relaxation of Covid lockdown rules. Ebb & Flo however have recently announced exciting plans for a brand new Water Sports centre to be built on disused land, site of the former Savoy amusement arcade, next to their existing premises.

225. The former 'Moon on the Water' live music venue and 'Ebb & Flo' water sports centre in the radically altered and heavily disguised former Taddy's public house building. Inset: Taddy's Public House in 1965 with the Savoy amusement arcade next to it.

Michael Foxon.

226 – *The massive promenade frontage of the Siemens Network Rail Train Maintenance Depot, site of the former Gayway amusement complex. Inset: The Gayway in 1965.*
Michael Foxon.

This is where footfall largely ceases along the North Promenade today, except for the Cleethorpes Indoor Market, for next to the shops is the open site of the former Savoy amusement arcade (1960), demolished about 1989, probably following the expiry of its lease. This 70ft frontage was Lot 17 in the British Railways sale. It was originally the central section of the Auckland Colonnade (1885-1955).

The long derelict Public Conveniences, constructed in about 1955 as part of the post-war Better Cleethorpes modernisation scheme, were not included in the British Railways Board sale of commercial seafront property as they were presumably local authority owned. This was originally the North end of the historic Auckland Colonnade of 1885 which housed Jackson's Dining Rooms (1885-1912), later Smalley's Restaurant (1912-c1930).

VALUABLE FREEHOLD AMUSEMENT ARCADE NORTH PROMENADE, CLEETHORPES
For Sale By Public Auction
On May 1st at 2.30 p.m. on the premises
(unless sold previously)
Comprising 90 ft. frontage with 45 machines, prize bingo, fully equipped American style fast food bar.
Full Planning Permission for Fish and Chip Take-away.
Genuine reason for selling.
Apply: GOUDES,
CHARTERED SURVEYORS,
AUCTIONEERS AND ESTATE AGENTS,
3, Town Hall Street,
Grimsby,
South Humberside.
Telephone 55391.

227. *The former Gayway up for sale again. The Stage 18th April 1985.*

The North Promenade Today

The massive 170ft promenade frontage of the Siemens Network Rail Train Care Depot has the greatest historical provenance on the North Promenade. It comprised the A, B & C parts of Lot 19 of the 1965 British Railways sale of commercial seafront property (see earlier chapter), being the former Gayway complex and its post-war annexes.

Twenty years later however, it was back on the market being advertised for sale in the 18th April 1985 edition of The Stage as a valuable freehold site with amusement arcade, complete with machines. This was clearly being aimed at an amusement operator, but was actually re-purchased by British Rail (Network Rail) for their enlarged Cleethorpes train maintenance depot scheme and alas, the splendid Art-deco (former Gayway) amusement complex, including the Ritz cinema and adjacent shops were swept away. This site has the most historic significance on the North Promenade, having previously formed a large part of the Pleasureland open air fairground (1909-1939) and scene of the 1932 fire which destroyed the Golden Dragons steam powered Scenic Ark. Previous to that it was the site of the Warwick Revolving Tower (1902-1909) and of the Fairy River (1902-c1935). Today, it breaks the line of buildings and has had the unfortunate effect of dividing the North Promenade into two parts, for beyond the Siemens Network Rail site, there is only the Indoor Market and the former Wonderland building.

228. *The Cleethorpes Indoor Market, formerly the Happidrome Amusement Arcade. Inset: Happidrome in 1965.*

Michael Foxon.

Miles of Smiles

Next to the Network Rail entrance is the 150ft frontage of the Cleethorpes Indoor Market, formerly the Happidrome Amusement Arcade, built in 1956 as part of the post-war modernisation scheme. This was Lot 18 in the British Railways sale. The site was previously part of Pleasureland which over the years hosted many fairground rides and attractions including the Wall of Death, the Famous Bowl Slide, the Sunrise Cafe and much more (Author's note: There is still much to discover about the Pleasureland open air fairground site during the period 1902 to 1939).

Remarkably, changing tidal patterns and shifting sands have uncovered the sawn off timber stumps of the Victorian Switchback Railway in the sands between the breakwaters opposite the Indoor Market and Wonderland. Clearly discernible is the square footprint of the boarding station and the path of the ride along the sands, enabling its exact position to be identified. The Tuppeny Switchback, seen in Edwardian coloured postcards and described in detail in earlier chapters, was the very first big ride attraction in Cleethorpes.

The final building on the North Promenade is the imposing 400ft frontage of Wonderland, constructed in 1926 and in use more recently as a Go-Kart track and Airsoft Paint Ball centre. It was part of Lot 19 of the British Railways sale of commercial seafront property. Following the demise of its original purpose, the buildings' potential has never been realised. Available for letting yet again (2011–2013), the Agent for that offering suggested possible uses might include its continuation as a Sunday Market, or as a leisure facility (example laser quest, indoor go-karting, soft play area, etc). Not mentioned was its potential as an indoor amusement centre! Wonderland in more recent times has been all of those things. Go-karting ceased in 2018 and the building in 2020 was a Nerf Wars indoor activity arena. With a Nerf Wars gun comes unlimited foam darts…! A visit during the spring of 2022 revealed half of the former Wonderland Great Hall being used for vehicle storage, repair and restoration, perhaps echoing its former use during WWII for vehicle assembly and maintenance,

Between 1981 and 2013, Wonderland has been variously a Sunday Market and an indoor games venue. It was of course the Great Hall of the former Wonderland Amusement Park, the largest covered amusement complex on the East Coast, created by George Wilkie in 1926. Before the Great War, it was the site of the Dip the Dips roller coaster (1913-1925) and even earlier, the Hotchkiss Bicycle Railway (1902-c1908).

Beyond the Wonderland building at the very end of the Promenade is today the Seaview Motorhome Stop-Over. This was also part of Lot 19 in the British Railways sale. Most recently it has been the Sunday Market car park (c2005-2019) and before that the site of Dudley Bowers outdoor amusements (1980-c2005). Most significantly however, this was the end of promenade site re-modelled by George

The North Promenade Today

Wilkie in 1926 for the new Wonderland (1926-1980) which included the Big Dipper, Boating Lake (Lakeland) and much more. In the earliest developments of the North Promenade however, this was the site of the Figure of Eight railway (1908-1925) and the Kursaal Bazaar & Cafe from c1906.

Chapter Twenty
VISIONS OF THE FUTURE

229. The vision of Dynamic Swirling Illuminations in the form of LED lights along the North Promenade with rapidly changing light sequences.

NELDC.

The Local Authority, aware of the Victorian heritage of the North Promenade, and with the benefit of Coastal Communities funding, is keen that the present generation should leave some lasting heritage for the future. To this end, they have drawn up plans to improve the North Promenade and increase footfall, the most ambitious (and controversial) being the erection of a 72ft high White Palm Tree on the promenade, opposite Wonderland. This would be taller, it is claimed, than the 'Angel of the North' and be illuminated artistically. Also in the plans is the provision of 'Exercise Furniture' along the promenade on which folk passing by can use, painting the shutters of the various buildings along the North Promenade to create the 'Longest Visual Art Gallery' and Dynamic Swirling Illuminations in the form of LED lights strung along the North Promenade with rapidly changing light sequences. Of course, such exciting plans are

Visions of the Future

230. Impression of how the controversial White Palm Tree might have looked.
NELDC.

likely to be disrupted in the light of Covid circumstances. At the time of writing, the exercise furniture had been installed and the Longest Visual Art Gallery completed, but the controversial White Palm Tree proposal had been abandoned.

Another radical proposal to further develop the North Promenade area of Cleethorpes at the time of writing is the 'One Cleethorpes' development of three high rise residential blocks close to the station. Again, viability and progress will be dependent on Covid circumstances but at the time of writing, planning permission had been granted.

Network Rail closed Suggitts Lane crossing on 'Safety Grounds' as part of their national plan to reduce the number of level crossings on the network. This had the unintended effect of further frustrating efforts to increase footfall (and development) along the North Promenade by making access more difficult for local folk, however following much representation, a new pedestrian footbridge over the line at Suggitts Lane has been constructed, which opened for use during March 2022, restoring a much used local thoroughfare to the North Promenade.

231. The new Suggitts Lane footbridge under construction from the seaward side. November 2021.

Steven Foxon.

Miles of Smiles

232. *The new footbridge viewed from Suggitts Lane. November 2021. Compare this taken from the same spot in plate 188.*

David Handy.

233. *An impression of the proposed 'One Cleethorpes' development of three high rise residential blocks overlooking the North Promenade, to be built on disused land behind the station.*

Cielo Reality.

Visions of the Future

234. Impression of the 'One Cleethorpes' development seen from the North Promenade.
Cielo Reality.

235. Impression of the new Ebb & Flo water sports centre to be built on the site of the former Savoy Amusement Arcade on the North Promenade
Ebb & Flo.

Miles of Smiles

Staycations

The current disruption and uncertainty around travel arrangements due to Covid has brought about fresh opportunities for British seaside resorts as Staycation breaks and holidays have increased in popularity. At Cleethorpes, all the elements of a successful resort are still in place. The pier has been revived as a high end Fish & Chip restaurant, a brand new water sports centre has been given the go-ahead and there are plans for illuminations with swirling flashing LED lights along the promenades, but best of all, there are the golden sands for which the East Coast is renown. The railway station is on the promenade and whilst it would be unrealistic to expect the crowds of trippers arriving by rail as in the past, there remains an excellent service to Manchester, Sheffield and the industrial Midlands from where many of those day trippers of the past originated. Indeed, Rail Company 'TRANSPENNINE EXPRESS' is in the process of introducing locomotive hauled, brand new Nova 3 train sets on Manchester services from the 2022 summer timetable. For those arriving by car, there is adequate car parking on Grant Street serving the North Promenade, on the Promenade itself, and by the Leisure Centre serving the southern part of the resort.

The new footbridge over the railway at Suggitts Lane will certainly encourage greater local footfall but the real answer to reviving the North Promenade lies in re-developing Wonderland again as a family entertainment centre, or similar. Now history does have a strange habit of repeating itself and the Great Hall still has the potential to become a modern indoor family amusement centre. Let us hope that the entrepreneurial spirit of George Wilkie is not dead and that his legacy can be re-awakened for a new generation of excited children. "Pleasure the weather can't spoil!"

Epilogue

The end of the North Promenade is a quiet place today. Gone are the screams from the Big Dipper leaving only older folk to remember, for here was not only the landmark roller coaster, but also the Miniature Railway, Boating Lake, Speedway Cars, Peter Pan Railway, Promenade Cafe and best of all, the Golden Galloping Horse roundabout with its magnificent organ playing rousing music all day, every day. Looking at the empty site today, how could so much pleasure have been crammed into such a small space?

Appendix One
ALTERNATIVE NAMES

East Coast Amusement Company advertising gives a good impression of the early development of Wonderland. Care however, needs to be applied in the precise interpretation of the rides as many are described as 'new' but perhaps with a subtle name change, thus *appearing* to be new!

In the days before stricter advertising standards, the names of rides and attractions would be subtly changed to make it appear something was 'new' but already existed. For example, it will be seen in Wonderland advertising that the Big Dipper was also known as the Giant Coaster, Scenic Coaster or even Scenic 'Supreme' Coaster over the years. Some Wonderland ad's even include both the Big Dipper and Scenic Coaster, which are actually the same ride!

Below are the common use names of various rides and attractions, followed by the 'also known as' (aka) variations used in Wonderland marketing and advertising in the body of the book.

Pleasureland 1925:

>DIP THE DIPS aka: *Dipping the Dips, Giant Mountain Dip the Dips, Ariel Scenic Railway, Flying Switchback.*

Wonderland from 1926:

>THE BIG DIPPER   aka: *New Dips, Giant Dipper, Giant Dips, Scenic Coaster, Scenic 'Supreme' Coaster.*
>DODGEMS aka: *New Dodgems.*
>CHAIR-O-PLANE aka: *Flying Chairs.*
>ELECTRIC SCENIC RAILWAY   aka: *Scenic Ark or Platform Scenic. Various themes inc. Noah's Ark, Venetian Gondolas, Cycledrome.*
>MIDGET MOTORS aka: *Custer Cars, Auto Cars, New Midget Motors, Kiddies Speedway.*

Miles of Smiles

SKATING RINK aka: *Roller Skating, Grand New Open Air Roller Skating Rink.*

GHOST TRAIN aka: *The Lost World.*

MOTOR BOATS (Lakeland) aka: *Speedboats, Water Dodgems (Not to be confused with post-war Electric Water Dodgems).*

LOOPS aka: *Cages, Looping the Loop, Over the Top In a Swing.*

BROOKLANDS SPEEDWAY aka: *Electric Speedway. Brooklands Racing Track, finally Indianapolis 500.*

BIG WHEEL aka: *Big Eli Wheel.*

ZOO aka: *Miniature Zoo, Monkey House, Animal House, Pet's Corner.*

WONDERLAND MINIATURE RAILWAY aka: *Lakeside Miniature Railway.*

CRAZY HOUSE aka: *House of Laughter.*

GALLOPERS aka: *Golden Galloping Horse Roundabout.*

JETS aka: *Hurricane Jets, Flying Jets.*

WATER DODGEMS (post-War) aka: *Electric Water Dodgems.*

CYCLEDROME (post-war) aka: *Silver Rodeo Ark.*

Appendix Two
TIMELINE OF WONDERLAND RIDES

Wonderland Rides - Time Line	1926	1927	1928	1929	1930	1931	1932	1933	1934	1935	1936	1937	1938	1939	1949	1951	1953	1956
New Dips	x	x	x	x	x	x	x	x	x	x	x	x	x	x	x	x	x	x
New Dodgems	x	x	x	x	x	x	x	x	x	x	x	x	x	x	x	x	x	x
Famous Bowl Slide	x	x	x															
Flying Chairs (Chair-O-Plane)	x	x											x			x	x	
New Whip	x	x																
Electric Scenic Railway	x	x	x	x	x													
New Circus	x																	
Midget Motors (Custer Cars)		x	x	x	x													
New Atlantic Flyer			x	x														
New Radio Cars			x	x	x													
Roller Skating Rink				x	x										x	x		
New Rapids				x	x													
New Caterpillar				x														
High Diver					x													
Death Riders (Wall of Death)					x	x										x		
Miniature Railway						x	x											
Ghost Train						x	x	x	x	x	x	x	x	x	x	x	x	x
Petrol Skooter's						x							x	x				
Auto-Cars						x												
Noah's Ark						x												
Boating (Speedboats, Water Dodgems)								x	x	x	x	x	x	x	x	x	x	x
Dickens' Art Gallery								x										
Scenic Coaster								x	x	x	x	x	x	x	x	x	x	x
Looping The Loop									x	x	x	x	x	x	x	x	x	x
Brooklands Race Track (Speedway)											x	x	x	x	x	x	x	x
Mirror Maze											x			x				
Kiddies Speedway											x							
Globe of Death											x	x						
Cycledrome												x	x	x	x	x	x	x
Big Eli Wheel												x	x	x				
Loop-O-Plane												x	x	x				
Water Shute													x	x				
Mont Blanc														x				
Aeroplane Rides														x				
Miniature Zoo														x				
Model Railway															x			
Lakeside Miniature Railway															x	x	x	x
Crazy House															x	x	x	x
Cartoon Cinema (Gayway)															x	x	x	x
Gallopers															x	x	x	
Frogmen																		
The Rotor																	x	
Electric Water Dodgems																x	x	
Hurricane Flying Jets																		x

Appendix Three

THE HOTCHKISS PATENT BICYCLE RAILROAD

The brainchild of American, 'Professor' Arthur Hotchkiss, it was first demonstrated in New Jersey with a line of track 1.8 miles long from Smithville to Mount Holly for the Mount Holly Fair in September 1892. It was envisaged as a practical people moving track, rather than for recreational purposes and was provided to transport workers to and from the Fair quickly and cheaply. The average rider was said to complete the journey in six or seven minutes. One was later installed at Coney Island where it was a huge success.

Now established as a fairground attraction, the first example in the UK was imported and installed at Great Yarmouth in 1895. Later, UK built examples began to find their way into Coney Island style resort developments, such as at Great Yarmouth, Blackpool and Cleethorpes.

Eastern Daily Press: 100 Years of Fun & Thrills. Great Yarmouth
10th September 2009

The Eastern Daily Press, in an article celebrating the centenary of amusements in Great Yarmouth refers to a contemporary report about the Hotchkiss Railway being the first in the UK:

> *As for his imported Hotchkiss bicycle railroad, it opened here in 1895 and comprised a 250ft diameter circle with two rails along which travelled odd-shaped cycles carrying one or two people. There could be racing although the inner circle was obviously shorter than the outer one. A leaflet about the 2d ride explained: "This system is perfectly safe, conducive to good health, has no tendency to demoralisation and places within the power of all the means of indulging in the exhilarating recreation of cycling."*

Miles of Smiles

It closed in 1909 after 14 years and moved to a pleasure ground in Huddersfield where it was still operating in 1936.

The one in Cleethorpes would have been almost identical.

Appendix Four

THE GREAT CENTRAL RAILWAY JOURNAL 1906

Places of interest on the Great Central No 3: CLEETHORPES
By Mr W.T. Bolland

Note: Grammar and Spellings as published.

"It would be very difficult for any man, no matter what manner of man, to visit Cleethorpes and return home without getting some good of his stay – in increased vigour, or capacity for enjoyment, or in the storing up of happy memories to tide him over a dreary winter; for placed as it is at the very mouth of the Humber, Cleethorpes enjoys the bracing breezes of the German Ocean, a particular immunity from rain-fall, and a plethora of sunshine. These and other natural features make it one of the most healthy sea-side resorts in England.

On no two days may a man's mood be alike; but there is everything here to answer every mood; and one may pick and choose day by day (even hour by hour) what one will see and do. Cleethorpes is truly variety.

From a stretch of promenade, and drive, nearly two miles in length, with sands shelving to the edge, the Humber with its sweeping waters, gathered from Yorkshire wold and moor may be seen to meet and lose itself in the unresting northern sea. All the day one may stand and view the dark hulls, and now the glint of a sail in the sun, as ships, about their lawful business, come from and go towards the big sea outside.

The fine sweep of sand, possibly unequalled in England for paddling in safety, is the children's play-ground. Here they may bathe, paddle and dig; building up, with elaborate care, what their fancy directs for the returning tide to quietly cover. In the shade of the long sea wall, mother sits, with watchful eye, and knits, and exchanges gossip with her neighbour, while father drowses over the morning's news.

Miles of Smiles

If one would frolic and be noisily gay, there is to be found away to the left "All the fun of the fair." Here there are merry-go-rounds, cokernut-shies, and "Aunt Sallies," which, like old friends, seem to have been with us always. A switchback is uncoiled for many yards along the sands, a fairy river runs its tortuous course, a bicycle railway circles around and there are things to be done and seen for the nimble penny, that no one may lack an exciting moment. From the top of a wooden tower one may sit upon a little mat and slide gloriously down a spiral way to the sands beneath. What man who has been a boy could resist it?

Intersecting the promenade and drive is the Pier, straddling, like some strange, many-legged animal across the golden sands. A little way down the Pier stands the magnificent new Pavilion in which Concerts and Entertainments are held daily, and Dancing, that enjoyment of our youth, is indulged in nearly all day long. The Pavilion, built only last year to replace the old one which was burned down in June 1903, is a commodious one and will seat over a thousand people. It has a large and well-appointed stage and accessories, and the floor, from the character of its construction, is admirably adapted for dancing, and in the morning, in the afternoon, and in the evening, the cadence of a waltz, or the ring of the lancers, floats away over the sands and sea.

Under the glass-covered verandah, hung with flowering plants, young men and maidens meet; and here one may marvel on the power of the youth with a smile, and the many ways of a man with a maid. To the right of the Pier are the terraced gardens and well kept greens, where is played the old-famed game of bowls and the more modern one of tennis. From the ivy-clad "Ross Castle", a long view of the river is to be had, and the distant gloom of that spit of Yorkshire land ending in Spurn Point. When the mists and shadows of night gather, like a mantle, over the waters the Light-house at Spurn points out its guiding beam for miles around.

Here one cannot help but comment on the very handsome and well-appointed bathing establishment on the Promenade containing sea-water baths and a large salt water swimming bath which are well patronized by many visitors.

Far away to the right past the new "Kingsway" and its sea gardens and its embattled front are the links and camping ground. Here one may play golf and lead the "simple life" in "smalls" and a tent, and keep ones bottled beer delightfully cool by burying it in the sand.

The country about Cleethorpes is remarkably flat; cycle rides, drives, and long walks may be enjoyed without inconvenience or labour. Through the beautiful avenue to the old church at Humberstone; to the Lock at Tetney with its inn and quaint group of cottages; the Park at Brocklesby with its prize cattle and its deer, and to Pelham Pillar so famous locally for its picnicking and junketing – these are but a few places of many.

Enjoy hours of holiday freedom by the sea and obtain a breath of its life giving ozone, at a charge which to our fathers would seem impossible. London to Cleethorpes and back again is upwards of four hundred and two score miles but four shillings and three-pence is the charge for the journey.

The Great Central Railway Company have over one hundred thousand pounds invested in Cleethorpes, will carry you from the other side of England, set around you every reasonable thing you can expect to minister to your comfort and pleasure and take you home again happier and healthier at a less cost than many pay for a bottle of wine for their dinner".

Appendix Five

THE CAGNEY RAILWAY AT WONDERLAND

The first passenger carrying miniature railway in Cleethorpes was the short lived Cagney railway which operated in Wonderland for a couple of seasons in 1931/2. Information on it is very sketchy but to make sense of what is known and its significance as a miniature railway, we need to look back some thirty years earlier to the Military Exhibition at Earls Court, London, in 1901. The miniature railway at Earls Court (and that at the Glasgow International Exhibition of 1901), are generally considered to be the first steam hauled passenger carrying pleasure railways operating in the UK. Norman Drake's book Railways for Recreation, published by the Narrow Gauge Railway Society in 2019 includes a photograph on page 12 showing the Cagney miniature railway at Earls Court before the exhibition opened. It was a simple out and back straight line and the locomotive a Cagney Model C, identical to the one that appears in the Grimsby Telegraph picture A Holiday Ride on the Miniature Railway at Cleethorpes on Monday 28th March 1932.

The Cagney Miniature Railway in Wonderland was very much a temporary affair. Doug Best (now in his 99th year!) remembers riding the Cagney Railway as a child and when shown the Grimsby Telegraph image, immediately recognised the driver as the person he remembered all those years ago! Doug recalls 'It was a US Cagney style steam 4-4-0 tender locomotive with several sit-in carriages. The gauge was probably about two feet and the ride cost 2d'. It started indoors by the Joiners Shop. The loco faced outwards towards the town and hauled its train of carriages a short distance out of the great hall and into the open, before propelling them back again. He recalled riding it several times in about 1932.

Having established this, we can conclude with some certainly that the locomotive was a Cagney Model C of twelve and five eighth (12-5/8) inch gauge, and that the carriages were four wheelers. The Cagney Railway at Wonderland ran from the back corner of the Wonderland Great Hall near the Mikado Cafe, adjacent to the joiners shop in a straight line out into the Pleaureland open air amusement area (behind what is now the Indoor Market) and terminated adjacent to the LNER steam locomotive turntable (now the Network Rail servicing facility), a distance of only about 60 yards. The locomotive was at the town end of the line and hauled the train away out of the great hall into the open, then propelled it back. Miniature railway authority Simon Townsend's writings include Ron Taylor's recollections of the Cagney engine at Cleethorpes. His father was an LNER engine driver and his family spent their holidays at Cleethorpes. His father got friendly with the driver of the Cagney loco who allowed him to drive it.

The Cagney Railway was operated by Fairdom Ltd. The miniature railway was advertised in a display advertisement in the Hull Daily Mail on Thursday 18th June 1931. It read: SCOOTER SUPREME on the Promenade. For the Kiddies THE MINIATURE RAILWAY IN WONDERLAND, the Smallest Engine in the Country, Fairdom Ltd.

Bringing together all the various snippets of information, we can conclude that the Cagney railway at Wonderland worked for at least two seasons in 1931/32, that it was a Cagney Model C Locomotive of 12-5/8 inch gauge and that the ride cost 2d. Less certain is whether it was the actual locomotive used at Earls Court in 1901, but 12-5/8 inch gauge was not common the UK, so it is tempting to think the first miniature railway to operate in Cleethorpes, may well also have been the first to operate in England?

Appendix 5a: The Cagney Railway System

236. Cagney Railroad advert c1905.

The Cagney Railway at Wonderland

The Cagney Brothers – A great name in steam railroading! In 1898, the Miniature Railroad Co (Cagney Brothers) of 74 Broadway New York City began marketing a variety of small live steam locomotives for amusement park use. The actual manufacturing was done, under contract, by the McGarigle Machine Company in Niagara Falls, a company closely connected to the Cagney Bros by family marriage and later absorbed by them. They were sturdy locomotives in miniature designed to do real work and were all loosely based on the famous New York Central and Hudson River Railroad 4-4-0 No. 999, the first steam locomotive in the world to travel at more than 100 mph. They produced several models. The Model C was the smallest at 12-5/8 inch (321mm) gauge, then the much more popular 15 inch (381mm) gauge Model D, and the even larger 22 inch (559mm) gauge Model E. Over the years, Cagney locomotives were supplied to four World Expositions including the 1939 New York World Fair. Many of these sturdy little locomotives worked seven days a week for long periods in amusement parks and pleasure grounds. Cagney locomotives and rolling stock were exported to Latin America, Russia, South Africa, Japan, Thailand, Australia and New Zealand; even a gold plated example to the King of Siam! Cagney railways in the UK operated at the Crystal Palace and Alexandra Palace miniature railways. One was even supplied in 1902 to the Blakesley Miniature Railway in Northamptonshire, close to Basset-Lowke's company Miniature Railways of Great Britain Ltd that went on to manufacture their own series of 15 inch gauge locomotives. No doubt the prominent UK miniature railway engineer, Henry Greenley would have examined it in great detail! Much later, a Cagney railway operated briefly at Wonderland, Cleethorpes. Cagney Brothers ceased trading in 1948, but many of their locomotives are still in use in pleasure parks around the world and have a loyal following, so much so, that brand new Cagney Class D locomotives to the original design are available from an engineering company in the USA.

Generally considered to be the first steam operated passenger carrying miniature railways in the UK were the Cagney railway's at the Glasgow International Exhibition and the Military Exhibition in Earls Court, London, both of which opened in May 1901. The Glasgow exhibition railway was of 15 inch gauge and quite ambitious with a circular track giving a long ride. It used a Cagney Model D locomotive. The Military Exhibition miniature railway in Earls Court was a more modest affair employing the smaller 12-5/8 inch gauge Cagney Model C locomotive and carriages. The Military Exhibition was on a grand scale, akin to the later World Fairs. Also operating on the site was a Chinese Dragon running on rails, subject of Norman Drake's book Railways for Recreation published by the Narrow Gauge Railway Society in 2019. A photograph on page 12 shows the Cagney miniature railway before the exhibition opened. It was a simple out and back straight line. Modest as it may have been, the Military Exhibition's guide book provides a very detailed description of the railway:

Miles of Smiles

The smallest steam railway in the world is not, as many might imagine, a toy. It is really a revelation in modern engineering and demonstrates the perfection attained in locomotive building. These marvellous railways consist of an engine and ten passenger cars. The engine is but 5 feet 4 inches in length, 18 inches wide and measures 28 inches from rails to the top of the chimney, The driving wheels are only 10 inches in diameter and the gauge is a little over 12 inches. Yet whist a child can operate it, the train is capable of 10 miles an hour carrying 20 passengers.

The diminutive cars each hold two passengers and an idea of the size of the engine can be gained when it is stated that the engineer has to take his place on the tender in order to operate it.

It is a distinct novelty to be able to take a comfortable seat in the smallest train in the world and whirl along the diminutive track. It enables one to realise the uncommon experiences of GULLIVER ON HIS FAMOUR TRAVEL. There is the Lilliputian station where the train pulls up panting fuming, for all the world like its familiar prototype.

Hitherto the miniature railway has been only for the fortunate few able to afford an expensive luxury. Now, at last it is for everyone to enjoy the peculiar experience. Grown up people, as well as the rising generation, patronise the railway in vast number and evidently extract a GREAT AMOUNT OF INNOCENT PLEASURE from the ride.

The train is in every respect an exact reproduction of a full-size engine and carriages. The same is taken in the selection of the materials and every detail of the ordinary passenger train is faithfully reproduced, even to headlights, whistle and sand box.

The miniature train bids fair to become a permanent attraction and a welcome addition to the outdoor recreations for the people.

Alas, this was not to be as the Military Exhibition closed on October 19th 1901 and was rapidly dismantled, such that most of it (including the Cagney Railway) was disposed of in a grand Sale conducted by London auctioneers, Chadwick & Sons, by order of the London Exhibitions Company on October 29th. Its subsequent history is unknown, but an identical (maybe rationalised) Cagney Railway operated at Wonderland, Cleethorpes for at least two seasons in 1931/32.

Comparing the already referred to photograph of the Cagney Railway at the Military Exhibition in 1901 with that in the Grimsby Evening Telegraph of Monday 28th March 1932 captioned A Holiday Ride on the Miniature Railway at Cleethorpes, (reproduced in Peter Scott's A History of the Cleethorpes Miniature Railway page 158), it will be seen that this too was a Cagney Model C with identical pattern carriages.

Appendix Six

CLEETHORPES SEAFRONT BUS SERVICES

An account by Norman Drewry reproduced from Brian Leonard's book Cleethorpes & District Remembered published in 2003:

"In 1925 the Provincial Tramway Company started a seafront bus service along the promenade at Cleethorpes. It started at the northern end of the promenade (Wonderland) and ran along it until it reached the Brighton Street slipway, then joined the Kingsway and terminated at the Bathing Pool. It operated at Easter, Whit Bank Holiday and then week-ends until the summer season began, when it ran daily.

The buses on it were called runabouts and were numbered in a separate series. The fleet numbers were prefixed with the letter 'R'. Two types of buses were used, the first being three Guy toast-racks which had no sides and seated four abreast, very small wheels, some having solid tyres. The second type was six wheeled Chevrolet's, which were normal twenty– seater buses, but with a canvas roof which in fine weather was folded back.

In 1936, Cleethorpes Corporation bought the tramways and buses from Provincial and renumbered the runabout buses into their own series of fleet numbers and repainted them from their original green livery into dark blue and cream.

At the outbreak of the war the service ceased and the buses were scrapped or used as civil defence vehicles. One Chevrolet survived the war to become a lorry for the Parks Department. Cleethorpes Corporation also inherited from Provincial a Guy twenty-seater bus with a canvas top and sometimes used it on the seafront service. During the war it was used by a private bus operator to transport workmen to and from air fields being built or extended".

BUMPY RIDE was the headline of a reader's letter in the Sheffield Evening Telegraph on Friday 18th August 1939: "The trip from the Bathing Pool to Wonderland, Cleethorpes, in the open bus had been shaky and bumpy, and I said so. What are you grumbling at replied the driver / conductor? It's as good as the Figure 8 and I've only charged you tuppence!" Interesting that the Figure 8 had been dismantled for some 13 years, so that must have left a lasting impression as well!

Appendix Seven

HIGHWAY HEAVYWEIGHTS VISIT CLEETHORPES

Al Capone's Bullet Proof Car

A brief visiting attraction in Wonderland during the thirties was AL CAPONE'S BULLET PROOF CAR, displayed in the Blacksmiths shop during its UK tour. Al 'Scarface' Capone's Armoured Killer Car was a 1928 Cadillac V-8 Town Sedan which was cleverly painted green to mimic the Chicago police cars of the day, complete with flashing lights, siren and even a police band radio. It carried 3000Ilbs of steel armour, had a one and a quarter inch thick windscreen, one inch thick bullet proof windows with holes through which machine guns could be fired and the rear window dropped for his henchmen to fire at chasing cars. Each door weighed 10 stone (140ibs). It weighed 3.5 tons and could travel at speeds up to 110mph! Its attendants demonstrated the special features of the car to visitors who paid a small charge to inspect it.

Hermann Goering's Armoured Car

At Lubeck in Northern Germany towards the end of the war, Major Maurice Tavinor, a Warwickshire Police Inspector seconded to the War Office, captured Goering's bullet-proof Mercedes-Benz car, which was discovered on the top floor of a brewery, guarded by German soldiers. It may be that the significance of the car had yet to be realised for it was afterwards moved to a large enemy vehicle compound containing some 30,000 vehicles. When its significance had been realised, it was recovered by the REME, restored to working order and shipped to the UK as a trophy. Commissioned by the War Office, it set off on an extensive tour of UK venues and garages to raise funds for the Soldiers, Sailors & Airmen Families Association (SSAFA).

Miles of Smiles

Note: This was Hermann Goering's Armoured Car and not the 'Blue Goose' which was his ceremonial car, recovered in South East Germany and used similarly by Allied forces.

The tour started in 1946 visiting Nottingham and Derby; later that year in Harrogate, Blackpool, Bath, Eastbourne and Plymouth. It is known to have been displayed at the Western Garage in Newton Abbot, spending a week there. Admission price to inspect it was 6d. Other venues included Boniface & Cousin's garage showroom in Fareham, Castle Garage in Cardiff, St John's in Great Yarmouth, Kennings in Sheffield, Caffyn's in Tonbridge and many more.

It visited Coventry, well known car manufacturing city, in the spring of 1947. The motoring correspondent of the Coventry Evening Telegraph on Saturday 29th March 1947 was enthusiastic in his reporting:

"GOERING'S CAR HELPS CHARITY & SERVES AS A GRIM REMINDER. Yesterday I had an experience which Hermann Goering would have given a breastful of medals to have enjoyed, writes an "Evening Telegraph" reporter. I rode in triumph through the heart of Coventry ensconced in the ex-Reich marshal's gargantuan bullet-proof car. I had persuaded Captain J. F. Thirlby, driver of the car on its tour in aid of Services charities, to take me for a run round the city. Seated in the front of the monster 7.7 litre Mercedes, grey like a battleship and wider than a 'bus, it seemed at first as if it could scarcely be accommodated in the narrow curves of Coventry's thoroughfares. The manner in which it could be manoeuvred through the traffic was, however, amazing. A wide lock, rapid acceleration, and a top gear speed range from walking pace to a proven 95mph, quickly gave a sense of complete control. Comfort was assured by independent front suspension, super-sprung seats, and an almost silent engine. Here indeed was power. The engine registers 155bhp without the supercharger, and 230bhp with; twice the maximum of the biggest lorries and 'buses.

THE SENSE OF POWER. People eyed us curiously as we made for Broadgate. The car was built to impress, but few probably realised that had events taken a certain turn it would have awed hostility, rather than puzzled curiosity that would have prompted their attention. The Nazi's certainly knew a thing or two about psychology. Maybe a subconscious knowledge of the drama surrounding the vehicle helped, but I could not fail to feel a peculiar sense of power as we made our way through the traffic to the London Road. Behind me was a retractable 'bullet-proof curtain; beneath my feet was a steel floor, proof against mine and grenade; at each side were the fixtures for the machine guns, without which no Nazi leader ever felt properly equipped. The very seat on which I sat could be cunningly tipped to form the platform on which the Falstaffian Marshal used to stand to acknowledge the siegheils of the mob. Just above my head, fixed to the top of the windscreen, was the handle in which he gripped in the process, lest pride should take a fall. The car's five-ply glass windows were spattered, but not shattered, with bullet-holes. This, Captain Thirlby said, had been done by exuberant 'Tommies' when the car was discovered in a German vehicle park.

COLD FEET PRECAUTIONS. Other damage, a missing door handle, odd bits broken off, had all been done by souvenir hunters while it had been on tour. As we sped up the by-pass, Captain Thirlby told me he had driven the car 3,000 miles and had visited 25 different centres in the past year. This week he is putting it on display at the Parkside Garage. A small charge will be made to inspect it, and proceeds will go to the SSAFA. It was on this derestricted run back that the full power at our command became evident. With an impressive scream from the supercharger speed mounted rapidly. Captain Thirlby effortlessly manoeuvred the monster round a traffic island. "Can't be too careful," he commented, "we've had an offer of £10,000 for her, and that's a lot of money to get smashed up." As we pulled into the garage he showed me one last gadget. A flick of a switch and a stream of hot air was wafted to the floor at the rear in case the Marshal ever got cold feet! A thoughtful race, the Germans, in some things anyway".

The tour continued throughout 1947 and following years calling at garages and exhibition venues in all four corners of the UK. It concluded with a tour of Ulster, the Scottish Borders and Scotland in 1951, having travelled some 20,000 miles in all. After its UK tour, the War Office sold the car at auction in 1952, when it realised £1,050.00 from a private buyer.

After the war, Major Tavinor returned to Police service and in 1946, as Inspector Tavinor, he was included in the King's Birthday Honours List by being awarded the Commander-in-Chief's certificate for outstanding service and devotion to duty during the occupation of Germany. He retired in 1950 as Inspector in charge of the Wilnecote sub-division of the Sutton Coldfield Division of the Warwickshire Constabulary.

Appendix Eight

WONDERLAND SUNDAY MARKET FINALE

Grimsby Telegraph 26th March 2013

After receiving just a week's notice that Sunday would be their last day of trading, sellers are "furious" that they will not be able to benefit from the Easter boost in trade.

Town & Country Markets, which has owned the site for about ten years, issued all traders with a letter stating: "We are now in a position where we have accepted an offer from a purchaser for the freehold of the site.

"This offer is for the land and the building which houses the market, but does not include the market as a going concern."

The site had failed to sell at auction, but the mystery buyer later made an offer of £302,500, which Town & Country accepted.

Michael Miller, from Cleethorpes, is the son-in-law of former Wonderland owner Dudley Bowers and has three stalls on the market.

He said: "My father-in-law would be very upset by what is happening.

"People won't come down this end of the promenade once the market has gone and it will spell the death knell for other businesses down here.

"It would be OK if the new company had another tenant, but they don't, it is just going to stand empty."

Diane Brown fears she could lose her home when the market closes.

"I've been selling here for 19 years and I am absolutely gutted we're being forced out with so little notice," she said.

"I'm worried I could lose my home without this money coming in.

"The worse part is that we haven't even got Easter Bank Holiday to sell because they're forcing us out straight away."

John Malik, who has had a stall there for 30 years, added: "We've stuck around through the bad weather and the poor winter months and we were hoping to recuperate some our losses over Easter, but now we've got no chance to do that."

Marie Padstow, who has had the Bits And Bobs stall for five years, added: "We've stuck by the market through an awful winter with no customers and now they're kicking us out before Easter, which is one of our busiest weekends.

"We're hoping that the council will find us somewhere else to operate from next weekend, but there isn't much time left."

Sweet shop stallholder Lee Sammut added: "It seems totally ridiculous that they're forcing us out when they haven't got any other use for the place yet."

Shopper Roger Roe has been visiting Wonderland since he was a little boy and takes his wife and daughters on Sundays.

He said: "It's sad because it's the end of an era. Places like this are dying out and it is going to be another tradition that's lost."

Wendy Fisher, head of assets at NELC, said: "We're currently looking at an alternative site where they might be able to set up on Easter Sunday and Monday."

Appendix Nine

MEMORIES OF WONDERLAND

Doug Best 2007

I remember some of the workers and staff who worked at Wonderland. At the top of the tree was Ma Wilkie. She had two daughters, Hilda and Bessie, who worked with her. Hilda's husband was Sid Smith who was Managing Director, and a very good boss. The electrician in the early days (post-war) was Frank May and after him came Noel Gray and his son John. Noel and John were followed by Cliff Colebrook and his son. The latter served his time as an apprentice electrician at Wonderland. I remember Barney Samuels, the manager of the Big Dipper, who had John Stone, foreman joiner, working for him. John, in turn, was assisted by Chris Beer. Arthur Taylor, who became Park Manager in later years, worked with Snowy Trash on the Speedway. They could pick up a car with two people in it with one hand and throw it several feet to get the cars moving again after they had piled up. Another young man who worked on the Speedway was Roy Drinkall. He used to throw the cars about as if they were made of balsa wood.

Jim Griffiths was Foreman of the Park. He could tell you stories about when he was a Fairground Traveller using a steam traction engine to move from place to place. He knew all the roadside watering places in the country where water could be topped up and overnight accommodation could be found. He told of one place, a doss house, which just had a rope across the room to rest your head on while you slept. In the morning the landlord would wake up people by releasing the rope! Jim had a gang of men to put rides up and take them down at the beginning and end of the summer season. He knew every nut and bolt on all the rides. During the season, he would look after the Cycledrome in the middle of Wonderland. I remember one worker who could jump on the ride when it was running at full speed with a mug of tea in each hand, one for Jim and one for himself and not spill a drop! Jim was always the cashier and driver of the ride, which was a good money spinner. The ride later became the Waltzer.

Miles of Smiles

Eddie Robotham managed the Gallopers. He would do anything for you. There was always plenty to fix on the galloping horses as, at the time, they were at least 80 years old. I frequently had to make new bearings for the universal couplings that enabled the horses to go up and down and the joiners often had to repair broken horse's legs. Sometimes we would have to dash to Savages of Kings Lynn, where the ride was originally built to get a new crown wheel or pinion for the main drive and one or other stay late at night so the ride would be ready for opening next morning. The Gavioli organ was the best sounding organ in the country. Organ Connoisseurs from miles away would come and listen to its special sound, enhanced by the addition of extra pipes from an old, but more modern organ that stood unused for years in the Wonderland paint shop. I think that, somewhere, the Gallopers are still going. The organ went to Screeton Bros at Barton on Humber. (Footnote: The wonderland Gavioli is now restored and operational in the USA).

Ralph Smith, who married Hilda's daughter Betty, was foreman painter. Cyril Creswell, a really good painter and artist worked with him. Cyril painted a lot of the pictures around Wonderland. Particularly good were those on the gallopers and ghost train. The Ghost Train manager was Harold Scherzlinger. His wife, Hilda, managed the cafe at the west end of the promenade. All the workers had tea breaks there.

Then there were the stall holders. Mrs Lockley ran the Laughing Clowns. She often came into the workshop to ask me to adjust the Clowns to reduce the number of top prizes being won! Ken Hood in Pets' Corner was a lot of fun and always had plenty of jokes to tell. Mr Scruton and his wife, both still working in their eighties, ran the Spider & Fly. Bill Shotton's stall was the Hammers where you could win a comb for six pence. George Blythe and his son Colin had several stalls and Peter Jones had a stall where you rolled a ball into numbered holes. Peter's prizes were not too bad. Norman Murgatroyd had the Westminster Shooter Gallery. Jack Peals worked for him. He was a good mannered man who used to ask, would you like a few more shots, sir? Then there was Reuben Felcey who said you could win a rugby ball or football on his stall. I don't think that anybody did. The best they got was a comb or a small stick of rock. There was a Coconut Shy and the Derby Racer owned by the Dearden family. You had to pull a knob to make the horses go round the track. I think that there were seven horses and the one that stopped nearest to the winning post was the winner. You got a good prize if you won. The best was a thick stick of rock about 18" long.

During several summer seasons, I managed the Photographic Department which included Wondersnaps and Jollysnaps. The cameramen of Wondersnaps took photographs of people on the rides. The cameras they used had flash units which required two six volt batteries. These were held in boxes as big as jerry cans. The boxes were carried all day, slung with straps on their right shoulders, by the cameramen. During this time, they would take as many as 900 to 1000 photographs and give out a card to each one of the holidaymakers snapped. Photographs were always ready for collection two hours after the pictures were taken. Jollysnaps gave holidaymakers the opportunity to have their photographs taken with their heads over or through a comic board, or in prison, or even on TV. During the winter, I worked in the fitting shop for Jack Newbutt who was Maintenance Manager. When Jack left to work down south, I became Maintenance Manager and my friend and right hand man in the Photographic Department, Colin Govis, took over the management of the department. Frank Carver also worked in the darkroom every summer when I was there. He became a BSc and PhD in Chemistry at Leeds University.

Appendix Ten

THE WONDERLAND MINIATURE RAILWAY

Michael Newbutt 2008

During 1949 my family and I moved from Kenton in Middlesex to Cleethorpes in Lincolnshire. I was 8 years old and my father had been, until this move, a fitter on the railway at Neasden loco sheds as well as part time engineering manager at Kenton Grange miniature railway. This railway was broken up in 1949 and much of the hardware sold to East Coast Amusements at Cleethorpes, including five of the locos. We went with it. My father purchased a house in Brereton Avenue and we arrived there in the late autumn of '49……

The sea front at the north end of the promenade at Cleethorpes was given over to amusements. 'Wonderland' was a large covered area of all the rides and amusements of the day. Just outside this and extending to the very tip of the promenade were a group of additional attractions including a Big Dipper, Boating Lake, Gallopers and Miniature Railway. The railway had recently been set up by a Mr. Woolley and ran around the boating lake, probably a distance of a quarter of a mile. The set up was not very substantial and the track and solitary locomotive not capable of coping with the heavy usage just beginning to happen at that time, caused by the large amount of holidaymakers using Cleethorpes for a seaside holiday.

This post war period saw an enormous rise in train excursions into Cleethorpes. 'The day tripper' and 'factory shut down week' holiday makers were out in force from the industrial towns of Yorkshire after the constraints of the post war period. Cleethorpes station is on the promenade so was ideally placed to deliver passengers into the amusements.

My father was now employed to not only take over the improvement and running of the miniature railway, but also to be engineer to much of the Wonderland amusements.

Miles of Smiles

Arriving as we did during a shut down period was obviously a help in getting to grips with the task. Assessment was made of the railway and it was decided to use 3 of the 5 Kenton locos and to sell the other two. The loco that had been used to run the railway was a fine scale Basset-Lowke 'Royal Scot' and was not substantial enough to cope with everyday running, but was kept for display.

The 3 locos chosen to run the railway were: A1 pacific, American pacific and the Hudson. The 4-8-4 was considered to have a too long wheelbase for the 40ft radius curves, so after being on display for the first year it was sold. The Kenton Scot was not in good condition and had a narrow firebox which would possibly have made the 10 hour daily operation with the variable coal available very difficult, it too was sold.

Now dad had to get to grips with a new skill: keeping the rides and other amusements running. Everything from Gallopers to rifle range; from tea kiosk to dodgems. Although I was only nine I wanted to spend as much time as I was allowed on the sea front with my father. After school summer evenings and weekends were all spent 'helping' with the railway. It was at this time that I met someone who has become a lifelong friend, Ray Crome. Ray was the same age as me and had the same interests in railways, steam and generally messing with things mechanical.

The railway was largely rebuilt, dad had help from Doug Best who, during the season, ran the photography department. The first season was difficult and really highlighted the difference between running a railway once a week or so for pleasure compared to running 7 days a week for profit! Wear and tear on rolling stock meant that wheels, bearings and all parts that moved were in need of attention even before the end of the season. Fine sand blown up from the beach also added to the wear of all moving parts, not to mention everyday maintenance needed to the stock, locos and track.

The mainstay of motive power was the Hudson, since it was easiest to keep going for the driver. It was also the most powerful and could handle the biggest trains. The two Pacifics were kept available and used more during the quieter week days. On particularly busy weekends Hudson and A1 were used to run two trains, using a passing loop to increase the number of trips.

The lessons of the first season were taken on board and new heavier duty coaches of the 'garden seat' pattern were built with ball race wheel bearings. The Hudson was rebuilt with new motion parts so that all the motion had ball or needle roller bearings, including axle boxes. Main frames stiffened with more staying and an extra feed pump fitted. The water supply for the locos had been taken from the mains, but this was very hard water and meant frequent washing out of the boilers so a rain water supply was arranged from a walled off area of the boating lake.

Luckily some great staff were employed during the season. I don't know how dad got them but they certainly kept the operations side of things going while dad kept

The Wonderland Miniature Railway

up with running repairs on the amusements as well as the railway. I can only recall the full name of Arthur Johnson (driver) and Bill Hart (driver), the others included Mrs. Brown (ticket kiosk), Jim (ticket collector and general help; ex-trawler man), a character known only to me as 'fat pump' (his name for a grease gun) general help & crossing keeper and Roy (driver and mechanic).

After the second season the railway ran very reliably. Dad and Doug Best working hard out of season to repair and improve all aspects of the railway and do the maintenance on the other Wonderland amusements. My friend Ray and I were now 11 or 12 and we were able to help out (as well as enjoy ourselves) both during the season as well as during the closed period. Doug Best although not a trained engineer or fitter became a valuable colleague and friend to dad, he had a natural flair for things mechanical as well as being a willing learner. I have a suspicion that they had a lot of fun as well.

It was around this time ('52) that for some reason that can only be described as 'showmanship' the A1 pacific had an A4 type streamlined casing added....to make matters worse it was Chrome plated! Dad and Doug made and fitted it and although it must have taken a lot of work to achieve. I only hope they are both a little embarrassed when they look back on it!

Wonderland was well equipped to manage itself with a fully equipped carpenters shop, electricians, paint shop and of course dad and Doug's engineers workshop sited within the miniature railway. This workshop was soon to be pushed to its limits. The Hudson was doing the lion's share of the work on the railway and the improvements and beefing up of its components really showed how inadequate the two other former Kenton locos' were for this sort of duty. Of the two pacific's the American outline one was of the lightest build and was little used, so in '53 it was sold to a Major Hext who was building a private railway on his estate in Cumbria. Doug Best and dad overhauled and converted this loco to look similar to a BR Clan class for Major Hext and delivered it themselves to the Coniston railway. Also in 1953 it was decided that the Hudson needed a brother, so the two Amigos in the workshop added to the work load of winter refurbishment of amusements to embark on the production of a new steam loco. This was to be a workhorse designed to be easily maintained and driver friendly as well as easy on the track. 'Grimsby Town' in honor of the local football team that had done something special that year was the name bestowed on the new 4-4-4 creation in 1955. Looking not very pretty, and not based on any prototype, the new engine was a great success. Indeed this loco continued running the railway alone under Doug Best's management when dad had moved on in 1959. During the building of 'Grimsby Town' in 1954, Major Hext purchased the A1 and so additional work was put on the duo to prepare and deliver this loco......without A4 casing.

Miles of Smiles

'Grimsby Town' and the Hudson (now named 'Henrietta' after my mother) were easily capable of running the railway and as Ray and I were entering our teens we were deemed old enough to take our turns on driving duty. Oh how we lapped it up. We each had our own favorite engine; Ray spent his summers on the Hudson and me on Grimsby Town. During the busiest times when running two trains using the loop, we would each try to arrive back at the station after our second circuit before the other had acquired a full train and set off. For several years our summers were spent driving and doing whatever maintenance we were capable of alongside the regular summer crew while dad ran around attending amusement emergencies. I especially remember a Mr. Murgatroyd who owned a couple of stalls in Wonderland who would come running to the workshop calling "Jack, Jack, Jack" when one of his rifle ranges was in trouble. Another person I remember during those summer months was Hilda in the end of prom café…she seemed to need quite a lot of maintenance to her water softening and tea making machines…(?!). So dad was kept very busy during the season, especially since Doug was not available because of him running the busy photographic side of the Wonderland operation. Ray and I meanwhile also had the task of helping to consume the left over ice cream from a nearby kiosk at the end of the day from what was then a new innovation….soft whipped ice cream. Apparently it could not be kept overnight.

In 1959 dad left the railway for a job in Amersham, Bucks. I suspect he could see the writing on the wall for a resort like Cleethorpes and at the age of 44 wanted a more secure future. Doug Best ran the railway from here on until he left in 1966. I think Henrietta had been dismantled because of boiler problems shortly after dad left and never ran again, until her rebuilding in 1976 by dad and me………… But that's another story.

Appendix Eleven

A GHOSTLY EXPERIENCE

Rob Foxon 2019

It was a normal day on the miniature railway at Wonderland some-time in the late fifties, when a call came of a problem on the Ghost Train. I was about ten or eleven years old at the time and eager to be involved in anything going on, so asked if I could accompany engineer Jack Newbutt and help (watch) with whatever the problem was. Of course, as apprentices do, I carried the tools! At the Ghost Train we met the operator, probably Harold Scherzinger, who explained the problem. It was one of those very rare occasions when one could enter the 'Lost World 'haunted cavern with the lights on. I remember it was actually quite small, the single rail winding around in many tight curves and skeletons hanging from crude scenery. It seemed much bigger when riding the car! Whatever the problem was, it was soon resolved and I was asked to help in testing afterwards, which of course I readily agreed to. I was asked to remain in the cavern and when called to put my foot on a treadle to check it was working correctly. The others left and I awaited the call, when the lights went out and it became the haunted cavern again. Standing in the dark frozen to the spot, it seemed an age before the shout; press the treadle now! I promptly obeyed and it set off one of the eerie ghost sirens and flashing lights! Now completely frozen to the spot, the lights came back on again and I was escorted back out into the main hall with a face as white as the shirt I was wearing, much to the amusement of all concerned! I never did ascertain what the original problem was, but am sure it had absolutely nothing to do with the treadle I was asked to 'test'. Clearly, it was one of those growing up experiences that all junior staff are subjected to at some time in their careers!

BIBLIOGRAPHY & FURTHER READING

Books

Reference has been made to the following:

Cleethorpes: The Creation of a Seaside Resort: Dr Alan Dowling. 2005. Phillimore & Co Ltd. ISBN 1 86077 343 5

A Chronology Of The Construction Of Britain's Railways 1778-1855: Leslie James, Ian Allan 1983 ISBN 0 7110 1277 6

Miniature Line at Cleethorpes: J. Newbutt & W. Hart. Model Engineer, 10th December 1959. p521.

English Fairs: Ian Starsmore. Thames and Hudson, 1975. ISBN 0 500 27070 8

Cleethorpes And District Remembered: Brian Leonard. Tempus Publishing, 2003. ISBN 0 7524 3003 3

Good bye To An Old Friend: Phillip Upchurch, 2007. The Key Frame, Quarterly Journal of The Fair Organ Preservation Society KF3-07 p10.

Trains to the Lincolnshire Seaside Vol3: Cleethorpes: A.J. Ludlam. Lincs Wolds Railway Society 2014 ISBN 978 0 9926762 4 7

The Railways of North East Lincolnshire; Part2, Stations: Paul King. Pyewipe Publications 2019 ISBN 978-1-9164603-1-7

Gresley's Coaches: Michael Harris. David & Charles, 1973. ISBN 0 7153 5935 5

Sale of Commercial Sea Front Property. Henry Spencer & Sons: By order of British Railways Board Auction Catalogue 17th September 1965.

History of the Kenton Miniature Railway: Eric L. Basire, 2015. ISBN 9 781514 189986

Railways for Recreation: Norman Drake, 2018. Narrow Gauge Railway Society. p12.

Cagney Bros 1901 Catalogue: Facsimile, 1998. Plateway Press, Fidalgo Reprints. Introduction by Simon Townsend. ISBN 1 871980 37 2

A History of the Cleethorpes Miniature Railway: Peter Scott, 2015. Minor Railway Histories No7, Chapter 10. ISBN 978 1 902368 41 2

Further Reading and Research:

Happiland: William Bedford, Heinemann, 1990. ISBN 0 434 05559 X. A work of fiction by a local author that includes a good impression of the life of the North Promenade in the fifties.

Other useful sources:

National Fairground & Circus Archive / University of Sheffield.
   https://www.sheffield.ac.uk/nfca

INDEX

Page numbers with illustrations are shown in **bold**.

Arcadia 107, 111, **113**, 114-115, **116**
Armoured Car 95, 133, 263-264
Atkins, Tommy 66
Auckland Colonnade 5, 6-8, 10-11, 14, **15**, 25-26, **27-28**, 31, **35-39**, 44, 62, **64**, 65-66, 73, 75, 77, **84**, 111, **112**, 119, 211, 219-220, 237-238

Barretti, Ben 163, 193
Beeching 203-204
Best, Doug 50, 55, 63, 73, 79, 88, 90-92, 93, 129, 133, 136, 145-146, 150, 152, 163, 169, **170**, 172, 175, 184-5, **187**, 188, 190, 193-195, **198**, 257, 269, 274-276
Bicycle Railway, Hotchkiss 8-9, **12-13**, 14, **15**, 22, **25-26**, 30, **35**, 45, 70, 240, 251, 254
Bioscope, American 14, 23, **39**, 179
Blakeman 113, 121, **215**, 216, 232
Boxing 93-94, 110
British Empire Exhibition 51-52, **53**, 55-56
Brooklands 51, 96-97, 99, **100**, 101, 103, 126, **128**, 139, 142, **158**, 159, **160**, 167-168, 172, 197, 248

Brown, H.B. Brown & Son 8, **38**, 70, 75, 77, 88, 113, 121-122, 213-214, 216, **217**, 230, 235
Bullet Proof Car 95, **96**, 133, **134**, 263, 264-265
Bus Service, Seafront 59, 71

Cagney Railway 90, **91**, 257, **258**, 259-260, 279
Cans 147, **178**
Captive Aeroplane 14, **22**, 23
Carriages 12-13, **18**, **25**, 57-58, 91, 113, **114**, 120, 131, **132**, 135, **136**, 138, 150, 168-169, **202-203**, 204, **205-206**, 257, 259-260
Casino, amusements 123, 215, 230
Chiappa, Victor 163, 193
Cleethorpes Advancement Association 56, 86, 102, 190
Cleethorpes station 1, **2**, **5**, 25, **28**, 202, 206, 273
Coney Island 47, 51, 154, 251
Coniston 275
Crazy House 131, 143, 147, **178**, 199, 248

Cripsey, Wall of Death 72-73, 79, 89, 110, 119, 177, 240
Crome, Ray 151, **170**, 195-197, 274
Custer Cars 48, 5-52, 55, 163, 193-194, 247
Cycledrome 97-99, 101, 129, 131, 135, 138, 143-144, **145**, **165**, 166-167, 185, **186**, 187, **189**, 226, 247-248, 269

Dearden's, juvenile Rides 52, 75, 90, 97, **98**, 99, 103-104, 131, 147, 175, **176**, 177, 199, 270
Dip the Dips **25**, 26, **27**, 44-45, **46**, 47, 61-62, 150, 240, 247
Dodgems, Electric, Water 48, 53, 55, 73, 90, 93-94, 97, 103, 124, 126, 128, **129-130**, **132**, 135-136, 139, 141-143, **145**, 153, 154, **155**, **158**, 159, 166, 167-169, 177, 183, 185, 188, 191, 199, 225-226, **227**, 247-248, 274
Doncaster 74, 81, 203

East Coast Amusement Company 25, **26**, 44, **45**, 46, **47**, 48, 51-53, 55, 62-63, 79, 94, 102, 110, 126, 131, 135, 142, 146, 150, 169, 185, 190, 193, 221, 247, 273
Empire Colonnade 8, **38**, 39, 70, 75, **77**, 113, 121, 235
Excursion trains 1-2, **3-4**, 23, **28**, 30, 43, 56-58, 86, 88, 94, 119-120, **121**, 200, **201**, **203-204**, 205, **206**, 207, 212, 273

Fairy River 9, 14-15, **17**, 18, **26**, 31, **36**, 63, **64-65**, 239, 254
Figure 8 Railway **19-20**, **21-22**, 27, 32, **37**, 38, 45, **46**, 61, 150, **154**, 262

Floods 30-31, 105, **113-117**, 118, 136, **137**, **195**
Flying Chairs (Chair-O-Plane) **29**, 44, 47, 51, 53, 55, 63, **64**, 97, 129, 159-160, **161-162**, 247
Frinton, Freddie 81

Gallopers 73, 128, **129-130**, 136, 139, **158**, 161, **162-164**, 166, **168**, 169, **171**, 172, 185, 192-194, **195**, 199, 224-225, 248, 270, 273-274
Gavioli 52, 129, 136, 161, 164, 194, **195**, 270
Gayway 83-84, 110, **111**, 119, 180-182, **202**, 203, 209, **220**, 221, 223, **238**, 239
Ghost Train 48, 90, 93, 96, 99, 101, 126, 147, 156-157, **158**, 185, 191, 197, 225-226, **227**, 248, 270, 277
Globe of Death 79, 97
Gondola Scenic Ark **25**, 91, **92**, 178, 247
Great Yarmouth 13-14, 251, 264
Griffiths, Jim 131, 138, 191, **192**, 269

Hancock's 23, **46**, 61, 66, **67-69**, 70, 74-75, **77**, 79, 87-88, 111, 114, 116
Happidrome 9, **111**, 119, 180, 211, **220**, **239**, 240
Hardy's 24, 75
Hawkey's Premier Cafe 8, 25, **38**, 75, 77, 81, 113, 121, 175, 211, **215**, 216, **235**
Hawkey's Capitol Cafe 5, 8, **38-39**, 74, 75, **77**, 81, 107, 111, **112**, 119-120, **204**, 211, **218**, **236**, 237
Helter Skelter 9, 14, **16-17**, **22**, 23, **26-29**, 31, **36-39**, **46**, 66, **67**, 74, 77, 121, 180, 226

Index

Hindenburg 79, **80**
Holiday Week Gala 135, **136**
Holley, Walter E. 111, 113
Hook-a-Duck 46, 177, 199
Hoskins, Mr W. 109
Hurricane Jets 138, **142**, 143, 159, **160**, **172**, 197, 225, 248,

Illuminations 87, 107, 203, **242**, 246

Jackson, Robert 7, 10, 14, 26, **37**, **39**, 238
Joy Wheel 22-23, **27-28**, **39**, **46**, 61, 66, **67**, 140

Kenton Grange railway 131, 169, 193, 273-274, 279
Kursaal Bazaar & Cafe **17**, 21, **22**, 23, **26**, 27, **37**, 53, 93, 110-111, 241

Lakeside Miniature Railway 126, 131, 135, 139, 147, **162**, 168, **171**, 191, 195, 248
Lakin, Robert & Co 48, 98, 131, 150, 154, 166
Laughing Clowns 147, 175, **176**, 198, 270
Lawrence Wright 63, **64**
Locomotive 'Henrietta' **138**, 168, 169, **170**, **195**, 197, 276
Locomotive 'Grimsby Town' 169, **170**, **196**, 275-276
Loop-O-Plane (Loops) 97, 99, 101, 146, 160

Mad Mouse 146, 153, 173, **224**, 225
Mancho Tables 48, **49**
Mermaid 2, 230, **233**
Mexborough 81

Mikado Cafe 56, 257
Mirrored Maze 48, 96-97, 103, 131, 179, 199
Monkey House 48, 66, **67**, 179, 248

Newbutt, Jack **120**, 131, **132**, 133, **138**, 152, 163, 169, **170**, 172, 185, **193**, **195**, 197, 271, 277
Newbutt, Michael **194**, 195, 196, 273
New Dips 21, 45, 47, 52, **53**, 55, 59, 61, 93, 126, 150, 247
New Whip 47, 51, 53, 55

Orton & Spooner Ltd 48, 141, 154, 167, 226

Parker, Albert 75
Pierrots 24
Peter Pan Railway 121, **131**, 141, 146-147, **163**, 164, **171**, 172, 185, **189**, 196, 224, 246
Pleasureland 25-26, 29, 44, 55, 62-63, **64**, 72-73, 79, 90, 239-240, 247, 258

Railnews 208
Rhyl 141, 153, 173, 224
Ritz Cinema **83**, 110-111, 119, **120**, 211, **220**, 221, 239
Rotherham 32, 81
Rotor **140**, 141

Samuels, Barney 73, 150, **194**, 269
Savoy amusement arcade 119, 211, **219**, 237-238, 245
Sea Cars 56, 60, 71, **77**, 121
Sheffield 1-2, **3**, 6-7, 15, 23, 30-32, 40-41, 43-44, **46**, **56**, **57**, 61, **62**, **66**, **71**, 73, **81**, 87, 89, 91, 93, **94**, 97, **100-101**, 108-110, **135**, 136, 145,

162-165, 172, 200, 202-203, 205, 207-208, 222, 230, 246, 261, 264, 280
Skee Ball 50, **65**, 177
Skating Rink 32, 55-56, 90, 126, 128-129, **131**, 136, **137**, 141, 151, 155-156, 161, **171**, 172, 248
Slater, Jimmy 81, **84**
Slot Machines 15, 115-116, 180
Smalley, Mrs Margaret 26, 65, **66**, 238
Smith, George 101
Smith, Sid 124, 126, 161, 191, 269
Speedway 51, 96-97, 99, 101, 103, 126, **128**, 129, 139, 142, **158**, 159, **160**, 167-168, 172, 180, 185, **189**, 191, **196**, 197, 224, 225-226, 246, 247-248, 269
Spider & Fly 147, 174, **175**, 191, 198, 270
Suggitts Lane 2, **12-13**, **19**, 21, 45, 105, 113-114, 118, 152, **203**, **243-244**, 246
Sunday Market 146, **225**, **228**, 240, 267
Sunrise Cafe 63, **64-65**, 94, 240
Supercars Ltd 48, 141, 150, 154, 171
Switchback Railway 3, 8-13, **15**, **18**, 19, **22**, 23, 27, **28**, 30-32, **35-37**, 59, 61-62, **64**, 66, 73, 89, 230, 240, 247, 254

Taddy's public house 111, **112**, 119-120, **219**, **237**
Taylor, Arthur **128**, 159, 185, 191-192, 197, 269
Trade Fair 142, **143-144**, 145
Two Stick Charlie 74, 77

Victor Colonnade 2, 6, **7**, **34**, **38**, 113, 122-123, 182, 207-208, 211, **212-214**, 230, **231-232**

Waltzer **145**, 159, **165**, 166-167, 177, 199, 224-226, **227**, 269
Warwick Revolving Tower 5, 7, 14, **15**, 21-22, 25, **26**, **35-37**, 84
Water Chute 12-13, 30, 90, 156
West, Walter **74**, 75, 113, 121, 217, 235
Wilkie, Mrs Elizabeth 'Ma' 126, **190**, 191
Wilkie, George **18**, **29**, **37**, 44, 47, 52, 55, 61, 72, 82, 84, 92, 94, 97, 105, 126, 157, 162, 190, 240, 246
Wonderland 3, 9, 12-13, 16, 21, **25**, **29**, **37**, 44-45, **46-47**, 48, **49-50**, 51-52, **53-54**, 55-56, 58, 61-63, **64-65**, 71-73, 75, **77**, 79, 81-84, 86, **89**, 90, **91** 92-94, **95-96**, 97, 98, 99, **100**, 101-106, 109-110, 114-115, **117**, 118-119, 124-126, 128-129, **130**, **132**, 133, **134**, 135-136, **138**, 139-141, **142-145**, 146-147, 150, **151**, 152, **154**, 157, **160-161**, 163-164, **165**, 166, **167**, 168-169, **170**, **172**, 173-174, **175**, 176-177, **178**, 179-180, 183-185, **186**, 190-200, **202**, 203, 208-209, 211, 220, 221-222, 224-226, **227-228**, 232, 239-242, 246-249, 257-261, 263, 267-270, 273, 275-277
Wondersnaps 127, **129**, 133, 147, **155**, **165-166**, 168, 183, **184-189**, 192-193, 195, 198-199, 270
Wright, Jack **132**, 147, **160**, 178, 199

Zeppelin 41, **80**

This book is printed on paper from sustainable sources managed under the Forest Stewardship Council (FSC) scheme.

It has been printed in the UK to reduce transportation miles and their impact upon the environment.

For every new title that Matador publishes, we plant a tree to offset CO_2, partnering with the More Trees scheme.

MORE TREES
LET'S PLANT A BILLION TREES

For more about how Matador offsets its environmental impact, see www.troubador.co.uk/about/